Music Theater and
Popular Nationalism in Spain
······ 1880–1930 ······

MUSIC
THEATER
AND
POPULAR
NATIONALISM
IN SPAIN
1880–1930

CLINTON D. YOUNG

LOUISIANA STATE UNIVERSITY PRESS · BATON ROUGE

Published by Louisiana State University Press
Copyright © 2016 by Louisiana State University Press
All rights reserved
Manufactured in the United States of America
First printing

DESIGNER: Michelle A. Neustrom
TYPEFACE: Vulpa
PRINTER AND BINDER: Maple Press

LIBRARY OF CONGRESS
CATALOGING-IN-PUBLICATION DATA

Young, Clinton D.
  Music theater and popular nationalism in Spain, 1880–1930 / Clinton
D. Young.
      pages cm
  Includes bibliographical references and index.
  ISBN 978-0-8071-6102-9 (cloth : alk. paper) — ISBN 978-0-8071-
6104-3 (pdf) — ISBN 978-0-8071-6105-0 (epub) — ISBN 978-0-
8071-6106-7 (mobi) 1. Musical theater—Spain—History—20th century.
2. Musical theater—Spain—History—19th century. 3. Zarzuela—
Spain—20th century. 4. Zarzuela—Spain—19th century. 5. Musical
theater—Political aspects—Spain—History—20th century. 6. Musical
theater—Political aspects—Spain—History—19th century. 7. Nationalism in music. I. Title.
  ML1747.Y68 2016
  782.10946'09034—dc23
                                                              2015011998

For my family: Mom, Dad, and Leah

Extraordinary how potent cheap music is.

—NOËL COWARD, *Private Lives*

CONTENTS

....

ACKNOWLEDGMENTS

. . . .

I f, as is generally acknowledged, the best part of writing is having written, then the best part of having written is having written the acknowledgments. Not only are they a symbol that one's work is almost complete, but they allow one to relive the best parts of a research project—the conversations that lead to new insights, the serendipitous encounters that change the course of your work for the better, and the intellectual excitement that comes from sharing ideas with a receptive audience. Acknowledgments are a reminder that one is part of a community, and I am grateful that I have had the support of a large and supportive community while working on this project. While I alone am responsible for the flaws in this book, it is vastly better than it might otherwise have been due to the support of the people I thank below.

My first thanks must go to Pamela Radcliff, my principal academic advisor at the University of California, San Diego. She is that rarity among graduate advisors, one who is willing to allow her students latitude to work in areas outside of her own specialized interests. Thanks to her, I have been forced to communicate musical ideas to people who don't read music—and this project wouldn't exist otherwise. She has also been a colleague since graduation; I especially want to thank her for allowing me to read some of her as yet unpublished work while I was finalizing the manuscript, which helped me crystallize my own thinking on the debates surrounding the Restoration. David Ringrose served as my coadvisor, and I am in his debt for his unstinting support and unfailing good humor. Other UCSD faculty members who gave advice and significant support during my time there include Rachel Klein, David Luft, John Marino, Jann Pasler, Kathy Ringrose, Cynthia Truant, and Danny Vickers. One of the great advantages of UCSD was the welcoming and intellectually vibrant community of students working on Spanish history projects. Of these, Hamilton Stapell and Ana Varela-Lago deserve special mention: as we all started the same year, they have given input into this project for virtually its entire duration. Somehow they managed to avoid overt visceral reactions to the word *zarzuela* after hearing it so frequently for so long. Other Hispanists at UCSD to whom I am indebted include Daniel Berenberg, Enrique Sanabria, and Daniel Stuber. Thanks are also due to the non-Hispanist friends I made in California, including Heidi Keller-Lapp, Sara Malena, Rachel Shaw (who merits special thanks for indexing the book), Don Wallace, and Jackie Zucconi.

I've had the great fortune to work with a number of smart and friendly colleagues since graduate school, all of whom have taught me a great deal about research and teaching. At Western Carolina University, these included Laura Cruz, David Dorondo, Mary Ella Engel, Gael Graham, Jim Lewis, Richard Starnes, and Vicki Szabo. While at the University of Arkansas at Monticello, I've treasured my time working with Richard Clubb, Richard Corby, John Kyle Day, Marie Jenkins, Bill Shea, Carol Strong, and Donna Taylor. I've also enjoyed working with students at both institutions: teaching them European history and research skills has strengthened my ability to communicate concepts more than they'll ever know. A special thanks goes to Dan Degges, whose interest in the Hispanic world went so far beyond that of most undergraduates that it has helped to inspire my next project. I've met great colleagues at the annual meetings of the Association for Spanish and Portuguese Historical Studies, whose existence is one of the great benefits of studying Spanish history. It was at these meetings that I met Scott Eastman and Andrew McFarland, with whom I have spent many fruitful hours discussing the nature of Spanish nationalism. Thanks must also go to all the members—too numerous to list, but most of whom will be found in the bibliography—whose questions and conversations at the annual meetings have greatly helped and influenced my own thinking.

Then there are the institutions that have supported my research. Researchers are extraordinarily dependent upon librarians and archivists to help us locate the materials we need. My thanks go to the librarians at UCSD, WCU, and UAM, all of whom have managed to find the odd books I needed to finish this one. The same thanks go to the staff of the Biblioteca Nacional de España (especially the staff of the Sala Barbieri), the staff of Archivo General de la Administración, and the staff of the Biblioteca Española de Música y Teatro of the Fundación Juan March, who were extraordinarily helpful in digging out rare scores for me. The original research for this project between 2001 and 2003 was undertaken as part of a J. William Fulbright Foreign Scholarship. I must give special thanks to Patricia Zahniser, the American Program Officer of the Spanish Fulbright Commission, who aided me in the intricacies of living abroad; thanks are also due to José Álvarez Junco, who supplied a critical letter of support for my application. The other end of the project has been supported by the staff of LSU Press, without whom this book would still be random digital files on a computer. Special gratitude goes to Alisa Plant, who kept asking about my work for several years and made the review process far easier than I anticipated. Thanks are also due to the reviewers of the draft manuscript, whose suggestions made this a better book.

Finally, this book could never have been written without the support of my family. They have encouraged me in my academic endeavors despite the fact it has meant my living thousands of miles away—sometimes on another continent. But my mother, Dyana, my father, David, and my sister, Leah, have never questioned what I have chosen to do (at least to my face) and instead have listened to my complaints, cheered my good fortune, and welcomed me home with open arms when I've been able to return to Oregon. My grandmother, Lois Greig, has also taken a great interest in my stories of academia and travels to Spain, and I regret that my other grandparents—Wallace Greig, Wayland Young, and Helen Young—are no longer here to see the fruits of their encouragement and understanding. Without the unconditional love of all my family, I don't think I could have found the strength to follow my chosen career path and do the work that I do. And for that, I will be forever in their debt.

Music Theater and
Popular Nationalism in Spain
······ 1880–1930 ······

Theater Music and the Problem
of Spanish Nationalism

February in Madrid can be fairly miserable. Cold winds sweep down from the mountains to the north of the city, chilling buildings that are designed to remain cool against the intense heat of a Spanish summer. For music lovers, February 1894 had added misery. On the morning of Monday the 12th, newspapers carried the obituary of Emilio Arrieta, who had died the previous day and who was one of Spain's most eminent composers. Arrieta was not only the composer of several operas and zarzuelas, he was also the director of the Escuela Nacional de Música y Declamación, one of the key institutions for developing new Spanish composers, singers, and instrumentalists. He had been a favorite of Queen Isabella II—having been her singing teacher in the late 1840s and early 1850s—and although this was not mentioned in the obituaries, he may have also been one of her lovers. His compositions attracted some of Europe's greatest singers: the premiere of his opera *Marina* in 1871 had featured Enrico Tamberlick, one of the leading tenors of the late nineteenth century. (Verdi had written the role of Alvaro in *La forza del destino* for Tamberlick.) Arrieta was more than a composer in mid- and late nineteenth-century Spain. He was an institution.[1]

Exactly one week later on the 19th, the same papers carried the obituary of an even more revered and beloved composer. Francisco Asenjo Barbieri had passed away at 1:20 that morning. Like Arrieta, Barbieri was a member of the Real Academia de San Fernando de Bellas Artes, which recognized the height of his accomplishment in Spanish artistic circles. As the compiler and editor of the *Cancionero musical de los siglos XV y XVI* (Songbook of the Fifteenth and Sixteenth Centuries), he was one of the fathers of the discipline of musicology in Spain. He was the founder of the Sociedad de Conciertos de Madrid, one of the earliest orchestras in Spain, and was its principal conductor for many years. During his tenure, he introduced Spain to important music by Mozart, Haydn, Rossini, and Beethoven. But most of all, he was beloved for his musical theater compositions. His zarzuelas *Jugar con fuego, Pan y toros,* and *El barberillo de Lavapiés* had been wildly popular at their premieres and were frequently revived. The depth of feeling aroused by Barbieri's death can be judged by the fact that the weekly review *Blanco y Negro* featured four photographs of his funeral cortege and noted that at the funeral service "women with shawls tightly wrapped around the body and kerchiefs on their head pursued [the coffin], moving their lips and letting tears fall before the cadaver." Arrieta's funeral had not attracted such attention or grief— or media coverage.[2]

Although Arrieta and Barbieri were both towering figures of nineteenth-century Spanish music, it was Barbieri whose death attracted the most attention. This was not merely because he died a week later. The real reason can be gleaned from four retrospective articles in the daily newspaper *La Época* evaluating the music of each man. These articles were written by Spain's most eminent music critic, Antonio Peña y Goñi. Peña y Goñi was well acquainted with each man and his role in Spanish musical history: in 1881, he had published *La ópera española y la música dramatica en España en el siglo XIX* (Spanish Opera and Dramatic Music in Nineteenth-Century Spain), a massive overview of the development of Spanish theatrical music. As Arrieta and Barbieri were both dramatic composers, they had featured prominently in the text. Although Peña y Goñi softened his criticisms of men who had just moved into a realm where they would be immune from music critics at last, his evaluation of the two composers had not changed since 1881. This would not be to Arrieta's benefit.

On the 12th of February, *La Época* published Peña y Goñi's "La música de Arrieta," which opens by comparing Arrieta's musical and dramatic sense with that of the Italian Vincenzo Bellini, the composer of the operas *La sonnambula, Norma,* and *I puritani,* some of the greatest examples of the bel canto vocal style that flourished in Italy in the early nineteenth century. This might seem like a compliment, since Bellini's operas had remained popular in Spain through the nineteenth century; Italian opera, and bel canto opera in particular, was the cornerstone of the operatic repertory at the Teatro Real, Spain's leading opera house. But for Peña y Goñi, Arrieta's Italian sensibilities disqualified him from being a truly "Spanish" composer. Peña y Goñi found Arrieta's zarzuela music "cosmopolitan" rather than quintessentially Spanish. Even more damning was the way in which Arrieta used Spanish popular songs, which were regarded as one of the hallmarks of zarzuela. Peña y Goñi eviscerates Arrieta's music with a metaphor: "Arrieta did not take from our popular songs the flowers they released, nor posies. He extracted the essence and presented the aroma." In a follow-up article the next day, the language slips a little and the point becomes even clearer: "Elegant and immaculate as a composer, he always wrote with a delicacy of touch and a feminine morbidity of pure Italian stock, the Maestro hated vulgarity and fled from it carefully."[3] It does not need Freudian analysis—or even much knowledge of the Spanish idea of machismo—to realize that Peña y Goñi found Arrieta's music to be technically advanced and enjoyable without finding it particularly Spanish. The picture he creates of Arrieta is that of the enervated artiste, lounging languidly and delicately sniffing the air before deigning to present his art to enraptured followers—a picture, it should be noted, that is completely unfair to Arrieta. Not that Arrieta's essential foreignness was a new theme for Peña y Goñi. Early in his career as a critic, he had complained, "Is there no manner— I thought—to *deitalianize* this man?"[4]

Contrast this treatment of Arrieta with the odors that came out of Barbieri's music: "The aroma of the music of Barbieri is a penetrating aroma, the sweat of the people, but of a clean and healthy people who sing in the open air, are bathed in sun and saturated in happiness, asking of a musical note an intensity of sentiment that cannot be found in the spoken word."[5] Setting aside the irreverent thought that Peña y Goñi's true calling might have been writing ad copy for deodorant, the reader will note that he claims Barbieri's music for the masculine and sun-drenched Spanish people. The critic titled his paean to Barbieri "El maestro seguidilla," the *seguidilla* being a traditional type of folk music from the region of Castile. (The most famous seguidilla is Georges Bizet's adaptation of the form for the seduction of Don José at the end of Act I of *Carmen,* "Près des ramparts de Séville.") Peña y Goñi lamented that the people of Spain had no idea how much Barbieri had done for them or for their music, concluding his evaluation of Barbieri's music with this: "your music, alive, witty, confident, has the colors of the national flag, and will live among us as an everlasting insignia of the national art." Even accounting for the fact that the music critic was a close friend of Barbieri, it is clear that for Peña y Goñi, the composer's greatness was to be found in his nationalistic tendencies. In another article the following day, Barbieri was bluntly portrayed as an emancipator of Spanish music with an "ideal [that] was purely and exclusively Spanish."[6] Nor was the contrast between the two composers based solely in Peña y Goñi's partisanship. The obituary of Arrieta in *El Imparcial* on 12 February noted that it was common for music critics to characterize Arrieta's music as more Italian than Spanish.

This discussion of musical theater styles is the necessary crux for understanding Spanish music in the nineteenth century: to talk about Spanish music of the time is to talk about theater music by default. Spain did not have the proliferation of symphony orchestras that drove musical development elsewhere in Europe. Spain's nascent bourgeoisie had neither the money nor the numbers to build an audience for symphonic music the way the middle classes were doing in England and France, nor did it have the court cultures that led to the development of orchestras across Central Europe.[7] (Spain's Bourbon monarchs—with the notable exceptions of Philip V and Isabella II—were not musically inclined.) Although Barbieri had been leading orchestral concerts in Madrid since 1859 and had founded the Sociedad de Conciertos in 1867, these orchestras were often ad hoc ensembles with no formal home and no firm financial foundation. Spain's first professional, full-time orchestra, the Orquesta Sinfónica de Madrid, would not be organized until 1910. The concert societies of nineteenth-century Spain tended to focus on introducing Spaniards to "European" music rather than to the compositions of their compatriots. So Spanish music was theater music, and any composer who actually wanted to hear his music performed became a theatrical composer by default.

But even in theater music, Spanish composers could not develop in the same way as their counterparts across the Pyrenees. In Europe, virtually all serious theatrical composers were opera composers. Serious composers shunned light opera and popular theater. (The one notable exception was England's Sir Arthur Sullivan, and even he was chagrined to realize that his reputation would rest not on his monumental attempt at opera, *Ivanhoe,* but on the lighter works that he penned with W. S. Gilbert.) Spain, however, was an operatic colony of Italy. This had been made exceedingly clear in 1850 with the inauguration of the Teatro Real, Madrid's main opera house and the only theater in the country subsidized by the Spanish government. The opera chosen to inaugurate the house was Gaetano Donizetti's *La Favorita,* another bel canto selection (albeit one that was at least set in Spain). The opera was chosen by the contralto Marietta Alboni, who sang the title role since it was part of her contract as the theater's prima donna.[8] All performances were sung in Italian as all the singers were Italian. Since the audience of the Teatro Real was composed of the aristocracy and the wealthy, there was no need to sing in Spanish for the benefit of a popular audience. The thirteen operas performed that first season were Italian: seven by Donizetti, three by Bellini, two by Rossini, one by Verdi. In later seasons, French and German operas were translated into Italian for performance. Spanish music conservatories taught singing in Italian but not in Spanish. On the rare occasions when the Teatro Real performed an opera written by a Spanish composer, the text had to be translated into Italian for the performances since the star singers were unwilling to learn Spanish texts. During the reign of Isabella II, only two Spanish operas were given at the Real: *Idelgonda* in April 1854 and *Isabel la Católica* in December 1855. Both were composed by Emilio Arrieta.

Thus Spanish composers turned by default to the one musical form that would be widely performed in Spain (and in Spanish): zarzuela. Today, zarzuela is something of a catch-all term that can describe Spanish works variously categorized in English as "light opera," "operetta," or even "musical comedy." At its core, zarzuela—like virtually all lighter forms of musical theater—is a musical theater genre in which the musical numbers alternate with dialogue. It does not have the continuous music or recitative of opera. The Spanish trace the history of the genre to the performance in 1657 of *El laurel de Apolo* by Pedro Calderón de la Barca, which featured extended musical numbers in the tradition of that new art form coming out of Italy, opera. The genre became known as zarzuela because the first works were performed at King Philip IV's hunting lodge just outside Madrid, the Palacio de la Zarzuela. (The palace itself derived its name from the numerous brambles—*zarzas*—in the countryside nearby.) Zarzuela remained an entertainment for the aristocracy until the accession of the Italianophile Bourbon monarchs to the throne, when opera became the entertainment of choice at court. In the early 1700s zarzuela moved into Madrid's popular theaters, where it abandoned the high-flown mythological plots that had predominated at court and began to take an interest in the life of average citizens (or at least stereotypes of average citizens). The Spanish playwright Ramón de la Cruz both popularized the *sainete,* a theatrical genre of short plays about everyday life, and wrote many libretti for zarzuela in the latter half of the eighteenth century. Although the stories of these zarzuelas were Spanish, their music was not. Composers still used Italian opera music as their main inspiration and model.[9]

Zarzuela underwent a drastic decline in the early nineteenth century, especially as the Italian operas of Rossini, Bellini, and Donizetti gained in popularity: their high-flown sentiments and lush music reflected the Romantic theatrical culture prevalent in Spain at the time. By the 1830s and 1840s, a number of Spanish composers began to try their hands at writing operas. To distinguish their works from the Italian bel canto imports that so bedazzled Spain, they dredged up the moribund genre of zarzuela and began to apply that term to their compositions. The late 1840s and the early 1850s saw the birth of the modern zarzuela, which in its earliest incarnation featured Italian opera-style musical numbers, spoken dialogue, and plots frequently "adapted" (a polite euphemism for "ripped off") from French light operas.[10] The seminal work for modern zarzuela was Barbieri's 1851 success *Jugar con fuego* (Playing with Fire), with an elegant verse libretto by the Romantic playwright Ventura de la Vega. Set in early eighteenth-century Madrid, the plot revolves around the scandalous love affair between a duchess and a commoner. Barbieri's major innovation was that he began to incorporate Spanish folk melodies into his music, especially in the choral numbers.[11]

Jugar con fuego is generally regarded by Spanish musical scholars as the first modern zarzuela. However, the works that followed it until the late 1870s sound to modern ears much more like operas than operettas. The complex, high-flown, and romantic music demands trained voices. (Spanish opera singers like Victoria de los Ángeles, Montserrat Caballé, and Plácido Domingo frequently programmed zarzuela music in their recitals.) The solo arias and duets not infrequently sound as if they could be transplanted into contemporary Italian operas. But from the early 1850s, zarzuela was regarded as a particularly Spanish genre of music theater. As Peña y Goñi's postmortem evaluations of Arrieta's and Barbieri's music make clear, much of this was rooted in Barbieri's innovation of incorporating Spanish folk music into his scores. But it was more than the mere use of folk music. Folk music was used primarily in the numbers sung by the chorus; Spanish music was used to characterize the Spanish people. The use of the chorus and choral music is so prevalent in many of these zarzuelas that some scholars have argued that the true protagonists of these types of zarzuelas are the Spanish people themselves.[12] None of this is unusual, for by the mid-nineteenth century numerous

European composers were becoming interested in incorporating folk music into serious concert works and operas. At approximately the same moment that Barbieri was revolutionizing zarzuela, Franz Liszt was transmuting Hungarian folk songs into the piano pieces he published as the *Hungarian Rhapsodies* in 1853. The development of zarzuela was part of the wider trend toward musical nationalism that engulfed Europe in the mid-nineteenth century.

The development of zarzuela as a nationalist genre of music had societal as well as musical implications. With the revival of zarzuela in the early 1850s, Barbieri and other Spanish musicians decided that a new theater should be built to showcase the genre. The new Teatro de la Zarzuela was inaugurated on 10 October 1856. The music performed that evening set the pattern for how zarzuela music would be interpreted in the future. Among the highlights of the evening was a cantata composed by Arrieta, who set lyrics extolling how genius and beauty inspire artists and musicians. The music was quite well received "although the listeners found little novelty" in Arrieta's work.[13] The evening concluded with the performance of a musical allegory simply titled *La Zarzuela*. In it, the Commedia dell'arte figures of Harlequin (representing Italian music) and Pierrot (representing French music) try to woo and conquer Zarzuela—who is female in this particular version of the allegory. They are stopped by the figures of Tacón (who represents the classical Spanish theater) and Figaro (who is from Spain, even if he was created by a French author and musicalized by an Austrian and an Italian), who persuade Zarzuela to follow her own inclinations and become something new and original—something Spanish.[14] The music for *La Zarzuela* was composed by three of Spain's leading composers of the day: Arrieta, Barbieri, and Joaquín Gaztambide (who conducted the orchestra that evening). Each man contributed to the idea that foreign music was taking over Spanish musical life and that foreign influences needed to be held at bay.

Aside from the music, the inauguration of the Teatro de la Zarzuela helped to form another crucial interpretive point about zarzuela and its role as Spanish music. The 10th of October had not been chosen at random to open the theater. The date was chosen specifically because it was Queen Isabella's birthday. However, the court and most of the aristocracy did not attend the inauguration of the new theater because they were at the Royal Palace celebrating the installation of General Ramón Narvaéz as minister.[15] Thus the audience at the Zarzuela that night was not the haut monde of Madrid who had helped to inaugurate the Teatro Real six years earlier; it was the upwardly mobile middle classes who sat in the new plush velvet seats that night. In retrospect, the audience loomed large in the claim that zarzuela was a Spanish genre of music. The aristocracy supported Italian opera, but the Spanish people attended performances of zarzuela. This may help to explain why Peña y Goñi would later characterize Arrieta's Italianate music as effete and enervated. It played into popular conceptions of a decadent aristocracy (headed by a queen who did not bother to cloak her wide-ranging sexual life with Victorian discretion) that supported Italian opera while the Spanish people were listening to good, solid Spanish music. Although it was primarily middle-class theatergoers who attended the performances at the Teatro de la Zarzuela, discussions of zarzuela inevitably characterized the genre as "música popular": in nineteenth-century Spanish parlance, "the music of the people." Both the music and its perceived audience made zarzuela quintessentially Spanish.

The fact that the most notable Spanish music of the late nineteenth and early twentieth centuries was being created for the popular theater and not the concert halls or opera houses that dominated musical life in other countries has serious ramifications not only for understanding Spanish music, but for understanding the history of Spain and the history of nationalism in general. Traditionally, the study of nationalism has focused on how European states in the nineteenth century constructed nationalism and national identities as a way of organizing their citizens. The traditional social order had been disrupted, fragmented, and reorganized by such shocks as the French Revolution, the Industrial Revolution, and the emergence of the working class in the political sphere. Nationalism, whether by imagining communities to organize people into, by inventing traditions for all social classes to take part in, or by turning peasants into Frenchmen and thus having them identify with the nation rather than social class or local origin (to pick only three metaphors that have come to form the foundation of the modern academic literature on nationalism), became the main vehicle by which governments coped with the transition to modernity that defines the history of the nineteenth century.[16]

If this top-down view of nationalism seems to lack nuance, it may be because the original scholars of nationalism tended to focus on the actions of the state in creating nationalism. But even if the state was the main actor in creating a sense of national identity among its population, the population did react to these projects in one fashion or another. The creation of national identity is not merely a state-driven, top-down process. The population being national-ized has a say in the process as well, often redefining national identity in ways that the state may not have had in mind. Local identities, ethnic identities, and religious identities—identities that nationalism was meant to replace—can prove powerful in helping to define what it means to be French or English or German or Spanish. Local populations and individuals have agency in determining what their identities actually are; they are not merely passive re-cipients of a state-driven agenda. People interpret their past and their culture to convince themselves that their "nation" has existed since time immemorial when, in fact, it hasn't been around much longer than the steam engine. Rec-ognizing that nationalism also has a bottom-up dimension does make the his-tory of nationalism much messier, but also gives the historian greater access to the lived experience of people during the rise of the idea of nationalism in Europe—what, for example, the peasants actually thought about being turned into Frenchmen.[17]

In no European country is the popular experience of nationalism more crucial to understanding its development than in Spain. Spain, unlike the northern European states and like its Mediterranean counterparts Italy and Portugal, had a weak central government in the late nineteenth and early twentieth centuries. Thanks to the relative poverty of Spain and its exceed-ingly limited industrial development during the 1800s, the Spanish govern-ment did not have the means to develop and sustain a nationalist project. Lack of money, for example, kept the state from mandating compulsory primary education and left most schools in the hands of the Catholic Church, which had condemned the secular power of the state and liberal ideals (which in-cluded the ideal that the nation and not religion should be the basis of iden-tity) in the 1864 Syllabus of Errors. Nor did the Spanish government have the will to develop a nationalist project. In the wake of the revolutions and politi-cal upheaval that occurred between 1868 and 1874, the Spanish government was focused on maintaining political stability and quiescence. Nationalist projects tended to involve citizens in political discourse, which led inevitably to that most cherished and dreaded phenomenon of the nineteenth century, mass democracy. Spain did not have the mechanisms to channel, harness, or divert this force as the northern European states did; nor did it have the au-tocracy to suppress it entirely, as Russia did. This left the Spanish state in an extremely awkward position. To seem like a modern country, it had to undertake nationalist projects like flags, postage stamps, national anthems, and historical celebrations. But the government did not want the outcome of such a project, and supported it with something less than outright enthusiasm.

In the standard narrative of Spanish history, the weakness of the state in the late nineteenth and early twentieth centuries led to a fragmented and weak sense of national identity. In particular, the absence of a state-oriented project of national identity was what led to the rise of regional nationalisms in Catalonia and the Basque Country. Over the course of the nineteenth century, a revival of interest in the Catalan and Basque languages and the medieval cultures of the regions had transformed into political movements demanding greater political representation and regional autonomy; the industrial bourgeoisie of each region used regional culture as an additional layer to an argument that the government in Madrid, in thrall to the agricultural interests of central and southern Spain, was actively impeding industrialization and economic growth in the northern regions of the country. In the classic top-down view of nationalism, the central state is supposed to eradicate regional identities, and the failure of the Spanish government to do so is considered prima facie evidence of a weak nationalist project. But powerful regional nationalisms that advocated for autonomy and independence could be found in the United Kingdom, France, and Belgium, as well as the polyglot Austro-Hungarian and Russian Empires during the same period.[18] Regional nationalisms are not evidence of a weak nationalist project. Rather, they are evidence of a nationalist project that has a significant popular, bottom-up component.

In Spain, more than in any other major European country, the development of nationalism and national identity occurred on the popular level. (In Italy, the closest comparison, the population was as reluctant as the government to develop a sense of nationalism, thanks to the condemnation of the Catholic Church. Although Spain was a devoutly Catholic country, the Church played a less active role in politics than it did in Italy.) In the absence of a powerful central state government during the late nineteenth century, nationalist ideas were developed in other venues—especially cultural venues. Painters like Emilio Sala y Francés, Francisco Pradilla Ortiz, and Antonio Gisbert Pérez created spectacular canvases of crucial moments in Spanish history like the expulsion of the Jews from Spain, the conquest of Granada, Juana la Loca mourning over her husband's funeral bier, or the execution of Spanish liberals on the beaches of Málaga. Fiction recast history in an exciting form: Benito

Pérez Gáldos, the most eminent Spanish novelist of the nineteenth century, wrote forty-six books known collectively as the *Episodios Nacionales,* which retold nineteenth-century Spanish history from the Battle of Trafalgar to the Bourbon Restoration. The *Episodios Nacionales,* published between 1872 and 1912, used romance and adventure to trace the development of the ideals of liberalism and Spanish unity born during the Napoleonic Wars. Spanish intellectuals such as Miguel de Unamuno and José Ortega y Gasset undertook extensive study and criticism of Miguel de Cervantes's seventeenth-century classic *Don Quijote,* which helped to make it the cornerstone of all Spanish literature. There were popular campaigns to build monuments to Cervantes across Spain. The Prado Museum was organized to create a home for Spanish painters, in the process canonizing El Greco, Diego de Velázquez, and Francisco de Goya as a sort of holy trinity in a Spanish school of art.

Such popular cultural nationalism was almost inevitably liberal in tone, using the model of the Italian *Risorgimento* rather than the German *Kulturkampf.* This sense of national identity located the formation of the Spanish people in the turmoil of the Napoleonic Wars (known in Spain as the War of Independence) when, as the myth goes, the Spanish people rose in a unified fury and waged guerrilla warfare to drive the French invaders from the Spanish soil.[19] Like all nationalist myths, this ignores a few salient points—some Spaniards welcomed the French as reformers bearing new ideas—and it elides the British invasion of Iberia entirely. The myth also inflates the importance of the Cortes of Cádiz, which claimed to rule Spain in the name of the people. While besieged by the French Army in 1812, the Cortes issued a radically liberal constitution. This constitution and its liberal ideals were rejected by a large swath of the Spanish people, led by the Catholic Church; horrified by the anticlerical tendencies of the French Revolution and nineteenth-century liberalism, conservatives proposed an alternate narrative that stressed Spain's role as the redoubt of Catholic faith. For the conservatives, Spanish history focused around the reign of Ferdinand and Isabella I (known in Spanish as *los reyes cátolicos*—the Catholic Monarchs) who laid the foundations for a vast and powerful Spanish empire with the necessary help of the Spanish Inquisition. Although this conservative narrative is usually considered a major variant of Spanish nationalism—herein are the roots of Francisco Franco's dictatorship, after all—this was less a nationalist project than an attempt to maintain a societal status quo.[20] Like its liberal counterpart, conservative nationalism in late nineteenth-century Europe was an attempt to reconcile a country's population with the dislocations caused by industrialization, urbanization, and modernization. Spanish conservatives, unlike their French or German counterparts, built a vision of a country unchanged since 1492.[21] It was Spanish liberals who were undertaking a recognizably nationalist project, creating the myth of a common past in order to prepare the nation for a common future. Popular Spanish nationalism was concerned with the modernization of Spain and how it could best cope with the future.[22] And nowhere was popular liberal nationalism more powerful or effective than in a realm normally associated with frivolity and divertissement: popular musical theater.

The deaths of Arrieta and Barbieri were not the only musical events of nationalist portent during February 1894. On the 10th, the night before Arrieta's death, the Teatro Real gave the Spanish premiere of Verdi's latest (and, as it turned out, last) opera, *Falstaff*. And, as if to make sure that the major musical event preceding Barbieri's death was as Spanish as the event preceding Arrieta's was Italian, fate allowed for the premiere on Saturday, 17 February 1894 of what would become one of the most beloved and popular of all Spanish zarzuelas: Tomás Bretón's *La verbena de la paloma* (The Festival of Our Lady of the Dove). The two works were not dissimilar in plot, as both center around the machinations of elderly men looking for feminine companionship—at least sex, if not love—and the younger folk who manage to find romance during a nocturnal celebration. Although as a composer Bretón was not in the same elevated realm as Verdi, he was a leading figure in Spanish musical circles. Bretón was the composer of numerous concert works and operas that garnered critical plaudits, although they were generally ignored by the public. He was widely respected—following Barbieri's death, Bretón would be elected to take his chair at the Real Academia de San Fernando— although his caustic personality meant he was not much liked in Spanish musical circles. (He had made an enemy out of Antonio Peña y Goñi, which failed to help the reception of his more serious musical works.) He was a staunch proponent of Spanish nationalist opera. Like all other Spanish composers, he wrote zarzuelas, although these generally failed at the box office. But *La verbena de la paloma* would be wildly popular. It is one of the key compositions in the development of zarzuela as nationalist music. But it looks and sounds like nothing else in the European canon of nationalist compositions—except for other zarzuelas.

To understand just how Spanish nationalism looked onstage and how strikingly different it is from other European music theater works, it is worth examining the opening of *La verbena de la paloma,* which is a five-minute-long musical scene. The curtain rises on a sweltering August night in a Madrid street with a pharmacy, a pastry shop, a house, and a tavern.[23] The shops are busy and the residents are enjoying the evening air:

> Don Hilarión and Don Sebastián are seated at the door of the pharmacy. The porter of the building and his wife are also seated, enjoying the night air. The wife has a small sleeping child in her lap. The pastry shop is full of people and there is much activity. At the door of the tavern, playing cards at a small table and seated on benches, are the Tavern-keeper and two friends of his. His wife serves them drinks from time to time. Julián, seated on a low stool and leaning against the wall of the tavern, sighs and complains.

It is a striking stage picture, and similar scenes can still be found from time to time in certain neighborhoods of the city during the summer. From the number of people in the scenario—especially the indications of activity in the tavern and the pastry shop—one might expect a standard ta-ra-ra-boom-der-e chorus extolling the joys of living in the vicinity. Instead, we hear a fidgety tune from the violins and piccolo, and one of the elderly gentlemen sitting in front of the pharmacy begins to sing:

> Castor oil
> is no longer unpleasant to take.
> They give it to you in little pills
> and the effect is still the same.[24]

If any other operetta opens with two elderly gentlemen singing about the effectiveness of purgative cures, I have yet to encounter it.

Bretón uses music to heighten the ordinary, everyday quality of the entire opening scene. The vocal lines in the opening number—especially those of Don Hilarión and Don Sebastián—verge very closely on being *sprechtgesang,* in which the words are spoken in time to the music rather than sung, much as Rex Harrison did in *My Fair Lady.* Bretón does indicate pitch for his vocal lines, but the musical range is so limited that the dialogue between the two elderly gentlemen often sounds as if it is being spoken. It is no surprise to discover that this opening is listed in the vocal score as "Parlante y escena," or literally "Speech and Scene."[25] This low-key avoidance of flights of song continues as Julián and Seña Rita (a barmaid working at the tavern) engage in a brief dialogue in which she chastises him for literally crying into his beer. This is then followed by some discussion between the tavern-keeper and his card-playing cronies. Although the music has become a little more involved, it is still parlando; the effect makes the entire introduction to *La verbena* sound like what one would encounter on the streets of Madrid. Rather than using the music to heighten the emotion of the moment as opera would, Bretón uses his music to heighten the everyday quality of the scene he is depicting.

This strategy continues even as the music of the opening scene becomes more song-like and we come to the first vocal solo in the work, "Julián's Song." For the first time we hear a vocal line with some actual range to it. This first "musical" moment in the score also announces the theme and plot of the work, for Julián's monologue sums up his emotional situation, which gives *La verbena* one of its subtitles, "Celos mal reprimidos" (Ill-Restrained Jealousy):

> Regular people
> have hearts as well,
> and tears in their eyes
> and ill-restrained jealousy.
> . . . .
> For a dark-haired flirt
> I am lost,
> and the courage I have stored up
> drains from my face![26]

This soliloquy is the first moment in the work wherein a character announces their state of mind, and it is appropriate that Julián should thus be the first character to burst forth in full-fledged song, the accepted method of performing internal thoughts in musical theater. Julián's outburst is followed by a sequence in which all the vocal lines heard thus far—Don Hilarión's praise of laxatives, the cardplayers' quarrel, Julián's laments—combine in counterpoint. Since all but the last vocal line are parlando, the naturalism of the opening scene has not been completely stripped away, and the musical realism is only heightened by what follows: as the ensemble ends, the strings in the orchestra pick up an enchantingly quiet figure while the porter and his wife discuss whether their infant son is asleep and how hot their apartment is likely to be.

This nine-bar interlude gives way with a crash to the chorus in the pastry shop. The orchestra roars out fortissimo, and now the chorus that a lesser composer might have used to open the work bursts forth. Orders of food and drink give way to one of the most famous choruses in the zarzuela repertory:

> Because it is the Festival
> of Our Lady of the Dove,
> a shawl from China-na,
> China-na,
> I will give to you.[27]

This chorus sets the scene and establishes that the festival is happening that night. It also establishes the identity of the chorus as the Spanish people, since Bretón uses the basic zarzuela template developed by Barbieri in *Jugar con fuego,* that of the Spanish people singing a Spanish piece of music. The chorus is a seguidilla, the first folk music idiom to crop up in the score. This chorus also ends the first musical scene quite effectively on a high note (as it were) that demands audience applause. As far as the demands of musical theater construction go, the opening of *La verbena de la paloma* alone would establish Bretón as a subtle genius of the highest caliber.

La verbena de la paloma depicts a Spanish neighborhood in its entirety, from the dirty old men on the corner to the excited patrons of the pastry shop. It is a slice of life of 1894 Madrid, where a lover's jealousy (which virtually every other operetta composer in Europe would deem sufficient for a plot) is only one part of the fabric of daily life. By focusing on daily life, Bretón was doing something extraordinary: he was creating a realistic music theater work, something that would not occur on a regular basis again until Stephen Sondheim reached his maturity in the early 1970s. A young man singing about his potential jealousy is not the sort of thing one runs into on a daily basis (even in Madrid). On the other hand, elderly men complaining about their bodily functions and how those might be regulated are hardly uncommon (especially in Madrid). Musically, this links with Bretón's intense use of quasi-parlando vocal lines and his attempts to minimize the "musical" effects of the opening number. Both the composer and the librettist are seeking to create a realistic depiction of street life in Madrid while working in a genre where realism is more often a detriment than a positive virtue. Of the numerous epithets hurled at musical theater over the years, "realistic" is just about the last word that springs to mind.

Yet *La verbena de la paloma* and many other Spanish zarzuelas prided themselves on their realism. Ricardo de la Vega, who wrote the script and lyrics for *La verbena*, was highly praised for this aspect of his work: critics and audiences viewed his characterizations as an accurate representation of daily life in Madrid. *El Imparcial* praised "the spirit of just observation that characterizes all the works of Ricardo de la Vega," which is the sort of critical notice more likely to be applied to a naturalist or realist novel. Even more astonishing was Pedro Bofil's review in *La Época* where he posed this question, with his tongue only mildly in his cheek: "What can follow, when the run ends of this specimen of *pérezgaldosismo* that began its theatrical reign last night?"[28] The equation of Ricardo de la Vega with Benito Pérez Gáldos, Spain's most eminent realist novelist, is surprising. Gáldos focused on the seamy and often tragic underside of life in Madrid, whereas Vega's script is a comic look at flirting and jealousy. Nevertheless, it does not take much imagination to see the potentially tragic implications of the heroine Susana's initial decision to take up with the elderly and lecherous—but well-off—Don Hilarión. Susana will eventually settle for the poor typesetter Julián by the end of the work and presumably settle down to a future of grinding urban poverty. Strip out the music and one might well have a plot suited for Gáldos's *Fortunata y Jacinta* or his contemporary Emile Zola's *Nana* or *Germinal*.

The evocation of Gáldos is appropriate for another reason that Pedro Bofil probably did not intend: the invocation of the author of the *Episodios Nacionales,* one of the literary touchstones of Spanish nationalism. Just as the chorus singing a seguidilla links *La verbena de la paloma* with the nationalist traditions of zarzuela, the direct citation of Gáldos in the critical response to the work is just one indication that this work and other popular theater pieces of the late nineteenth century were part of a popular nationalist project. Musical theater, like literature and the visual arts, was creating a sense of Spanish national identity. To the modern spectator of *La verbena*, this can seem like a counterintuitive statement. It takes place in an urban neighborhood during a period in which the majority of the population were still rural agricultural laborers. It has no obvious nationalist themes or references to Spain's past. Instead, *La verbena* is a decidedly small-scale drama about which man—an old lecher or a lovesick young wimp—is going to escort Susana to the local festival. There is nothing that nationalist theater composers like Verdi or Richard Wagner would recognize as celebrating a nation's past or developing a myth about a national group of people. (It should be noted that Bretón was capable of such traditional grand gestures, having done it in several operas himself: his operas *Los amantes de Teruel* and *La Dolores* were chock-full of folk music and nationalist tropes.) To those accustomed to the full-bodied romantic nationalism of late nineteenth-century European music, *La verbena de la paloma* would seem to have no claim to being nationalist.

But zarzuelas like *La verbena de la paloma* were the most nationalist cultural artifacts turned out in Spain in the years around the dawn of the twentieth century. Even more than grand historical paintings and literary creations, musical theater was what enabled Spaniards to come to grips with the vast modernizing changes taking place in their country. Spain was slowly but surely urbanizing and industrializing from the 1880s through the 1920s, and zarzuela did more than reflect these changes: the genre demonstrated to Spanish society what such a nation could look like. It might have been difficult for a citizen in Burgos, for example, to picture the rapid changes taking place elsewhere in Spain. But when that citizen saw a production of a zarzuela or heard zarzuela music played in a local band concert, they had another way of grasping how the national community was changing. Zarzuelas were like dictionaries and newspapers: all were ways in which countries could be unified conceptually to form a new national imagined community. Traditionally, the seguidillas had been a regional folk dance native to Castile, the province in the heart of Spain. It would not have been danced by peasants in Andalucía to the south nor by the inhabitants of Catalonia on the Mediterranean coast. But zarzuela provided for the integration of regional differences. Regional folk dances like the seguidillas, the *jota,* or the flamenco could be used to characterize the Spanish people. In fact, later in *La verbena,* Bretón uses one form of flamenco music—the soleá—even though the work is set in Madrid and not Andalucía.

Zarzuela could even be used to represent the fact that as Spain modernized, it was adopting more customs and ideas from other European countries. One of the musical numbers in *La verbena* is a mazurka. The mazurka was originally a Polish folk dance that had become popular in Madrid's dance halls and salons during the late nineteenth century; along with the waltz, the polka, and the schottische, the mazurka was one of the early forms of popular music. (All could be considered very early forerunners to swing, rock-and-roll, or rap.) Even though none of these dances was Spanish, they made their way into zarzuelas. Dance music became a form of urban folk music, and thus had an equal claim with the seguidillas and flamenco to being considered Spanish music. All of the reformers who composed these works did so in the name of strengthening the Spanish nation. Zarzuela had been built around popular music, and once popular tastes started to shift, zarzuela music did as well. If folk and popular music represent "the people," then zarzuela too represented the massive shifts in understanding how the Spanish people viewed themselves during this time period. Nationalism appears to be static in order to give the impression that the nation has always existed, yet it is a constantly shifting phenomenon. Zarzuela simply made such shifts audible and musical.

The process by which zarzuela became the main way in which Spaniards understood their national identity began with the revival of the genre in the 1850s. The zarzuelas of Arrieta, Barbieri, and other composers began to incorporate Spanish folk music and melodies, usually sung by the chorus. In these zarzuelas, the chorus often took on significant roles in the plot, which usually involved the leading characters fighting a corrupt government or decadent aristocracy. Already the roots of the division between what José Ortega y Gasset would later call "vital Spain"—the people—and "official Spain"—a sclerotic government—were taking hold in theater music. In the wake of the Revolutionary Sexenio of 1868–1874, "official Spain" wanted to promote political quietism, and zarzuela obliged by shifting away from the politically engaged plots of the 1850s and 1860s and focusing more on the age-old tropes of romantic love. But during that same period, the Spanish theater was developing a new system for staging plays: the *teatro por horas,* which featured one-act plays designed to appeal to a mass audience. This system would be at the core of zarzuela's development as a nationalist genre.

The teatro por horas encouraged the development of zarzuela's *género chico,* one-act plays that tended to be set in Madrid and focused on urban life. The género chico portrayed the new urban working classes onstage, and it also used the dance music that was featured in urban leisure activities to create a new type of folk music for the new type of Spaniard being portrayed on-stage. Thus zarzuela became one way that Spaniards could imagine a new national community in which cities were playing an ever-increasing role. At the same time, género chico maintained continuity with previous conceptions of Spanish identity by creating shows with historical settings. These works, which were primarily set during Spain's occupation by Napoleon between 1808 and 1813, continued the tradition that the Spanish people (or *pueblo*) were the true repository of the values and ideals that made up the Spanish nation. This liberal idea increasingly turned into jingoism in the late 1890s as tension between Spain and the United States led toward the disastrous War of 1898.

In the wake of Spain's defeat, zarzuela became the repository for a new idea: regenerationism, the need to reform Spanish government and Spanish society along more modern and European lines. Following the theatrical success of foreign hits like *The Merry Widow,* zarzuela embraced waltzes and other forms of central European dance music; in the process, such music became defined as Spanish. However, calls for reform also met with resistance. In the decade after 1900, género chico works set not in the city but in the countryside began to appear regularly on Spanish stages. These works developed the idea that a true and uncorrupt Spanish nation could only be found in the *patria chica* (roughly, "little homeland"), away from the modernizing influences of the major cities. This was not mere nostalgia. Spain's political elites could only maintain their control through a corrupt electoral system that relied on mechanisms of patronage and control in rural areas. Zarzuela had a multivalent nature that meant that it could encompass multiple visions of the nation at the same time.

This multivalent nature stemmed from zarzuela's position as one of the few forms of truly popular culture in fin-de-siècle Spain. But in the early years of the twentieth century, zarzuela took steps away from its mass audience. As part of the regenerationist ideal, zarzuela began to adopt musical tropes and ideas from opera. But zarzuela had originally forged its nationalist identity on the argument that opera was a foreign musical theater genre. Even the power of musical modernism could not overcome this essential betrayal of one of the central tropes of Spanish nationalism. Zarzuela's retreat from popularity continued in the 1920s as the dictatorship of General Miguel Primo de Rivera made it dangerous to be politically engaged. Since zarzuela's claims to represent the nation were frequently grounded in political critique, the genre turned toward apolitical adaptations of classic Spanish literature and nostalgic glimpses into Spanish history. This move turned the genre into toothless kitsch. The collapse of nationalism in Spanish zarzuela foreshadowed the ultimate collapse of Spanish nationalism that would eventually lead to the Spanish Civil War in 1936. Between 1880 and 1930, zarzuelas could mean many different things. Their one constant was that these works of musical theater show us how the Spanish theatergoing audience conceived of the shifts taking place in their national identity. In the absence of a strong nationalist project from the state, zarzuela shows us how the Spanish people forged their own sense of national identity at a time of momentous historical change.

Theatrical and Political Revolutions
in Nineteenth-Century Spain

Two revolutions occurred in Spain in 1868. The first will be familiar to everybody with even a cursory knowledge of Spanish history: the political revolution that dethroned Queen Isabella II and set off the chaotic interval known as the Revolutionary Sexenio. Between 1868 and 1874, Spain would experiment with various styles of government. Two attempts were made at enticing members of the European aristocracy into replacing the House of Bourbon as monarchs of Spain. The first attempt, which would have placed a member of the Hohenzollern family on the throne, inadvertently triggered the Franco-Prussian War of 1870, while the second enticed a member of the House of Savoy to reign in Spain as Amadeo I. He quickly abdicated, claiming that the Spanish were ungovernable. When that attempt at monarchy failed, the Spanish had a go at republican government that lasted eleven months. There were various caretaker military dictatorships, and after a politically exhausting six years, a final reversion to the Bourbon monarchy in 1874 in the person of the English-educated Alfonso XII, Isabella's son.

The second revolution of 1868 does not appear in books on the political history of Spain, as it took place not in the corridors of power but in the Café el Recreo in Madrid. It did not involve people shooting at each other or the fall of governments; instead, it involved people finding new ways to stage plays and profit from the theater. It was the birth of a unique theatrical system that flourished in Spain in the late nineteenth century. By the 1880s it would come to be known as the teatro por horas, the "theater by hours." The idea was simple. Rather than staging a full-length play, theaters would stage several one-act plays per evening. What made the idea revolutionary was the fact that a separate admission fee would be charged for each play, and the audience would come and go as they pleased without having to sit through the entire evening's bill, as is common when one-act plays are normally staged. Even with lowered prices—one could hardly charge full price for a forty-minute play—the potential profits for a theater were greater than if they had simply staged a full-length work.[1]

The birth of the teatro por horas was the birth of popular culture in Spain. Theaters would suddenly be responsible to a popular audience, and the survival of theatrical works would increasingly depend upon their box office appeal. One of the ways in which popular culture sought to maintain its hold on audiences and consumers was by presenting the world in a dramatic and spectacular fashion. Because of its need to attract audiences from across social boundaries, popular culture became one of the ways in which the rapidly shifting class structures of nineteenth-century Europe were portrayed and negotiated. And popular culture became one way in which people came to understand themselves, as material consumerism became a new marker of identity.[2] The revolution of the teatro por horas would take some time to fully change the culture of zarzuela, however. The major works of the 1870s and the 1880s consisted of what has become known as the *zarzuela grande,* full-length works with complex musical scores set against historical backdrops. But the zarzuela grande was running counter to the slowly developing ideas of popular culture: not only did it operate outside of the new system of the teatro por horas, there was an increasing disconnect between zarzuela and life as it was lived in Spain. Zarzuela, which had established itself as a nationalistic and essentially political genre in the 1850s, increasingly retreated from such stands after the Bourbon Restoration of the 1870s. It would be this withdrawal from the political that would allow the shorter works that developed under the teatro por horas to develop a new vision of Spanish nationalism.

Such musical nationalism would come from Spain's capital, Madrid. On the surface, this might seem odd, since the musical capital of Spain was arguably Barcelona. The Mediterranean port city, with its extensive rail and sea transport links, had much closer connections with musical life in France and Italy than did the relatively isolated capital. Barcelona's main opera house, the Teatre del Liceu, dates from 1838 while the Teatro Real in Madrid only opened in 1850. Barcelona was a center for choral and symphonic music, and boasts one of the most architecturally stunning concert halls in the world, the Palau de la Música Catalana—which opened in 1908 and remains one of the finest examples of Catalan *modernisme.* In any study of serious art music, Barcelona would have to take center stage. But outside of choral music, the musical life of Barcelona centered on Italian opera.[3] In contrast, Madrid was the center of Spain's popular theater, which featured works by Spanish authors and composers. Like the Broadway theaters of New York City, Madrid's theaters were the epicenter of popular theatrical production. Zarzuelas premiered there and would tour the country after their initial successes. Barcelona fostered the growth of art music and high musical culture in Spain, but the heart of the popular theater was in Madrid. And that popular culture was bound up in the success of the teatro por horas.

The teatro por horas system was an outgrowth of a rapidly burgeoning theatrical culture that had begun with the economic boom of the 1850s. The number of theaters operating in Madrid rose from ten in 1850 to sixteen in 1875 to twenty-six in 1900—more than doubling the city's theatrical capacity in a mere fifty years.[4] In addition to formal theaters there were the *salones-teatros,* where the shows had modest production values (only a few actors, and perhaps only a piano to provide music) and where the profits were augmented by serving as a café. Madrid's theatergoing audiences were also served by large multipurpose venues like the Circo Price, which, as the name implies, housed spectacles like circuses as well as theater and opera performances. The burgeoning European bourgeoisie was looking for places to spend its leisure time, and theaters were one of the many venues that catered to the newly emergent middle classes. But the bourgeois audience led to a subtle change in the subsidiary function of the theater. While the primary purpose of a theater was still to house the performances being staged, during the nineteenth century theaters lost their function as places where aristocrats went to see and be seen. Theaters evolved from being sites of sociability to being sites of economic activity.

The decline in theater as a nexus of sociability seems to have begun in Paris during the French Revolution and solidified with the increased bourgeois presence in theaters there during the 1830s.[5] The wider bourgeois audience caused basic changes to theater construction: the number of seats increased, foyers and staircases grew in size to accommodate more spectators, cafes were often built into theaters, and private rooms were built for subscribers to relax in before performances. Improvements in lighting technology, as theaters graduated from candlelight to gaslight to electric light, allowed house lights to be lowered during the performance. These changes in lighting shifted the audience's attention increasingly toward the stage, enhancing the theatrical illusions being portrayed there while turning one's attention away from other audience members.[6] All of these changes were designed to draw a paying audience into the theater. The teatro por horas was a particularly Spanish aspect of the increasing commercialization of the theater.[7]

The popularity of the teatro por horas was augmented by the introduction of another theatrical novelty to Spain. On 23 September 1868—the same week that General Juan Prim led the revolt that toppled Isabella II—the Teatro de Variedades premiered *El joven Telémaco* (Young Telemachus). This was the first play in the so-called *género bufo,* the Spanish version of what Jacques Offenbach had done at the Bouffes-Parisiens in Paris. Offenbach had used classical mythology to satirize the people and the mores of his day, and had succeeded by combining this satire with his tuneful music. The Spanish version aimed a little lower. The emphasis was not on the satire and the music, but on the physical charms of the chorus girls. Singing ability was not required as long as the prospective chorine was willing to appear half-undressed in "classical" gowns. (Most of the performers were untrained, and many were seamstresses put out of work by the rise of the sewing machine.)[8] The shrewd political humor of Paris was replaced by slapstick and nonsensical jokes. In any event, the *Bufos Madrileños* (the original company set up to produce not only *El joven Telémaco* but Spanish translations of other Offenbach's operettas) proved wildly popular to theatrical audiences looking for entertainment. Almost all of the pieces written in the género bufo style were short, one-act works, and they formed a vital part of the early repertory of the teatro por horas.

For the first two decades of its existence—from the late 1860s through the late 1880s—the teatro por horas was dominated by nonmusical works. While the development of the teatro por horas was based on economics and the desire to maximize profit, it is important to note that the system was predicated upon Spanish theatrical traditions that emphasized shorter plays. Beginning in the seventeenth century, Spanish theaters performed *entremeses*—short plays that were performed as curtain raisers or between acts of full-length plays (hence the name). Keeping the audience entertained was a necessity, as Spanish theaters catered to a specifically popular audience, much like the English theaters of the period and unlike the court theaters on the rest of the continent. The *entremes* was a crucial component of this system. By the eighteenth century the popular nature of Spanish theater meant that the most memorable plays being performed were shorter works. Arguably the central

Spanish playwright of the eighteenth century was Ramón de la Cruz, whose plays would have a vast influence on the nineteenth-century teatro por horas system.[9]

Ramón de la Cruz specialized in a genre of play known as the *sainete.* The sainete is a short play, always comic, usually set among the lower classes. Its dramatic emphasis is built on depicting the customs and habits of the population. Unlike full-length plays, these short works rarely have the time or space to develop a plot or fully drawn characterizations; thus the dramatic interest in the sainete falls to the depiction of local customs and the use of language—especially colloquialisms and slang. Cruz's works were always set in Madrid or its environs. Some of his contemporaries expanded the reach of the sainete to depict regional customs in other parts of Spain, particularly Andalucía. Notably, many of Cruz's sainetes also featured the use of music. Cruz was the undoubted master of the sainete, and after his death in 1794 the genre underwent a decline that lasted until the rise of the teatro por horas system.[10]

The sainete was one of the genres that would dominate the teatro por horas system. Its short format was obviously appealing for the economics of the system, as was the fact that sainetes could usually be performed by small casts with a limited number of sets and costumes. But the genre's emphasis on language and the depiction of everyday life also dovetailed quite nicely with the predilections of a new group of writers and journalists whom Nancy J. Membrez has dubbed the "*Madrid Cómico* Generation." [11] *Madrid Cómico* was a magazine that specialized in satirizing the news and society of the day, frequently in verse. Most of the writers who submitted their work to *Madrid Cómico* also wrote for the theater, and their ability to transmit a picture of society in verse was equally at home in the theater as it was on the pages of the satirical newspapers. The requirements of the sainete demanded writers with a keen ear for language, humorous jokes, and accurate depictions of everyday life. These were traits that the *Madrid Cómico* Generation had in abundance. The sainete was theater that was precisely keyed to the group of popular writers who made their home in Madrid during the 1860s and 1870s—figures such as Felipe Pérez y González, Javier de Burgos, and Ricardo de la Vega.

If the sainete was well situated to take part in the festive journalism of the late nineteenth century, it was also situated to take part in one of the more substantial European literary movements of the period: naturalism. On the surface, it doubtless seems a little odd to place one-act operettas into the same category as the work of Emile Zola and his compatriots. But in fact the sainete was built on much the same principles as naturalism. Both sought to portray daily life, especially daily life as lived by those classes that were not normally the subject of literature. Both rejected the tenets of high romanticism and its emphasis on style over substance. There is, of course, one major distinction between naturalism and what the sainete was doing. Naturalism sought to depict the often brutal aspect of lower-class life, usually with the goal of stimulating some sort of social change. The sainete tended to present a rather sanitized view of lower-class life; social change was hardly a part of its agenda.

Like the Fred Astaire–Ginger Rogers musicals during the Great Depression, the sainete and the teatro por horas could be accused of providing light entertainment while ignoring the social realities swirling outside the theater doors. The teatro por horas was born in a time of political and social upheaval. The 1868 Revolution was more than just the removal of a monarch from the throne. It was also the first eruption of mass politics in Spain. In order to help drive Isabella II from the throne, General Juan Prim had formed an alliance with Spain's Democratic Party—the most radical parliamentary faction of the 1850s and 1860s. The Democrats advocated a federalist republican form of government, pushing the party much further to the left than Spain's traditionally liberal Progressive Party. The Progressives had become disenchanted with Isabella during the 1860s due to her refusal to appoint liberal ministers, but the party remained staunchly monarchist. Prim's creation of the Progressive alliance with the Democrats in 1868 opened the way for the appearance of even more radical political groups, and the subsequent six years of upheaval politically mobilized an ever-increasing number of Spaniards.[12]

Although Prim allied himself with the Democrats, he had no intention of turning Spain into a republic. The subsequent search for a new monarch proved less than successful. Prim's first choice, Prince Leopold of Hohenzollern, triggered the Franco-Prussian War of 1870 when Napoleon III objected to having two Prussian monarchs on his borders. The crown eventually fell to Amadeo of Savoy, the younger son of King Victor Emmanuel of Italy. Amadeo was king for a little over two years and apparently hated every minute of it. That his main supporter, Prim, was assassinated the day the new king arrived in Spain seems to have influenced Amadeo's view that Spain was a cauldron of chaos and political discontent. He was not far wrong. The Democrats gained increased political power vis-à-vis the liberal Progressives during Amadeo's reign. This was especially true at the local level, where they won elections in twenty provincial capitals including Barcelona and Seville. Republicanism grew as a political force, and working-class leaders were galvanized by a Congress of the First Communist International in Barcelona in June 1870. Increasingly radical ministries came to power as the Progressives were unable to come up with a workable government, while representatives of Spain's major political parties encouraged Amadeo to abrogate the constitution. The reign of Amadeo I lasted less than three years, torpedoed by the unwillingness of Spain's political parties to operate within a constitutional framework.

After the collapse of the Savoy monarchy, the only governmental alternative was to establish a republic. It is indicative of the chaos that ensued that the First Republic had four different presidents during its short life. The attempt to run Spain as a republic worked no better than the attempt at constitutional monarchy had. The summer of 1873 saw several risings against the central government, many of which were organized by members of the First International. To complicate matters, Spain's ultramontane political faction, the Carlists, chose this same moment to launch a civil war against the Spanish government; the Second Carlist War would drag on into late 1874, deepening the country's chaos. By December 1873 the First Republic had collapsed and a military dictatorship took over. In December 1874 a group of young army officers staged another pronunciamiento against the generals in charge of running the war and the government. They backed a restoration of the Bourbon monarchy in the person of Isabella's son, Alfonso, who was then completing his education at Sandhurst Military Academy. As Alfonso XII, he returned to Spain in January 1875 while his mother remained in exile in Paris.

On the surface, it might seem as if the Bourbon Restoration of 1874 was a return to pre-1868 politics with a veneer of constitutionalism attached. Spain returned fairly smoothly to a parliamentary government with two competing parties under the control of a Bourbon monarch. There were, however, two major differences. In the 1850s the political parties had alternated in power only due to military intervention; the Restoration removed the military from the political process. This arrangement would work until 1923. The second major difference was that the primary architects of the Restoration political system, the politicians Antonio Cánovas del Castillo and Praxades Sagasta, were looking for ways to demobilize the people of Spain. The six-year interregnum had stirred up a hornet's nest: the idea that people other than the political elites could take part in politics. The Revolutionary Sexenio had also introduced radical political ideologies like republicanism and socialism to Spain—and had even made republicanism possible (if not practicable). When structuring the political system of the Bourbon Restoration, Cánovas and Sagasta had one overriding goal: political stability. The last thing that Spain's politicians wanted was a replay of 1868 or 1873.

The entire premise behind the Restoration government was to promote political quietism and avoid the consequences of popular political mobilization that had become evident during the Revolutionary Sexenio. Cánovas and Sagasta set up what became known as the *turno pacífico* ("peaceful turn"), a process by which the Conservative and Liberal Parties alternated in power on a regular basis—regardless of the demands of the electorate. Under the turno system, the king, in conjunction with the party leaders, would determine when elections were to be held and which party was to "win." The Ministry of the Interior would then determine how many seats each party was to hold. The beauty of this system—at least in the eyes of mainstream Spanish politicians—was that it excluded undesirable elements and political parties from the Cortes. Built around a classic two-party system like that in England, the turno excluded the new political forces that had so destabilized the country during the Revolutionary Sexenio. Newcomers to politics like the Republicans were excluded from the system thanks to the way that the government arranged for the desired results to be brought in from the voting urns.

When the elections were held, the results were mediated (or rigged, depending on how one views the situation) by figures known as caciques. Caciques were men of local prominence, usually large landowners, who controlled patronage of jobs and land throughout rural Spain. This meant they were in a position to arrange the votes in their areas so that results tallied with what was expected in Madrid. Caciques would distribute jobs and favors based on how the peasantry voted in elections. The caciques would also engage in tactics that discouraged men from voting—thus making it easier to stuff the voting urns; it was common practice to place polling stations in undesirable locations, such as pigsties or tuberculosis wards. Thanks to the manipulation of the system, what appeared to be a democratic political system on the surface actually engaged in political bossism and control that would have been envied at Tammany Hall.[13]

The shift toward greater political quietism was reflected in the zarzuelas that were written and performed in Spain between the 1860s and the 1880s. Although the teatro por horas had developed a new theatrical system, the majority of zarzuelas performed during these decades were the traditional full-length works of the zarzuela grande (a term that will distinguish them from the *género chico* discussed in the next chapter).[14] The zarzuela grande had been a politically engaged genre of music during the 1850s and 1860s, but due to the Restoration's push for political stability, zarzuela plots retreated from politics and came to focus on questions of romantic love instead. To get a sense of the political and aesthetic shifts that the Bourbon Restoration and the turno system engendered, it is best to pull apart the message of two works with music by Francisco Asenjo Barbieri, who was even then regarded as Spain's leading theater composer. The first work is *Pan y toros* (Bread and Bulls—an obvious play on the Roman idea of bread and circuses), an 1864 zarzuela with libretto by José Picón. The second is 1874's *El barberillo de Lavapiés* (The Little Barber of Lavapiés), with libretto by Luis Mariano de Larra. These two pieces are generally regarded as Barbieri's best works and have several features in common. Both have plots built around key events in eighteenth-century Spanish history, and each manages to work a romantic subplot into the historical drama. Each has important musical and dramatic roles for the chorus as a personification of the Spanish people. But the differences in the way these ingredients are used to construct each zarzuela are crucial to understanding the dramatic and political shifts that took place during the Sexenio and the Restoration.

Barbieri's *Pan y toros* is the musical work most exemplary of the prerevolutionary period, both musically and politically. The work is set in the early 1790s amid the intrigues surrounding Godoy, the Count of Aranda and favorite to the queen, and his attempts to end war with France. The plot centers around Captain Peñaranda, who is attempting to bring news of the army's wretched condition to the king. He is aided by several friends, including the artist Francisco de Goya and the Princess of Luzán—who have plans of their own to install Gaspar Melchor de Jovellanos as the king's chief minister. They are opposed by the mayor of Madrid, Quiñones, and his femme fatale sidekick Doña Pepita. Their goal is to keep the population of Madrid calm, and they do so by distracting the populace with bullfights, thus giving the zarzuela its title. History and politics are set at the forefront, for while there is a love plot of sorts as the princess falls for the captain, the most extended "love" scene in the piece is an attempted seduction of the captain by Pepita to keep him from reaching the king. The importance of history to the authors becomes most noticeable in the finale: the curtain does not fall on a final chorus celebrating the love of Peñaranda and the princess (as might be expected) but on a long, nonmusical speech from Jovellanos, who has just been named minister. Jovellanos speaks of the need to reform Spain's empire and asserts that the Spain subverted by the government's policy of *pan y toros* will act heroically when blood needs to be shed for the *patria*.

Pan y toros is written with a historical accuracy that other operettas never managed, in Spain or elsewhere. This comes not only from the identifiable historical characters who inhabit the work and play major roles in the plot (Goya, Quiñones, Jovellanos, and the three bullfighters Pepe-Hillo, Pedro Romero, and Costillares), but the care with which the historical backdrop is portrayed. Godoy's machinations and the problems with the army are not mere plot devices; they were major political problems in the 1790s. Picón and Barbieri even get the minor details right, such as the tone of reactionaries like Quiñones, who fulminates against Enlightenment thinkers such as Rousseau and Voltaire, whose followers "bathe in their poison."[15] Picón even manages to merge the love affair of Peñaranda and the princess into the historical fabric of the third act. She is planning to enter a convent because she thinks he has been murdered, but her followers manage to call the populace of Madrid to arms to prevent this, portraying the event as part of a plot by Quiñones and his minions—reflecting various political riots of the 1790s.

In contrast, *El barberillo de Lavapiés* relegates history to the background in the interest of furthering the love plot. *El barberillo* is set in Madrid during the reign of Charles III. Although never explicitly stated, it takes place sometime between 1766 and 1776, for the historical backdrop to the play is the attempt to oust one of the king's Italian ministers, Grimaldi, and replace him with the count of Floridablanca. For the purposes of the work, the historical Jerónimo Grimaldi has been conflated with another Italian minister, the marquis of Esquilache; the zarzuela also dramatizes a riot similar to the one that finally forced Charles to dismiss Esquilache.[16] This setting is the motor that drives the plot, which centers around the ultimately successful attempts of Lamparilla (the barber of the title) and his girlfriend Paloma to aid La Marquesita in toppling Grimaldi. Complications are provided by La Marquesita's love interest, Don Luis, who is an agent of Grimaldi's. In *Pan y toros,* it is the love interest that adds complications to the historical plot. In *El barberillo,* the situation is reversed and it is the historical situations that complicate the love story. The best example of this is the Act II finale: La Marquesita is threatened with arrest as a conspirator against the government. When Don Luis is unable to save her (the soldiers sent to arrest the conspirators insist on arresting everybody), Lamparilla proceeds to arrange for a riot that shatters the street lamps in the neighborhood and allows La Marquesita to escape under cover of darkness. Historically, this did happen—but the historical riot was in protest of one of Esquilache's edicts, and it led to the fall of the minister.

In part, the differences between the libretti of *Pan y toros* and *El barberillo* stem from their differing dramatic functions. *Pan y toros* is a serious drama. *El barberillo* is a comedy that verges on farce, and it is natural that the 1874 work should focus on the love plot. But this shift in dramatic emphasis takes on a very different tint when considered against the vicissitudes of the Spanish political situation in the late 1860s and early 1870s. *El barberillo de Lavapiés* premiered on 19 December 1874, a mere ten days before the military pronunciamiento that reinstated the Bourbon monarchy. By this point Spain had suffered from six years of political chaos: short-lived governments, military coups, a draining search for a new monarch, an experiment with republican government, and an outbreak of civil war in the Basque Country. *Pan y toros,* by contrast, was a product of much more politically secure times. Although there was mounting opposition to the Bourbon monarchy throughout the 1860s and constant interference in parliamentary government by both the crown and the military, the governmental system itself was relatively stable. Although Picón's libretto can be read as a criticism of the Isabeline monarchy—indeed, the zarzuela was temporarily banned in 1867 by the crown, seemingly for this very reason—it is very much a product of a period when public and intellectual interest in politics was quite active.[17]

By the time *El barberillo de Lavapiés* reached the stage, the political and intellectual climate was vastly different. The six-year interregnum of the Bourbon monarchy had exhausted the political elites of Spain. When Antonio Cánovas del Castillo undertook the restructuring of the Spanish monarchy and political system in 1874–1875, he did so with the primary aim of preserving the advances that liberalism had made while eliminating what he viewed as the new and unstable element in Spain's political system, popular mobilization.[18] The primary concern of the framers of the Restoration political system was not with political participation, but with political stability. *El barberillo* is a foretaste in operetta form of the developing turno pacífico. The historical and political events are relegated to the background; the emphasis is taken away from the political participation implied in the libretto and put on more mundane matters, like love. The politically active world of *Pan y toros* had come to life in 1868, and Spain's ruling elites had not been pleased with the outcome. The shift from the public to the private realms in the zarzuela plots reflected a desire to put the genie of mass political participation back into the bottle. The vision of the Spanish nation portrayed onstage correspondingly shifted from one in which the people were crucial political actors to one in which the people were barely present.

Key to understanding this shift is the contrast in the musical construction of each of Barbieri's works—specifically, how the chorus is used in each zarzuela. It is worth remembering that during the zarzuela revival of the 1850s, the chorus had come to represent the Spanish people. *Pan y toros* is packed with work for the chorus. Of the twelve numbers in the vocal score that involve sung text, eight involve work from the chorus. Of the remaining four numbers, two build the historical portion of the plot (the Abate's "Canción" in Act I and the Act II quartet), leaving only two numbers to advance the love story (the Act I duet and the princess's *romanza* in the second act). Musically, the choral and ensemble numbers gain emphasis as the work progresses: by Act III, the private sphere has virtually disappeared from the work.[19] *Pan y toros* makes heavy use of extended musical scenes that mix together solos, ensembles, and choruses to advance the plot. In lighter musical works, this technique is usually applied only in the act finales, when the plot must be advanced to a point where it can be halted for intermission or to bring down the final curtain. (Gilbert and Sullivan use this sort of construction consistently throughout the Savoy operas.) For the most part, when the chorus participates in extended musical scenes, it is in a supporting role. Admittedly, the amount of work the chorus does in *Pan y toros* can be overstated: with the exception of the Act I finale and the two choruses that open Act III, the choral work is intermixed in each number with various solos and ensembles. Although the chorus seems to be a large part of the musical construction of *Pan y toros,* it is not always the center of musical or dramatic interest when it is onstage. However, it is present.

This distinction is important to remember because the chorus is more frequently not present in *El barberillo de Lavapiés*. The chorus does turn up for the introduction and finale of each act—as is typical of operetta construction in general—but virtually disappears between these points. Paloma's famous entrance song has some choral support, "Como nací en la calle" (How I Was Born in the Street), but this is the only time in which the chorus sings between the opening and conclusion of an act in the work. Technically, the chorus participates in the middle of an act at one other point: No. 9, the seguidillas manchegas in the second act. However, as this leads directly without pause—both musically and dramatically—into what the score indicates is the "Final del Acto II" (No. 10 in the vocal score), it can legitimately be considered a part of the Act II finale.[20] The participation of the chorus is severely reduced in both scope and musical content compared to *Pan y toros*. Again, the decreased use of the chorus has the effect of reducing the importance of historical events vis-à-vis the love story, since the chorus plays the role of the Spanish people. A zarzuela that gives emphasis to the chorus by definition gives emphasis to the actions of a broad section of the population. It is a better vehicle for historical drama than is a zarzuela that gives its emphasis to the soloists, which is more suited to intimate stories than to the broad brushstrokes of the historical panorama.

While *Pan y toros* and *El barberillo de Lavapiés* provide audible evidence of zarzuela's depoliticization—a shift away from political engagement toward the more standard operetta concerns of romantic entanglements—they are hardly unique. The zarzuelas of the 1850s and 1860s are explicit in their political engagement, something that was built into the revival of the genre. While most of the libretti were not as directly politically charged as Barbieri's major works, they often dealt with a situation that was even more incendiary: the corruption of the aristocracy and the rising power of the nonaristocratic classes. The zarzuela that sparked the 1850s revival of the genre, *Jugar con fuego* (Playing with Fire), although essentially a plagiarized version of a French opéra comique, deals at its core with the corruption of the aristocracy. For having the temerity to fall in love with an aristocrat, the romantic hero Félix is committed to an insane asylum against his will. This was also the first time that Barbieri used Spanish dance music (in this case a popular song, "Habas verdes") to characterize the chorus as the Spanish people—who are only present as the inhabitants of the asylum.

The theme of conflict between the aristocracy and the Spanish people occurs in most of the major zarzuelas of the 1850s and 1860s. The problem of intermarriage pops up again in Cristóbal Oudrid's *El Postillón de la Rioja* of 1856, in which the baroness of Olmo finds herself falling in love with a lowly postilion. Although she discovers after their marriage that the postilion is none other than her intended fiancé the marquis of Alvardo, the couple is forced to flee to France because of his previous involvement in a duel. These plots of aristocratic disguise and identity reach their dizzying pinnacle in Joaquín Gaztambide's *Catalina,* first staged in 1854, where the plot is built around the love of barmaid Catalina for shipbuilder Miguel—who happens to be Czar Peter the Great of Russia in disguise. Catalina eventually becomes the czar's bride after she goes undercover as a Cossack recruit and uncovers a plot by Colonel Ivan to aid a Swedish invasion of Russia that will dethrone Peter. Although the plots of these zarzuelas inevitably end with both partners discovering or acquiring noble status, the sheer number of such plots in the 1850s and 1860s is a reflection of the increasing tension between the Spanish bourgeoisie and the Spanish elite, which controlled the political system.

After the Bourbon Restoration of 1874, the political overtones of zarzuela plots evaporated. Zarzuelas dispensed with history and politics almost entirely to focus on the traditionally private concern with romantic love that is the hallmark of musical theater, thanks to the need for political demobilization in the wake of the Bourbon Restoration. This was the logical outcome of the shift in the importance of the role of the chorus between *Pan y toros* and *El barberillo de Lavapiés.* The chorus ceases to function as the Spanish people completely, and their political role becomes a strictly musical one; no longer could the chorus be considered equal to the protagonists of the plot or even function as the protagonists. The dramatic focus of the zarzuela turned toward the individual, and as individuals became the protagonists of the zarzuela plots, the political concerns of the works declined. In the place of political drama, librettists provided exotic locations and stunning coups de théâtre to attract theatergoers.

One classic example of a demobilized zarzuela during the Bourbon Restoration is *El anillo de hierro* (The Iron Ring), with music by Miguel Marqués. The plot is a melodramatic farrago reminiscent of the zarzuelas of the 1850s and 1860s: orphaned fisherman Rodolfo loves Margarita, the daughter of the local lord, who is also being pursued by Rutilio, the baron of San Marcial (who is not above blackmailing her father for her hand in matrimony). In the end, naturally, Rodolfo turns out to be the son of an aristocrat who was murdered at sea by his servant—Rutilio. Just as naturally, the iron ring Rodolfo wears on his finger proves that he was betrothed to Margarita at birth. Librettist Marcos Zapato termed the work a "fable," although exactly what sort of lesson he was trying to teach is unclear. The closest the work ever gets to deep meaning is Margarita's realization that "True nobility / is written by God on the soul!"[21] In the classic tradition, such nobility of the soul only comes to those who were of noble blood to begin with—and one might also be forgiven for thinking that Rodolfo shows a little less than true nobility when he tries to murder Margarita late in the third act for betrothing herself to Rutilio in order to stop the baron from blackmailing her father.

The work was given a rapturous reception upon its premiere at the Teatro de la Zarzuela on 7 November 1878. Whatever the faults of the libretto, Zapato's writing was well received: the critic for *La Correspondencia de España* called the verses "magnificent" and noted that the audience "did not tire of applauding, frequently interrupting the performance."[22] (It also cannot be denied that no matter how hackneyed the plot, many of the stage pictures are dramatically effective—the use of lightning to reveal Rodolfo's knife during his attempted murder of Margarita, for example.) However, most of the critics turned their attention to Marqués's music. Given the composer's stature in Spanish musical circles, this is perhaps not surprising. Marqués was considered the leading Spanish symphonist of his day and had been one of the few composers of his generation to have studied abroad in Paris, where he befriended Hector Berlioz.[23]

Marqués's score is sophisticated and inventive. What most of the critics seemed to note is that the work reflected his predilection for symphonic composition. The critic for the *Crónica de la Música* saved his highest praise for the "Sinfonía" that opens the work and noted a "certain vacillation in the writing for the voices"—although he was more than willing to qualify this by noting that the work had made great strides forward compared to Marqués's previous attempts at vocal writing. In the same vein, *La Correspondencia de España* noted that the pieces receiving the most applause and that had to be repeated were the preludes to the first and third acts.[24] What the critics did not notice was the fact that Marqués does not indulge in traditionally Spanish dance or folk music. The only popular musical form Marqués uses is the barcarolle, which is traditionally associated with seafaring and sea songs, appropriate for a seaside drama. The score returns to this form again and again, helping to portray the coastal setting through the music. The barcarolle is the basis for the opening chorus, the tenor's music in the first act duet, and the opening of the second act finale.[25] Abandoning Spanish folk music is a potent example of the way in which zarzuela went out of its way to avoid questions of political mobilization by dropping any potential musical references to the Spanish people.

The melodrama of *El anillo de hierro* occurs in other zarzuelas like Ruperto Chapí's *La tempestad* (The Storm), which also places a premium on stunning theatrical effects. This time the love between fisherman Roberto and orphan Ángela is blocked by her guardian, Simón—until a wealthy returnee from the Indies, Beltrán, promises Roberto a well-paying position. At this point Simón recognizes Beltrán as the man accused some twenty years previously of murdering Ángela's father. All ends happily, however, when Simón has a nervous breakdown during the titular storm and confesses to the murder. Miguel Ramos Carrión's libretto has one fairly deft psychological touch: the link between Simón's guilt and stormy weather, which makes the climax seem less like the work of a plot-driven deus ex machina than it otherwise might. The fact that the opening night reviews were not all favorable did not stop audiences from embracing the work. The review in the *Crónica de la Música* felt that the libretto did not live up to the author's potential, even as it noted the ovation the author received on opening night.[26] *La tempestad* was popular enough that it served as the opening work of the season at the Teatro de la Zarzuela several times during the 1880s and 1890s.[27]

Both *El anillo de hierro* and *La tempestad* have certain dramatic devices in common. Both are situated in non-Spanish locales (Norway and Brittany, respectively), and both are built upon melodramatic plots. In neither work is there any reason the setting should not be Spanish—but neither is there any reason the setting *should* specifically be Spanish. In *El anillo,* the secondary comic couple is at least Iberian (he from Cádiz, she from Portugal); in *La tempestad,* there is no definitively Spanish character (although audiences might have associated Beltrán, newly arrived from America with great wealth, as an *indiano* immigrant).[28] The melodrama of each work is pronounced. Perhaps to distract attention from the dog-eared plots, each work has a stunning dramatic scene at the climax. *La tempestad* features a musical pantomime depicting Simón's crime and subsequent feelings of guilt, while *El anillo* has a mysterious, all-knowing hermit and its own attempted murder in the middle of a thunderstorm. The melodramatic plot constructions of these two works remove both from the established conventions of the 1850s and 1860s. Instead of turning on political events, the worlds that Zapato and Ramos Carrión created are intensely private, revolving around questions of parentage and identity rather than the public questions of liberty and political freedom that pervade *Pan y toros* or *El barberillo de Lavapiés*. Depoliticization may explain why the authors chose to remove the settings of these zarzuelas from Spain. By eliminating any reference to Spain, they were able to avoid the fraught question of popular politics that had arisen in the 1860s and that Cánovas del Castillo was so eagerly trying to put to rest under the Restoration.

Even when authors turned to Spanish history during the Restoration, the results were more melodramatic than political, as Chapí and Ramos Carrión proved when they returned to the Teatro de la Zarzuela five years later with *La bruja* (The Witch). In comparison with *El anillo de hierro* and *La tempestad, La bruja* almost seems realistic—providing one overlooks the main plot device, that of a relatively benign witch being transformed into a beautiful young woman through the power of love. The libretto is set in the closing years of the reign of King Carlos II, popularly known as "Carlos el hechizado" or "Charles the Bewitched." In the time frame of the libretto, sorcery and witchcraft were still common beliefs, and the libretto gains most of its dramatic mileage from this fact. Indeed, when Carlos's death is announced at the final curtain, it is explicitly linked with the death of popular superstition and the dawn of the modern, rationalist age: "Along with the bewitched king, there will also disappear from Spain superstition and fanaticism . . . the recluse that occupies this cell will be the last witch."[29] Within the context of the story this shift is used to remove Blanca, the innocent and beautiful incarnation of the title character, from the danger of the Inquisition.

The libretto for *La bruja* follows the conventions of pre-1868 zarzuelas. The work is set in Spain—here the countryside of Navarre—with actual historical events like the death of Carlos providing the historical backdrop. However, unlike *Pan y toros* or *El barberillo de Lavapiés*, the historical background is not central to the action of the work. Removing the historical portions of the book would not cause the plot to fall apart, so long as the character of Leonello has a reason to remove himself from the scene for the extended period of time between Acts I and II, thus proving his love for Blanca. The only event with political overtones in the plot is the arrest of Blanca by the Inquisition in the Act II finale, which seems to be predicated on the idea that it is she who is bewitching Carlos II. However, this motive is only alluded to briefly, in dialogue between Tomillo and the villagers early in the second act. When the Inquisitor announces her arrest, he accuses her only of "magical spells, / enchantments and witchcraft," not political treason.[30] The historical and political concerns of the plot have been superseded by melodrama.

Like the libretto, Chapí's score also adopts the stylistic model of older zarzuelas: the multipart musical numbers, extensive use of the chorus, and concertante finales are all present. Chapí also seems to revert to the use of popular idioms. The heavy presence of military forces in the libretto calls for a *pasacalle* and a rataplan (nos. 8A and 16 in the vocal score). As for folk music, a jota is the basis for the first-act finale, and the *zortziko*—a Basque folk dance—is a prominent motif throughout the second act (nos. 8C and 12A in the vocal score).[31] In addition, the character of Rosalía is given a mock-Moorish number in the opening sequence, the "Romanza morisca," which at least one critic found to have "a genuine Spanish tint."[32] This is a return to the Barbieri model, but it completes the political demobilization of the chorus that was evident in *El barberillo de Lavapiés.* Each of these self-consciously "Spanish" numbers is essentially diversionary. While they help establish the setting and thus provide local color, they do not establish the chorus as a politically active unit. It is worth noting the treatment of the second-act zortziko in this respect. The village celebration that the music embodies breaks off abruptly as the Inquisitor enters—the private concerns of the people give way to the political authority represented by the Church. The political demobilization of the zarzuela was complete.

An often-overlooked fact about European operetta in the nineteenth century is how politicized it was. Today, the word *operetta* conjures up images of Jeanette MacDonald and Nelson Eddy warbling away about the sweet mystery of life against a palpably artificial-looking scenic backdrop. Theatrical audiences during the nineteenth century would not have had a similar conception. The operettas of Jacques Offenbach, who invented the genre, regularly twitted the excesses of Second Empire France; *Orpheus in the Underworld* even goes so far as to introduce Public Opinion as a character in a thinly veiled satire on the licentious tendencies of Emperor Napoleon III. The Savoy Operas of Gilbert and Sullivan regularly mocked the British aristocracy: *Iolanthe* portrays the British Parliament as a sclerotic institution that can only be reformed under the influence of a magical fairy who can compel the MPs to do his bidding. Spanish audiences—especially the bourgeois ones that made up the bulk of the audience for zarzuela—also had a political experience when they attended musical theater performances in the mid-nineteenth century.

But in Spain, the problem was that the tradition of politically engaged musical theater—and specifically, a vision of the theater based in criticism of the elites and the idea that the Spanish people were protagonists of the nation's history—was anathema to the Restoration government. England's developing democratic traditions could tolerate the idea of government critique, and Gilbert's barbs were offset by patriotic songs that he and Sullivan incorporated into their scores. In France Offenbach's musical theater was embraced by the bourgeoisie as an example of their growing sociopolitical power.[33] But in Spain, politicians like Antonio Cánovas del Castillo and Praxades Sagasta were trying to create a world in which the elites still controlled the country and the people would be prevented from intervening in politics as they had done during the Revolutionary Sexenio of 1868–1874. The atmosphere of political quietism promoted the theatrical tendency toward Romantic operettas; coups de théâtre replaced coups d'état on the Spanish stage. But works like *El anillo de hierro* or *La bruja* were coming to seem old-fashioned to Spaniards not only because they refused to engage with the political tradition of the Spanish theater. As full-length works they did not fit with the emerging teatro por horas economy.

The 1870s and 1880s were a period of transition for musical theater in Spain. The teatro por horas was increasingly the center of Spain's theatrical economy. During the 1870s very few of the one-act works of the teatro por horas were musical. This began to change during the 1880s when even Barbieri, the bastion of traditional zarzuela, dabbled in shorter musical works. As composers embraced the idea of shorter musical works, the teatro por horas would blossom and come to dominate theatrical economics in Madrid and then in the rest of the country. And with these shorter musical works, zarzuela would once again embrace the idea that Spanish musical theater should represent the Spanish people. But just as the teatro por horas was a very modern form of theatrical economics, zarzuela would come to represent a very modern form of the Spanish people. No longer would musical theater works be set solely during the eighteenth century, and no longer would the Spanish people be charming villagers who sang traditional folk music. Zarzuela would embrace the fact that Spain was modernizing, and that its people were increasingly to be found in the melting pots of Spain's major cities. The genre would embrace the fact that these new urban denizens had wider musical tastes than just the seguidilla or the jota. Zarzuela was on the verge of learning how to articulate a new vision of what it meant to be Spanish—a vision that the elite politicians of the Bourbon Restoration were not willing to acknowledge.

2

Urban Life on the Spanish Musical Stage

The introduction of music to the teatro por horas happened almost by accident. The playwright Ricardo de la Vega (son of Ventura de la Vega, whose libretto for *Jugar con fuego* had been instrumental in the rebirth of zarzuela in the 1850s) had written a short play called *La camisa de la Lola* (Lola's Shirt) to be played as a curtain-raiser. The original impresario turned down the work, citing the racy title. Vega did some rewrites, turning the play into *La canción de la Lola* (Lola's Song). But in the meantime the impresario had decamped to Latin America, and Vega couldn't interest another producer thanks to the glut of one-act plays on the market. Vega then had the inspired idea of turning to an up-and-coming composer by the name of Federico Chueca to interpolate musical numbers into *La canción de la Lola*. The novelty of a play with "graceful music" created a smashing success in the late spring of 1880.[1]

But Vega's script for *La canción de la Lola* was not his father's zarzuela. Gone were the historical figures, the high melodrama, the fixations on the difficulties of romantic love. Instead, the cast of characters includes the local blacksmith and a fireman. We are introduced to the main character not in the midst of a romantic dilemma, but as she is being berated by one of her neighbors for having gone two years without washing her face or hands.[2] Nor did the work sound like the zarzuelas that had come before it. Gone were the quasi-operatic arias and the high-flown duets. Instead the musical numbers were "of the best that we know in the popular genre": a polka, a waltz, and other up-tempo numbers fill the score—all the numbers have tempo designations of either allegro or allegretto.[3] Chueca's musical inspiration was not opera, nor was it even traditional Spanish folk music; it was the cafés and dance halls of Madrid with their music straight from Central Europe. This combination of dance music and lighthearted plots was soon to be acknowledged as part of the zarzuela heritage by its new nomenclature. Vega and Chueca had reduced the extravagance of the zarzuela: hence, what they had invented became known as the género chico, or the "little genre" of zarzuela. (Technically, the género chico included both musical and nonmusical works, but for the purposes of this book I am using the term to refer to género chico zarzuelas only.)

The género chico flourished on Spanish stages from approximately 1880 until about 1910, and would continue to crop up until the Spanish Civil War killed off the production of new zarzuelas entirely. The dominance of the género chico at the turn of the century meant that Spanish musical theater looked like nothing else in Europe at the time. European operettas were dominated by full-length works—either the satirical jabs of Jacques Offenbach and Gilbert and Sullivan, or Franz Léhar's romantic flights of fancy. In contrast, Spanish theaters were dominated by one-act musical playlets that rarely had time to develop deep characterization or much of a plot. The subject matter of some of these shorter works was also radically different from that of their European counterparts. A significant number of género chico zarzuelas had contemporary urban settings. Set among Madrid's working classes, these were operettas with what would be described today as having a hip, contemporary feel. This alone makes them different from other European operettas of the period: almost none shared the modern urban setting of the género chico. Spanish music theater was unique in this regard. Only France portrayed urban life on the music stage to a similar extent, but in the opera house rather than in popular theaters.[4]

The urban setting of many of these género chico works is crucial to understanding the role of zarzuela in the dissemination of Spanish nationalism. During the latter half of the nineteenth century, Spain was beginning the slow and painful process of transforming from a rural, agricultural society to an urban, industrial one. Although the majority of Spain's population would remain rural until late in the twentieth century, the dynamics of urbanization were rapidly changing the country—and changing the meaning of what it meant to be Spanish. Musically, this would mean significant changes as well. "Spanish" music in an urban setting would not be the traditional folk styles that Barbieri had used in the 1850s and 1860s to demarcate the Spanish people. The music that defined urban life tended to come from central Europe: waltzes and polkas dominated the aural world of urban Spain, and they came to dominate the aural world of the Spanish stage as well. Not only did this dance music depict what would have been heard daily in Spanish cities, its simplicity helped to make zarzuela popular and more appealing to a mass audience. The género chico eliminated the operatic romanzas and elaborate concertante numbers that had populated the scores of earlier zarzuelas like *Pan y toros* and *El anillo de hierro*. The género chico relied primarily on actors who sing (or at least make a pretense thereof). The reason for this can be found in which part of a lyric theater work—the words or the music—provides the main dramatic impetus. In opera, it is the music that provides most of the dramatic action, and the casting requires singers who can make the most of the score. In operetta, the plot is generally carried forward in the spoken dialogue portions of the libretto. Thus, the casting is concerned with finding actors who can sing and who will not be hampered by the dialogue.

As a necessary result of the preference for actors over trained singers, the music of the género chico became simpler than that of its predecessors. The music often has a limited vocal range; the use of "through-composed" musical numbers declines drastically in favor of strophic songs in which the music is repeated (often with different lyrics), making it easier to memorize and perform. This is partially the result of an increase in the use of popular musical material. Traditionally, popular folk and dance forms had been restricted to the chorus, but with the género chico, the majority of the musical numbers became based in dance rhythms. The orchestral underpinnings of género chico music change as well. There is a greater tendency for the vocal line to be doubled in the orchestra, which again makes matters easier for the singers. The size of the orchestra also decreases somewhat, usually by reducing the number of string players, which has the consequence of making the winds and percussion more important. All of these were features of European operetta music in general, and Spain was not the only nation whose lyric theater was beginning to sound different in the later nineteenth century.[5]

Spain's musical theater began to sound different because the country was changing. Zarzuela reflected one of the most crucial changes to take place in Spanish identity: urbanization. Although Spain was still not an urbanized society like England, France, or Germany in the later nineteenth century, it was taking on the shape of one. By the end of the nineteenth century, Spain had no fewer than six cities with populations of over 100,000: Madrid, Barcelona, Valencia, Seville, Málaga, and Murcia. In the last twenty-five years of the century, the population of Madrid grew by 35 percent, and this was mild compared to the rates of growth for cities whose identity was more firmly rooted in industry like Bilbao (154 percent) or Barcelona (114 percent).[6] Still, Madrid was the most populous city in Spain, and like the industrial cities, by the end of the century nearly half of its citizens would not have actually been born in the city itself. As the city grew, so did the number of industrial workers, which expanded from 11,000 in 1850 to over 68,000 in 1905 (in a city with a population of approximately 500,000).[7] The presence of industry and industrial workers was becoming more and more obvious in all major Spanish cities under the Restoration.

In addition to rapid growth, the very shape of Spanish cities was changing. The late nineteenth century saw a dramatic expansion in the physical size of Madrid with the incorporation of two new neighborhoods, Argüelles to the north of the city center and Salamanca to the east. The upper classes were attracted to these new, modern neighborhoods; their subsequent relocation consolidated the lower middle class and the working classes in the older neighborhoods of southern Madrid, especially Lavapiés and the areas between the Puerta del Sol and the Puerta de Toledo. (Other major Spanish cities carried out similar urban reforms, most notably Barcelona.) This class consolidation reflected the political power of the Restoration. Those in the new neighborhoods held the political power, while the marginalized working classes were increasingly concentrated in the city center. It may be this, as much as anything, that helped to implement a proletarian consciousness and laid the preconditions for mass political mobilization in Spain.[8] Given these drastic political changes to the Spanish city, musical theater works that purported to portray Spanish national identity would have to find some new way to bridge the increasing gap between the bourgeoisie and the working classes, to show that they were part of the same nation.

This idea was central to the work that established the género chico as a force to be reckoned with: *La Gran Vía* (The Grand Boulevard), which was subtitled a "Comic-Lyric, Fantastic, Street-Smart Madrid Revue in One Act." The loose review structure of the work was successful at both celebrating Spain's growing urban culture and satirizing the problems that confronted the new urban nation. The opening number featured the female chorus singing a lively patter-style song establishing the urban milieu of the piece:

We are the streets, we are the plazas
and the alleyways of Madrid
because of a magical recourse
we are congregating here today.[9]

The chorines were dressed as the various streets they represented or as an ironic commentary on those names. Thus the Calle de la Primavera—Spring Street—wore a garland of flowers, the Calle del Tesoro—Treasure Street—was dressed as a beggar, and so on, although the main point of the costumes seems to have been the very short skirts that emphasized the chorines' legs, if the sketch in the 10 July 1886 edition of *Madrid Cómico* is any indication. The point of their song is to welcome La Gran Vía to the city. And thus the authors announced the improbable hook of their revue: urban reform. How many other musical theater works list Gaslight and Petroleum in the cast of characters?

The real Gran Vía was an idea whose birth arose from a confluence of urban developments in nineteenth-century Madrid. During the latter half of the century the urban bourgeoisie—as in most other larger European cities—began to move out of the congested historic center of the city and into newly constructed residential neighborhoods. In these new neighborhoods the buildings were larger, the streets wider and rationalized (laid out in a grid plan, rather than the haphazard jumble of central Madrid), and more trees and parks refreshed the inhabitants. The historic core of the city became the location of commercial establishments and government offices. This core needed to be connected with the outer neighborhoods to facilitate traffic, and reformers proposed building new boulevards through central Madrid in the style pioneered by Baron Haussmann in his reconstruction of central Paris. The new boulevards would improve both traffic flow and public health by ridding the city of its narrow and pestilential streets. The plan approved in January of 1886 consisted of one main avenue that would run between Argüelles and Salamanca through the north-central part of Madrid; due to cost overruns, construction only commenced in 1910. The first leg of the Gran Vía was opened to traffic in 1917, although construction ultimately dragged on into the 1950s.[10] The only thing that endured from the 1886 plan was *La Gran Vía.*

While the opening number of the revue and its closing tableau suggest a celebration of urban progress (the curtain falls on a celebration held on an idealized Gran Vía with statues honoring such abstractions as Liberty, Science, Justice, Work, and Virtue in the foreground), the majority of the songs and sketches satirize Madrid society even as they celebrate the promise of urban life and urban living. The most famous musical number from *La Gran Vía* demonstrates how the authors manage to combine social satire with a depiction of urban life. The song is a tango sung by the Menegilda, a serving girl:

> Poor girl
> who has to serve!
> You would be better off
> if you were dying.[11]

The song is an unvarnished picture of what life was like for many lower-class serving girls, a story of the drudgery of low-paid domestic labor such as ironing and sewing. Eventually she is thrown out of her post without warning and finds herself being propositioned by a gentleman from one of the large cafés. As with the main plot of *La verbena de la paloma,* if the Menegilda's story were in a realistic novel, it could only end tragically. But the tango ends with an ironic twist: she is employed by an elderly gentleman and comes to be his housekeeper, ruling the roost.

If the authors have sympathy for the serving maid, they proceed to satirize her former employer, a woman ironically named Doña Virtudes (Mrs. Virtue), who sings a complaint—set to the exact same tango—about how difficult it is to have a servant working for you:

> Poor mistresses
> who have to suffer
> from these wily tricks
> of their serving maids.

She goes on to complain about her servant's bad manners, idleness, and propensity to theft:

> I am missing two earrings
> of superior jet,

and finally, of all things,
I am missing my husband, which is the worst of all.[12]

The bourgeoisie as a whole comes in for plenty of ridicule in *La Gran Vía*. Another of the sketches features three ladies who boast about their vacation plans while leaving out key qualifying phrases. Thus one appears about to swan off to the beach resort of San Sebastián, neglecting to mention she's traveling to San Sebastián de Alcobendas, a very landlocked village just to the north of Madrid—in other words, she's going nowhere.[13] In fact, this ambivalent attitude of satirizing those who were buying at the box office can only be explained by the insistent populism of the género chico. As a nationalist genre, the género chico's sympathies were with the servants and not their masters. The Menegilda may be a thief and a home wrecker, but her slow and mournful tango is designed to get sympathy from the audience.

The satire of *La Gran Vía* was a reflection of the fact that urbanization was changing the class structure in nineteenth-century Spain. The advent of the teatro por horas system and the subsequent drop in ticket prices allowed the working class to attend theatrical performances for the first time. The cafés-cantante where the teatro por horas had begun would only charge the price of the food or drink consumed; the performance itself was free. By the 1880s most theaters had a working-class presence in their audience; how many members of the working class varied by the location of the theater. There was a distinction between theaters that catered primarily to the aristocracy and bourgeoisie—the Teatro Real, the Teatro de la Zarzuela, the Teatro Apolo; those that catered to a primarily working-class audience—the Teatro Novedades, the Teatro Barbieri; and those that managed a mixed audience—the Teatro Variedades, the Teatro Calderón.[14] This partially reflects the geographic location of the theaters. The Zarzuela and the Apolo were located in central Madrid, the traditional entertainment district of the city. The Teatros Novedades and Barbieri were located south of the Puerta del Sol, the traditional working-class neighborhood. There was a distinct sense in the press that the teatro por horas and the género chico were catering to the working-class elements in the audience due to the geographic locations of the theaters that performed género chico works.[15]

This appeal to a popular audience would certainly explain another of

Chueca's hits, *El año pasado por agua* (The Past Year Underwater), an 1889 review built around news stories of the day, such as the heavy summer rains and flooding that gave the work its title. One sketch involves a young married couple who reside in a working-class district of Madrid. The humor in the sketch comes from the description of their living conditions in a small back room on the fifth floor of their building. The god Neptune (who has left his fountain in the ritzy Paseo del Prado) asks incredulously if there is an elevator. The man replies in the negative, but does mention a mezzanine—putting them on the sixth floor. Neptune then asks how on earth visitors can knock at the street door and make themselves known. The reply is, "It's really quite simple: three knocks and a ring, a ring and three knocks, four separate knocks, three kicks, a scream, and a pistol shot," to which a figure portraying The Year 1889 adds unbelievingly, "and the trumpet of the Day of Judgment."[16] The implication is that Madrid's working class is stuck in a system of poverty that will take until the end times to get out of. But by placing the working classes and their misery onto the stage, zarzuela composers and librettists were providing a way for theatrical audiences to envision these groups as part of a new nation. Urban reforms might separate the working and the upper classes in ways that they would not have been separated in rural villages, but zarzuela was the tool for integrating social classes together.

This was important as the upper classes remained the core theatrical audience, and it was to them that theaters catered. Virtually all of the premieres of género chico works by important composers and authors—those most likely to be widely played and become established as part of the general repertory—took place in the establishments frequented by the bourgeoisie, such as the Teatros Apolo, Zarzuela, and Eslava. Furthermore, it was the middle and upper classes that had both the leisure time and disposable income to make theatergoing a regular habit. Finally, the structure of the teatro por horas evolved to favor the habits of the bourgeoisie. In most formal theaters, there were four shows per evening: the curtain times were usually 8:30 or 8:45, 9:30, 10:30, and 11:30 or 11:45. The fourth section was usually reserved for the most popular recent hits, which starred the best-known actors of the day. Earlier shows were where older and less popular works received their airings, although smash hits early in their runs might also play during the first section as a way of boosting attendance. Thus the most popular shows were easily accessible to the upper classes, whose occupations did not require them to be up and about early in the morning. This became especially true at the famed fourth session of the Teatro Apolo. By the 1890s this had become the place to see and be seen for those in high society, and frequently the rites of society in the lobby delayed the curtain time until after midnight.[17]

Zarzuela composers, who came almost exclusively from bourgeois backgrounds, would be the bridge between the working classes portrayed on-stage and their upper-class audiences. The few composers who came from the lower classes (Tomás Bretón, who originally was an apprentice to a shoe-maker, is the best example) very quickly assimilated to the bourgeois milieu of the theater. The reason for this class homogeneity is not hard to explain. Most composers and librettists needed at least a modicum of education before they could succeed in the theatrical world, and it was the middle classes that had the money to educate their children. The aristocracy had this money too, but their children were prepared for careers in the service of the state— diplomacy or leadership in the armed forces. Many of the composers of the género chico were originally intended for professional careers in fields other than music, usually engineering, medicine, or law, and almost all the librettists had journalism experience at some point or another. The fledgling Spanish bourgeoisie were in the best position to synthesize the various class experiences onstage.

Nationalism aims to achieve universality within a country, so how did bourgeois composers create music that would bridge the tastes of the bourgeoisie and the working class? Through dance music. Dancing was at the core of Madrid's leisure life in the later nineteenth century. Even more so than theater, dancing was a leisure-time activity that appealed across classes and social groups. Most dance venues catered to very specific social groups—aristocratic balls for the elite, dance halls for the lower classes—but there were venues for everybody to dance in. Dance halls and salons were the common venues for leisure-time dancing, and these forums imported the latest and most up-to-date dances from across Europe to attract their patrons, including polkas, mazurkas, schottisches, and waltzes. Dancing was also the main attraction at Madrid's traditional festivals, the *verbenas.* Here, social classes would inter-mingle in the open-air evening dances that traditionally climaxed the festivities, where the atmosphere was more permissive than in the socially segregated dance halls and salons.[18] Urban dance music was what united Spain's increasingly divided social classes, and dance music could therefore represent the Spanish people. Zarzuela already did this: Barbieri had used folk dance forms like the seguidillas to characterize the chorus and set it apart as a representation of the Spanish people, as discussed in Chapter 1. Género chico zarzuelas would simply use different types of dance music to portray this new urban world. While the seguidilla and the jota would never disappear completely, they increasingly shared time with the strains of waltzes, polkas, and other popular dances of the day.

The importance of dances to Madrid's leisure and social life can be measured by how often dances turn up as settings and plot devices in género chico works. In both *La verbena de la paloma* and *La Revoltosa*, a dance is the crucial scene in which the main dramatic conflict takes place and the lovers finally fall into each other's arms. The desire to attend a dance with the lady of one's choice is the motor that drives the plots of *El santo de la Isidra* and *Agua, azucarillos, y aguardiente* (and the climactic scene of the former takes place at the dance as well). Clearly, festival dances retained their traditional function as a place of sociability and celebration even as they were translated from rural to urban areas; what changed was the nature of the music. The traditional folk dances, the seguidillas and the jotas, were replaced by dance music that reflected a more urban sensibility. Dances in rural festivals were about celebrating community life. Dances in urban settings were more intimate and romantic, less focused on creating community than on creating romantic attachments.

The result is that the género chico, by adopting into its aural world this urban dance music with its various associations, helps to create an atmosphere of what Ramón Barce has dubbed "urban folklore." This interest in the habits and customs of urban life is hardly surprising, given the necessary shift in dramatic emphasis undertaken by the género chico. It also helped to give the necessary feeling of authenticity that the realist ethic demanded and that the género chico catered to.[19] But most importantly, urban dance music increasingly took the place of traditional folk music on the Spanish lyric stage. Whereas traditional folk music had depicted the Spanish people in zarzuela, the new demands of the género chico required a different sort of music. The género chico was the theater of urban Spain; what it required to depict the people of this new vision of Spain was urban folk music. Just as the zarzuela had originally turned to dance music to depict the pueblo, the género chico followed suit. The difference was that this dance music is hardly what one associates with traditional rural Spain. What was crucial for the composers of the género chico was that it did reflect the ambiance of urban Madrid.

It should come as no surprise that the music for the first of the género chico works was written by a composer who specialized in dance music. Federico Chueca, who would become the most popular and successful of the género chico composers following the success of *La canción de la Lola,* was one of the few who was born and raised in Madrid. From the beginning he was a child of urban Spain, unlike most of his fellow zarzuela composers who immigrated to Madrid from provincial centers.[20] Most of Chueca's musical experience and education came from his early years as a café pianist, playing popular music in the forms of waltzes, polkas, and the like. Although he did study briefly at the Conservatorio de Madrid, academia had little impact on his career. Instead, Chueca's flair was for pianistic improvisation. He apparently found that spinning off melodies on the piano was easy, even if the art of composition was difficult. It is not surprising that the majority of Chueca's stage output consists of the popular music that he first improvised in Madrid cafés. And these songs were generally based on Central European dance music.

Chueca's scores are a case study in how Spanish composers naturalized this new urban folk music, making it "Spanish" and thus as organic to zarzuela as the seguidilla. Many of his scores have been referred to as suites of dance music, and an examination of how he and his librettists structured their works demonstrates how Spaniards conceptualized urban nationalism. For our purposes, the best of his zarzuelas to examine is *Agua, azucarillos y aguardiente* (Water, Sweets, and Spirits) with a libretto by Miguel Ramos Carrión, first performed in 1897. Subtitled a *"pasillo veraniego"* (summertime walk), the work is set in the Recoletos Gardens, a popular park in Central Madrid. (Today Recoletos is the main north-south automotive thoroughfare through central Madrid; however, a few cafés and a tree-lined pedestrian walkway still allow one to recall gentler days through the automobile exhaust.) The ostensible plot revolves around the romantic intrigues of Serafín, a young bourgeois cad, and how these are thwarted by beverage seller Pepa and her fiancé Lorenzo. But the musical interest revolves around the various types who frequent the park and take their refreshment at Pepa's stand. Chueca's music deftly integrates central European dance music into a Spanish form of identity by celebrating a leisurely evening in Madrid.

It is significant that the first scene of *Agua, azucarillos y aguardiente,* which lays out the broad outlines of the plot—such as it is—has no musical numbers in it whatsoever (aside from some orchestral underscoring).[21] Although the scene is a deft parody of lower middle-class mores and bad poetry, it is little more than a setup for what follows. The dramatic concerns of the first scene (Doña Simona's precarious financial situation and the engagement of her daughter Asia to the untrustworthy Serafín) become submerged in a second plot (the conflict between Pepa and rival beverage seller Manuela) and the depiction of a typical summer evening in a turn-of-the-century Madrid park. The second scene—the heart of the work—opens with a scene of children playing games while their nannies look on. Chueca mixes two types of folklore in this opening chorus. The first is the songs sung by the children, which were not composed by Chueca but are in fact traditional children's songs from the period.[22] The second is an evocation of traditional Galician bagpipe music, and at least one of the children indicates his nurse is actually from Galicia.[23]

This opening chorus (No. 2 in the vocal score) provides both visual and aural evidence of the impact of urbanization in late nineteenth-century Spain. The children are unquestionably of the urban upper classes and have been shooed out of the house in the company of their nurses for fresh air. But the nurses themselves are immigrants, sent to the city to earn a living and clearly unhappy about it, as the refrain to one of their choruses indicates: "When will I go / to my hometown, / that insistently calls since I went away?"[24] Chueca's evocation of Galician bagpipes in the orchestra (actual bagpipes are not used, but the sound is mimicked by a combination of violins and muted trumpet) not only suggests the unhappiness of the transplants to Madrid, but is arguably an aural representation of the integration of the rural population into city life, as the music moves back and forth easily between the contemporary children's music and the rural past. There is a sense that Ramos Carrión and Chueca are evoking the urban future with the upbeat children's music and contrasting it with the slightly mournful music that represents the countryside.

This linking of urban life with cheerful and upbeat music continues with the next musical number, the Chorus of the Barquilleros (No. 3 in the vocal score). After several extended book scenes that advance the plot(s), the stage is invaded by a female chorus dressed as young boys who sell *barquillos,* waffle-cone and cream concoctions enjoyed during the Madrid summer before the advent in popularity of ice cream. Set to a march-rhythm, the chorus is a catalogue of the poorer neighborhoods in Madrid where the urchins live—la Ronda, Embajadores, Lavapiés—and the slightly more upscale locations where they vend their wares—the Prado, the Plaza de Colón, the Puerta de Alcalá, the Plaza de Cibeles (the last is given a very *madrileño* pronunciation as the "plaza *la Cebá*" in order to fit the rhyme scheme somewhat more smoothly).[25] The number is a simple celebration of urban life and urban pleasures: either the ability to purchase a barquillo or the ability to mock some of the slightly snootier customers, depending upon which side of the transaction one is on. To musically characterize this slice of urban leisure life, Chueca uses a *pasodoble,* one of the more popular dances of the period.

It is the extended finale to *Agua, azucarillos y aguardiente* that cements urban life as the new basis for Spanish nationalism. This ten-minute scene is a kaleidoscope of various types of popular dance music. It opens with a mazurka-style chorus by a theater audience happy to escape the roasting confines of the auditorium for the cooler night air—a serious problem in the days before air conditioning. They encounter an Italian street musician who entertains them with a popular song. This is followed by a *panaderos* (a type of flamenco music) in which Pepa and rival refreshment seller Manuela climax the turf war they have been carrying on throughout the play by slagging each other like fishwives. This duet evolves into a quartet in which their fiancés try to resolve the argument. Vicente and Lorenzo are able to do this by changing the music to a pasacalle reminiscent of music played before bullfights and by giving the women their Manila shawls (which had been pawned); all is forgiven and the four make their way to a verbena. Chueca has one last musical joke in hand. Serafín falls asleep in the park (having been drugged), and three robbers make off with his clothing to the orchestral music of Chueca's own "Jota de las Ratas" from *La Gran Vía,* which depicted the problems of urban crime. Serafín is arrested for indecent exposure (another typically urban crime, come to think of it), a suitable punishment for his attempted seduction of Asia. All ends happily.

The finale to *Agua, azucarillos y aguardiente* functions as a microcosm of the musical construction of the work as a whole. Chueca mixes together popular songs, traditional folk music (the panaderos), and urban dance music (the mazurka and the pasacalle) to create what might be referred to as urban folk music. This mixes both the traditional rural folk music of inhabitants new to urban life and the dance music that increasingly filled the function of sociability that folk music had for rural society. But the use of this new urban folk music expands somewhat from its use in the Barbieri-style zarzuela grande. No longer is it used merely to characterize the chorus as the Spanish people as it had been in Barbieri's works; it is used to characterize everybody, since even the principals get to sing waltzes and mazurkas. Appropriately enough for the dawning of the age of mass culture, there is no longer an assumption that the Spanish people are of a different class or social standing from the protagonists of the drama. Urban folk music characterizes everybody in the género chico because everybody—Doña Simona and Asia as much as Pepa and Manuela—are a part of the nation. Class differentiations are no longer to be denoted musically.

Nor is *Agua, azucarillos y aguardiente* unique in its treatment of urban dance music. The majority of Chueca's scores function in a very similar manner, consisting of collections of dance music.[26] The concept appears in an embryonic form in the seminal *La canción de la Lola,* which uses the polka as its main musical theme and then proceeds to work in a popular waltz. By the time Chueca had composed the score to *La Gran Vía* six years later, he had more or less perfected the idea of the zarzuela-suite. The score to that work contains polkas, waltzes, a tango, and the schottische. *El año pasado por agua* has a mazurka, a waltz, a pasacalle, a habanera, and a number that mixes a zortziko with a schottische. The zarzuela-suite was the standard compositional format of Chueca, who was in turn the most quintessentially urban of zarzuela composers. Doubtless, this is at least partially a heritage of his musical education in the dance halls of Madrid, but Chueca was not the only composer to pursue such a strategy—even if he was the one who pursued it most noticeably and most aggressively.

Both Tomás Bretón and Ruperto Chapí were more sophisticated and subtle composers than Chueca, but even their género chico works betray the influence of the zarzuela-suite method of composition. Bretón's *La verbena de la paloma* features an instrumental mazurka (which is used as the onstage music for a dance sequence) and a habanera. While the mazurka is played as a relatively straightforward piece of dance music, the habanera is developed instead as a concertante number (in fact, the vocal score gives it the title "Habanera concertante"—No. 5B) that displays the operatic possibilities of strophic dance music.[27] The main melody is almost ridiculously simple: the vocal line alternates between two notes (A and F#) in a limited rhythmic pattern (the phrase is based on two sixteenth notes and an eighth note that is repeated three times; this larger phrase repeated twice over makes up the basic melody). The simplicity of the tune should not be underrated: "¿Dónde vas con mantón de Manila?" ("Where are you going in your Manila shawl?") is one of the most widely remembered melodies not only from *La verbena de la paloma,* but from the zarzuela repertory in general.[28] This insistent musical phrase is batted back and forth between the characters of Julián and Susana until the entrance of the rest of the cast moves the score along. Even as the vocal textures thicken and become more complex, Bretón continues to keep the relatively simple habanera rhythm going in the orchestra with the strings and woodwinds until the end of the number, thus tying together the excesses of what is happening onstage with a simple and repetitive musical line in the orchestra pit.

Ruperto Chapí's *La Revoltosa* (The Mischievous Maid) from 1897 has a similar construction. Here the urban dance music is pared down to a single form, the waltz. But again, the dance music crops up in the two most important numbers in the score, the quartet (No. 2) and the love duet (No. 4). Waltz rhythms also turn up at several points in the musical scenes that comprise No. 5 in the score, which also feature a reprise of the theme from the love duet.[29] While much of Chapí's score consists of a flexible combination of song and sprechtgesang, these two numbers stand independently and serve to encapsulate the two key dramatic moments of José López Silva and Carlos Fernández-Shaw's libretto. The quartet consists of titular troublemaker Mari-Pepa's teasing of the three married men who are seeking her favors. She is having none of their promises and outlines the necessary attributes of a woman in search of love:

> A woman
> ought to have . . .
> Pupils to distinguish with,
> and a heart to love with,
> and good taste to choose with . . . [30]

Chapí uses the waltz to underscore the nature of urban love. On the one hand, Mari-Pepa points out the advantages of romance in the big city: with a little common sense a woman can choose with whom she will fall in love and eventually marry, an option not always available in the highly regulated sexual world of rural Spain. On the other hand, the situation is a warning, since the adulterous context of the quartet would hardly be so open in any but an urban setting. The love duet, appropriately, will also use the waltz. But here the lyric nature of the waltz form is used to emphasize the passion between Mari-Pepa and Felipe.

Bretón's and Chapí's use of urban dance music is more restricted than Chueca's, and the notion of the zarzuela-suite might not stretch far enough to cover the score of *La Revoltosa*. This is not to say, however, that Bretón and Chapí drew the line at using dance music at the outskirts of Madrid. They continued to use traditional forms of folk music—the seguidilla especially—in tandem with the waltzes and mazurkas, just as Chueca incorporated the sound of Galician bagpipes and the panaderos into *Agua, azucarillos y aguardiente.* What is most interesting about the way that Bretón and Chapí used folk music is the fact that such music is either used for the choruses—hardly surprising, given the heritage of Barbieri—or at moments of diegetic singing. The assumption is that the music people found most familiar was urban dance music. As with Chueca, everybody—regardless of class and station—sings music associated with the Spanish people, although that music was not what might have been traditionally thought of as "Spanish." A redefinition of what constitutes Spanish identity is well underway in the género chico works of the 1880s and the 1890s, a redefinition built around the realities of everyday life in an urbanizing society.

It was not simply the dance music that made the género chico representative of Spain's growing urban culture. The works themselves portrayed the new urban landscape in what contemporaries felt was a realistic manner. The localities in which these works took place would also have been instantly recognizable to the theatrical audience in Madrid. Just how faithful the scenic representation would have been onstage is something of a matter of conjecture. Due to the expense of constructing scenery, most theaters had a selection of stock sets (a street, the interior of a shop, the courtyard of a house) that would serve for almost any theatrical piece. Thus, most stage directions feature fairly generic settings—such as "a street in Madrid." However, works by more established composers and works that the impresarios projected would be hits would have new sets created (often by the team of Bussato and Amalio

Fernández, who were the leading set designers of the day) that depicted what audiences accepted as a theatrically accurate representation of the streets they traversed on a daily basis. The review of *La verbena de la paloma* in *El Imparcial* is illuminating: "All of the action takes place in the neighborhood where the Paloma Chapel is located, and there are scenes in the open air, at the door of a tavern . . . the style is that of an exact imitation, a faithful picture that is not even lacking a single detail, which appears before the view of the audience."[31] Even if we assume that the sets were hardly exact replicas of the street scenes in Madrid, the audience accepted the overall reality and accuracy of the scenes portrayed onstage.

In fact, the realism of the settings became crucial to the audience perception of these works. Consider Carlos Arniches's first staged play, *El santo de la Isidra*. When the work was first staged on 20 February 1898 (five days after the USS *Maine* blew up in Havana harbor), the libretto was roundly panned for a number of jokes the critics held to be in poor taste. On the other hand, the music by Tomás López Torregrosa was the saving grace that made the work wildly popular ("happy, frisky, very Madrilenian" is how *El Liberal* described it).[32] But the settings were integral to the plot. Two of the sets were representations of well-known Madrid landmarks. The second scene was set in front of the Toledo Bridge. The third scene was titled "La Pradera de San Isidro el día del Santo" (The Holiday at St. Isidore's Meadow), representing not only another familiar Madrid landmark, but showing how it appeared during a verbena: Arniches's stage directions call for banquet tables, vendors, and carousels. This representation of a festival in Madrid is crucial to the denouement of the plot, as neighborhood rake Epifanio has declared that only he will dance with Isidra at the festival that honors her saint's day. (San Isidro also happens to be the patron saint of Madrid itself, which adds a few layers to the plot.) However, shy neighborhood tailor Venancio is in love with Isidra. Eventually Venancio contrives to dance with Isidra at the festival and exposes Epifanio's philandering, which wins him Isidra's hand and the approval of her parents. In essence, Arniches has created a classic carnivalesque plot in which the standard order is overturned during the carnival or festival. Thus, the naturalism of the setting is crucial to the main theme of the plot, for without a traditional festival setting, Arniches's dramatic mechanisms would make much less sense.

But it is the first scene of *El santo de la Isidra* that purports to show the new urban face of Spain. Although the stage direction begins with a generic description, Arniches quickly becomes much more detailed:

> A small plaza in a working-class neighborhood. At the rear of the stage are two houses separated by an alley which leads to the Calle de Toledo, beyond which we can see the Plaza de la Cebada. The house on the left has functioning doors and on the ground floor, a shop selling imported goods. . . . The other house, on the right, has a tavern with a sign that reads: "No. 8, Wines and Liquors, No. 8." The door of the tavern opens into the alley and faces the audience. On the right wing of the stage is a house of modest construction, and in the corner where the house meets the tavern is the storage room of a shoemaker. On the left wing of the stage is another building, whose ground floor contains a furniture store, some of whose merchandise has been placed in the door. The sign of the store reads: "The Rocking Chair, Chair-Makers and Upholsterers."[33]

Arniches's setting may be imaginary, but the stage direction does all it can to establish the reality of the scene, from the precise address to the signs in the shop windows. Both the Calle de Toledo and the Plaza de la Cebada are well-known locations in southern Madrid, which means that the location that Arniches describes would be somewhere around the current La Latina metro station. I have not been able to determine whether or not the small plaza Arniches describes actually existed in 1898. Nothing like it appears on Madrid street maps of the period, but even today this part of Madrid has a number of small streets and plazas—any of which Arniches could have used for inspiration. The modest shops are the sort that still litter the neighborhood, and the *"tienda de ultramarinos"* (import shop) is a telling touch: the neighborhoods around the Calle de Toledo were populated by a number of immigrants from Latin America. Arniches's request for the practical doors, windows, and balconies would have heightened the realism since most género chico sets of the period consisted of painted backdrops, which forced the actors to make all entrances and exits from the wings, not from the buildings themselves.

It is an open question whether or not Arniches actually persuaded the set designer to create such elaborate scenery during the first run of *El santo de la Isidra.* The review of the work that had the most to say about the sets was that in *El Heraldo de Madrid,* which commented that "Señor Muriel has painted for *El santo de la Isidra* two pretty sets, which represent Toledo Bridge and St. Isidore's Meadow."[34] No mention is made of the complex set described for the first scene. Keeping in mind that at this time Arniches was a new and relatively unknown writer, the impresarios of the Teatro de Apolo probably chose to use a stock set for the first scene, as nothing in the dramatic situation absolutely demands the detailed realism that the author calls for. Doubtless Arniches was writing for an idealized production. Nevertheless, he could not have been too displeased about the verisimilitude displayed on the stage. As the reviewer for *El Liberal* asked, "*El santo de la Isidra* will figure for many nights on the boards of the Apolo, because the last scene is very Madrilenian, and who has left Madrid without seeing St. Isidore's Meadow—the last scene of the work—represented by a most beautiful set from Muriel?"[35] Whatever the flaws in *El santo de la Isidra,* it captured the spirit of Madrid, its citizens, and its environs in a way that the audience and the critics recognized as accurate.

Urban realism in zarzuela did not stop with the scenery. The most surprising aspect of Spanish zarzuela lies in its depictions of social hierarchy: only Spanish musical theater had the temerity to place a singing representation of the urban working class onstage. The workforce of traditional European operetta was traditionally squeaky clean peasant farmers and minor nobility that seemed to have stepped out of a Fragonard painting. The workers in Spanish zarzuelas of the 1890s were still squeaky clean—the realist trend had hardly extended to placing the grimy miners of Zola's *Germinal* on the stage—but they were recognizably members of the working class. Perhaps as one way of keeping things reasonably clean on the stage, the género chico tends to focus on female workers. Men worked too, but factory workers were perhaps less musical than female laborers, such as the nannies who supervised the children in the Recoletos Park from *Agua, azucarillos, y aguardiente,* or the ambulant water-sellers who carried their cool drinks in clay jugs and sold cups of water in the summer for a few centimes, depicted later in the same play.[36]

One of the most prevalent female workers in late nineteenth-century zarzuelas is the type that probably would also have been most prevalent in real life: the laundrywoman. These women took in washing from the bourgeois households in Madrid that did not have their own laundry facilities. Composers often tended to use this group of women as part of a chorus, and with good reason. The laundrywomen of Madrid congregated in the same area to do their work, on the banks of the Manzanares River, providing a logical reason to bring a large group of people together. The use of the laundrywomen as chorus is used to best effect in Chueca's *El chaleco blanco* (The White Vest). Here, the cheerful women's chorus is used to set up an ironic contrast with Ventura's despair that he has lost his winning lottery ticket. In fact, the opening of the second scene of *El chaleco blanco* presents a typical tableau of the workday along the banks of the Manzanares. The laundrywomen sing (not whistle) while they work; itinerant hairdressers and bread-sellers are on foot hawking their services and wares; policemen pass by making misogynistic comments; and buglers wander by to flirt with the women. (The area of the Manzanares in which the women did their laundry was not very far from the Royal Palace, and the buglers would have been from the guards stationed at the Palace.) Not only does the laundrywomen's chorus depict a tableau of daily life in Madrid, but it allows for a little mild mocking of the bourgeoisie, whose habits provide the laundrywomen with an occupation. Holding up a pair of socks, they state with amusement:

> These are the socks
> of a playboy,
> of a playboy.
> Oh, what a cold winter
> the poor boy has had!
> He has vents
> in front and behind.
> Be still my soul,
> that is how high society is![37]

If anybody can see through the pretensions of the middle classes—especially the social climbers—it would be the women who clean their underwear.

One suspects this mockery was far more prevalent and far more vicious among the real laundrywomen of the Manzanares River. The picture Rámos Carrión and Chueca present is exceedingly sanitized. In reality, these women were poorly paid and worked under conditions almost unimaginable today. A small vignette from the novelist Arturo Barea, whose mother was one of these laundrywomen, serves to blow apart the romanticized portrait of *El chaleco blanco:*

My mother's hands were very small. As she had been washing since sunrise, her fingers were covered with little wrinkles like an old woman's skin, but her nails were bright and shining. Sometimes the lye would burn right through her skin and make pin-prick holes all over her fingertips. In the winter her hands used to get cut open; as soon as she took them out of the water into the cold air, they were covered with sharp little ice crystals. The blood would spurt as though a cat had scratched her.[38]

Doing laundry for a living was hardly the idyllic romp that the sainetes portrayed. It aged the women prematurely and exacted a high physical toll: not merely the hands soaked in lye and coated in ice, but the constant bending and lifting of heavy loads that would hardly pass modern workplace safety standards.

Obviously, the argument that musical theater can be considered realistic and naturalistic can only be carried so far before the absurdity of such an argument becomes clear. Leaving aside the fact that musical theater cannot be realistic almost by definition—sane people do not break into song at key emotional moments in real life, although we all might be better off if we did—it is clear that zarzuela only rarely even attempted to grapple with the grittier aspects of working-class life in 1890s Madrid. In spite of this shortcoming, zarzuela composers and librettists were attempting to depict a new vision of the Spanish nation through the género chico. That vision was a picture of Spain that was urban, not rural; industrial, not agricultural; and modern, not backward. Even if the género chico could not be utterly naturalistic, it did seek to carry some level of realistic discourse within it.

In considering what the composers and librettists of zarzuela were attempting to accomplish, it is worth considering the arguments that Benedict Anderson makes about the way national communities are envisioned.[39] He links the rise of nationalism with the rise of mass literacy and likens the national community to the people who read a daily paper: none of the readers may actually know any other reader, but they can imagine a group of people from other walks of life who are reading the same newspaper at the same time. Nothing tangible links these people. They are a community only through the virtue that they can picture others doing the same thing they are doing. If popular literacy is one way to imagine a community, why not popular music?

After all, virtually all urban dwellers (and presumably most people who visited an urban area) were familiar with the new urban forms of dance music. Like folk music before it, dance music became a way of connecting people who had never met each other but who listened to the same melodies. It also proved an ideal vehicle in a time when urban culture was becoming more prominent than it had been before in Spain.

The perceived naturalism of the género chico was also crucial in this project of helping to create a new, imagined community for an urbanizing Spain. The daily life of the working classes would have been something of a mystery to the bourgeoisie that made up the majority of the theatrical audience. What better way to help these audiences imagine the newest members of the Spanish community than by literally placing them center stage? Such sanitized representations helped to diminish any threat the bourgeois audiences might have felt from the working classes. Turning a social question into entertainment romanticizes the issue as a matter of course—but then again, which foundations of national identity aren't romanticized fictions? And it was natural for theatrical composers and librettists to have their works turn on issues of class, since theater was a vehicle for social advancement for talented provincials who moved to Spain's growing urban centers. The idea of "art for art's sake" aestheticism that flourished in England, or the debates over serious music that flourished in Paris, Berlin, and Vienna, are not to be found in the musical world of 1880s and 1890s Madrid. This is perhaps a natural consequence of a musical world that was so underdeveloped as to inhibit the performance of new works by Spanish composers, who were thus forced into the commercial theater in order to make a living in their chosen profession. Even the most serious composers had to churn out commercial theater pieces to pay their bills. Such composers had few illusions about their audiences, and wrote works that would appeal to a broad spectrum of taste.

Thus the authors of zarzuela faced a potential trap: in order to have their music heard at all, they had to create entertainment for the bourgeois theater audiences—who doubtless would not have found the lice-infested realism of a Galdós novel to be worth the price of a ticket. (Warts-and-all social drama fared better on the legitimate stage: witness the success of Joaquín Dicena's 1895 *Juan José*, which is the realist drama that the género chico aspired to be.) On the other hand, once zarzuela composers had established themselves as the purveyors of nationalist lyric drama, they had to continue to supply nationalist works—even as the basis of Spanish national identity was beginning to change. And whatever ethical qualms one might have about the social function of depicting the working class onstage, it cannot be denied that zarzuela composers carried out their task supremely well with music that rises far above the at-times pedestrian plots. Whatever these works might be, they are undeniably entertaining.

The género chico helped Spaniards come to grips with the changing nature of national identity wrought by nineteenth-century urbanization, integrating Spanish theatrical audiences into this new vision of the nation. The runaway popularity of works based in urban dance music like *La Gran Vía; Agua, azucarillos y aguardiente;* and *El santo de la Isidra*—zarzuelas which still form the core of repertory today—indicates that audiences enthusiastically accepted the vision of an urban Spain. But national identity tends to present itself as something essential and eternal, even as it is constantly shifting. How did zarzuela composers and librettists convey the sense of an eternal Spain at a time when the country's demographics were rapidly changing? Through the portrayal of history onstage. As we saw in Chapter 1, zarzuela frequently used historical backdrops and intrigue as a motor for its plots. As the género chico embraced Spanish history, it would use the dance music that had proved so popular in urban works to entice audiences into the theaters. That dance music would help to link the Spanish people of the present with the *pueblo español* of the past and create the continuity that is so essential to the construction of national identity.

3

Staging History,
Staging National Identity

Imagine a performance of *West Side Story* in which all the music sung by the lovers Tony and Maria has been removed. No "Maria," no "Tonight." They're still on stage, they're still in love, they just don't sing. You would still have a pretty decent piece of musical theater with the Sharks and the Jets rumbling to Leonard Bernstein's music. But you wouldn't have a love story. You'd have a musical treatise on gang warfare, which isn't the sort of thing anybody would put on stage to attract audiences and make money. And yet, in 1886, composer Federico Chueca and playwright Javier de Burgos did something very similar: they created a musical treatise on liberal constitutionalism. *Cádiz* is not a musical love story, as most operettas are. It displaces the traditional motor of musical theater plots, that of young love, and replaces it with a musical representation of the birthing pangs of Spanish liberalism: *Cádiz* has as its protagonists the Spanish people themselves. As zarzuela became the vehicle by which the Spanish people came to articulate their sense of national identity in the 1880s and 1890s, historical subjects became again common on the Spanish lyric stage. Even as the country was moving forward toward an urban future, zarzuelas used the past as a further way of unifying the Spanish people.

The creation of a common historical narrative is crucial to the forging of national identity. It was one of the two defining factors outlined by Ernest Renan in his 1882 lecture "Qu'est-ce qu'une nation?," which gives one of the seminal definitions of nationalism. Modern scholars have also stressed the importance of a historical narrative that creates a shared national mythology to help bind the heterogeneous elements of a country's population together. Normally, this is done through formal channels by the state—primarily through elementary and secondary education. Throughout the nineteenth century, governments created state-funded educational systems, and one of the goals of these systems was to inculcate students with appropriate historical narratives. Spain was one of the major exceptions to the creation of widespread elementary education. Due to the poverty of the Spanish government, most of the educational system in the country remained in the hands of the Catholic Church, which had a very different agenda in terms of creating a communal identity.[1] As with other attempts to build a Spanish national identity, the effort of creating a nationalist historical narrative was going to have to come from outside the state.

The librettists and composers of the género chico zarzuelas of the 1880s and 1890s were not interested in the entire sweep of Spanish history. History on the lyric stage meant the War of Independence, the struggle against the Napoleonic invasion of 1808–1813. In spite of Spain's rich historical legacy, it is not surprising that this was the seminal moment for composers with nationalist aspirations. The War of Independence was the cornerstone of Spain's liberal nationalist historical narrative, in which the people of Spain rose up against a foreign invader, reclaiming the country when the conservative forces of the Catholic Church and the Bourbon monarchy could not.[2] The War of Independence was the perfect setting for stories that were not only historical romances but that also glorified the Spanish people, the bedrock of a liberal nationalist identity. The popular understanding of the Napoleonic invasion, in which the Spanish people rose up *en masse* to drive out the French (giving the world the term guerrilla in the process), became a central myth of Spanish history much as Valley Forge became a central myth of the American Revolution. But whereas Americans tend to obsess about George Washington, the Spanish glorified the average soldier. Zarzuela played the crucial role in making the average Spaniard the focus of the popular historical narrative.

The seminal work of historical zarzuela—the one that served as the model for virtually all the others—was the brainchild of Javier de Burgos and Federico Chueca: *Cádiz*. The project presumably originated with Burgos, who was originally a newspaperman from Cádiz. Burgos was another one of those men, so prevalent in Restoration Spain, who lavished their time and their ink equally between the theater and the periodical press. He had served as the editor of *La Palma de Cádiz* from 1866 to 1868, and he specialized in writing about Cádiz; his most memorable works are set in and around the city.[3] Burgos gave *Cádiz* only the thinnest of plots. The year is 1810, and the French are besieging the city. Elderly Don Cleto is eager to escape, and plans to abduct his ward Carmen in order to marry her. She is in love with Fernando, who will manage to rescue her from the fate worse than death by the end of the play. In order to flesh out this story, in several scenes the people of Cádiz declare their determination to fight the French invaders. And in a spectacular tableau, the Constitutional Cortes—the rump of the Spanish parliament, which was meeting in the besieged city—presents the constitution that they have drafted to the Spanish people.

However, the plot is essentially beside the point—which is made manifestly clear by the fact that Carmen and Fernando are the only two leading lovers in the history of operetta not to sing a note. Instead, the work is much closer to the revue style that Chueca had used in *La Gran Vía* earlier that season. None of the numbers actually advance the plot in the sense of expanding our knowledge of the characters or causing a shift in the dramatic action. All the numbers are essentially diversionary, and almost all are performed by the chorus or a large vocal ensemble. (The exception is No. 9, the "Canción del ciego"— the "Song of the Blind Man"—which was written specifically for the actor Julio Ruiz in order to allow him some satirical comments on the topics of the day.)[4] This does lead to an obvious question: if the traditional love plot to *Cádiz* is ephemeral and none of the musical numbers is necessary to the plot, what is the dramatic motor that actually drives Burgos's script and makes it work theatrically?

The answer lies in the voices that Chueca is writing his music for—it is virtually all chorus and ensemble work. Chueca and Burgos have turned the dramatic action over to the chorus. In this they continue the zarzuela heritage of casting the chorus as both the Spanish people and the protagonists of the plot. Burgos's libretto makes this especially plain as the figures at the center of the action are the Spanish people, not the cardboard lovers Carmen and Fernando. The very first stage direction spells out Burgos's plan: "As the curtain rises there appear in the plaza various groups of people belonging to distinct classes of society."[5] The opening chorus proudly proclaims that the French

> will need to send more Frenchies
> than there are grains of sand on the beach;
> Because the elderly, women, little children
> and all the classes of society
> will fight them with rocks, with sticks,
> with lead shot, with nails, and with their teeth.[6]

The message is clear. The politicians and the army cannot save Spain from the invaders; salvation lies in the hands of the people. But while Burgos has reinstated the Spanish people as historical actors, he fails to reinstate the strong historico-political plots that characterized the zarzuela grande. The political overtones to the Carmen-Fernando-Don Cleto love triangle are both underwritten and detached from the historical action. Don Cleto is an absolutist reactionary, while Fernando is a liberal constitutionalist. (One can only imagine what Picón and Barbieri could have done with this raw material.) This characterization is doubtless the result of the revue-style plot—which Burgos presumably constructed to suit Chueca's particular talents as a composer after the runaway success *La Gran Vía,* which opened only a few months before *Cádiz.*

If we are going to determine what Chueca and Burgos were trying to say about the nature of the Spanish people, a look at the musical construction of *Cádiz* becomes necessary. As with the zarzuela grande model, it is folk music that serves as the backing for the choral numbers. Where Barbieri tended to rely on a mere one or two forms—usually a jota and a seguidilla—to characterize his chorus, Chueca and Valverde change forms with virtually every number and sometimes even within a given musical number. *Cádiz* contains a seguidilla, a *sevillanas,* a *caleseras,* a barcarolle, a pasodoble, a flamenco, a zapateado, a polka, a tango, and a jota. Not all of these, admittedly, are Spanish folk forms. The polka is included as a comic interlude to characterize and mock some English visitors, while the tango (technically a Latin American dance) is performed by a pair of mulatto visitors to the city. Even with these removed, there is still a plethora of purely "Spanish" dance forms. By using such a vast number of folk and dance forms in *Cádiz,* Chueca seems to have been attempting to create a self-consciously "Spanish" musical idiom. Certainly the reviews of the work interpreted it in this manner. The review in *Madrid Cómico* noted that *Cádiz* "is spiced with seguidillas, caleseras, tangos, street songs, and patriotic hymns; it is, in sum, Spanish and, that is to say, Barbieriesque." A little further on, this speaker's companion notes that the comparison to Barbieri is the "highest praise" that could be given to a composer. *La Época* termed the music of the work "happy and Spanish" (as opposed to dour and German, perhaps).[7] Nobody could doubt the patriotism of the piece.

This self-conscious Hispanism was set against a historical plot that, as has been noted, was different in construction from the carefully constructed plots set by Francisco Asenjo Barbieri. The historical works of the género chico also feature a temporal shift. The zarzuela grande of the 1870s and 1880s had been set firmly in the eighteenth century. *Cádiz* moves itself forward only about fifteen years from the setting of *Pan y toros,* but by moving across the divide into the nineteenth century the work picks up a whole new set of political concerns. Where *Pan y toros* frames its major political battle in terms of Enlightenment rationalism versus absolutist rule, *Cádiz* ups the ante by making its heroes participants in the birth of Spanish liberalism. The most notable historical moment during the siege of Cádiz was not military: it was the meeting of the Cortés of Cádiz and that body's adoption of Spain's first constitution, the cornerstone of Spanish liberalism for the rest of the nineteenth century. Late in the second act of *Cádiz,* Chueca and Burgos have the Cortes march on to the strains of a military march and present the constitution to the population. (This is actually somewhat anachronistic as the setting clearly indicates the year is 1810, but the constitution was not penned until 1812.)[8] There is absolutely no dramatic reason for this scene in the plot of *Cádiz.* Clearly the authors felt that a presentation of the siege of Cádiz would not be complete without a dramatic reference to the constitution and its enthusiastic reception by the Spanish people.

The emphasis that *Cádiz* places on the Spanish people can be better understood by placing the work into relief with the 1890s writings of the philosopher Miguel de Unamuno, a figure not generally associated with light opera. Beginning in February 1895, Unamuno published a series of essays in the review *La España Moderna,* which he would later collect and republish in 1902 under the title *En torno al casticismo.*[9] Unamuno's goal in this series of essays was to uncover the true nature of Spanish identity. His conception of the nature of Spanish identity remains somewhat controversial today due to its emphasis on the specifically Castilian and Catholic components of that identity. But crucial to Unamuno's train of thought was a conception of history that he called *intrahistoria.* Intrahistory emphasized the actions of the people of Spain over a narrative of high politics. The Spanish people were not merely the primary force in history—they were the only force. Unamuno sweeps all other conventional historical forces aside to focus entirely on the pueblo.

For Unamuno, the spiritual center of Spain was the pueblo. This conception of the Spanish populace functioned as more than a quasi-Romantic "spirit of the people": Unamuno believed that the pueblo was the embodiment of the social contract by which people consented to be governed. Although he cites Rousseau in the development of his thinking, it is probably no surprise that Unamuno interprets the social contract a little differently than the Swiss philosophe. In Unamuno's vision, intrahistoria underlies the social contract. But this social contract is not meant to be the instrument of a state, but of local communities.[10] These local communities provide the basis for the nation in its broadest context: Unamuno's vision of nationalism was predicated on an assumption that national identity could not be built out of narrow and parochial notions of what constituted a people. Instead, it had to develop out of and exist in an international, cosmopolitan context. In this historical view, an event like the Napoleonic invasion of Spain was not necessarily a wholly negative phenomenon, as it brought new ideas and innovations with it: it enabled the pueblo to become part of a wider and more universal community.

Unamuno was hardly alone in his identification of the pueblo as the basis not only of Spanish national identity but of Spanish history as well. Angel Ganivet, Pío Baroja, and the essayist Azorín also found in the pueblo the crux of their concerns about Spanish history and identity.[11] However, when it comes to understanding the musical conceptions of history on the Spanish stage, Unamuno is the critical intellectual figure of the 1898 generation. In the Barbieri model of zarzuela, the people of Spain (the chorus) are important and even crucial actors, but history ultimately operates along well-established tracks of high politics. The subject matter of both *Pan y toros* and *El barberillo de Lavapiés,* after all, is essentially the replacement of a government minister. In the historical works of the 1890s, high politics disappear completely. It is *Cádiz*—the seminal work of género chico historicism—that is the key to understanding the nature of zarzuela history. Most other works fall back on the classic love-conflict-as-plot construction, but Federico Chueca's and Javier de Burgos's work minimized this. The nature of the episodic plot construction of the género chico significantly changes the political dynamics of the drama. By curtailing the amount of time any one character actually spends onstage, the género chico moved away from a drama based on individual actions and instead depicts a broad panorama of daily life, behaviors, and customs. It is exactly this—what others termed mere "folklore," which upset Unamuno tremendously—that is the basis of intrahistoria and the true basis of Spanish identity.[12] This is reinforced even further in the one scene of *Cádiz,* which verges on the depiction of standard history: the presentation of the Constitution of 1812 to the citizens of Cádiz. Even here Chueca and Burgos de-emphasize traditional history. The only historical figure to appear is the governor of Cádiz, whose name is not given in the libretto. Instead, Burgos merely informs us that this figure is the "Governor, who represents a very illustrious man from the historical fact we are celebrating." The emphasis of this tableau is on the reaction of the people of Cádiz, who "fill the balconies and windows, waving their hats, handkerchiefs, and fans."[13] The importance of the Constitution of 1812 is not in that document itself, or even those who created it; it is in the reaction of the populace to the idea of the new liberal order.

This liberal spectacle helped to cement the popularity of *Cádiz* and the financial viability of the género chico in general. *Cádiz* premiered on 20 November 1886 at the Teatro Apolo, sharing the bill with *La Gran Vía*, which had moved from the outdoor Teatro Felipe at the end of the summer theatrical season. It was this combination of two wildly successful plays that helped to establish the musical género chico as a theatrical force to be reckoned with. More importantly, it was the success of these two works that helped to create the identity of the Apolo as the "Cathedral of the Género Chico." The Apolo had been built in 1873 but had failed to attract audiences due to its location (on what was then the outskirts of central Madrid), the high ticket prices necessary to offset the costs of the luxurious interior, and certain construction flaws that let snow into the lobby during the winter. As a result, the theater changed impresarios frequently.[14] The Apolo had started performing género chico works in 1883. However, it was the two Chueca pieces that turned the theater into the dynamo that drove Madrid's theater scene for the next two decades.

The Napoleonic invasion that forms the historical panorama against which *Cádiz* is set was the foundational myth for liberal Spanish nationalism in the nineteenth century.[15] But the lavish theatricality and pageantry of *Cádiz* would not be a model for other historical zarzuelas. When Burgos managed to recapture the rapture of that work with the similarly modeled *Trafalgar* in 1891 (with the composer Géronimo Gímenez supplying the music), the critics were pleased. *El Heraldo de Madrid* summed up the work best by noting that *Trafalgar* was "a glorious defeat for our country and will be a beneficial triumph for the management of the Apolo."[16] But *Trafalgar* is not exactly a reworking of *Cádiz* set on the high seas. Burgos drops the episodic review-style format that shaped the libretto of the previous work and develops the work in a manner similar to the one used for *El barberillo de Lavapiés*. Romantic intrigue mingles with history. Further explorations of history in the género chico re-vert to this time-honored format. The historical zarzuelas of the 1890s pick up on this idea and radically foreshorten the amount of the plot turned over to the historical side of the work. This was mostly done out of necessity, for the one-act structure that dominated the teatro por horas meant that something had to go, and most librettists no doubt felt they could get more mileage out of romance than out of politics.

Still, it would be a mistake to dismiss the historical panorama of the Na-poleonic invasion as the equivalent of a painted drop cloth against which the drama is played out. This is essentially the charge Carlos Serrano levels at works like *La viejecita* and *El tambor de granaderos,* calling their Peninsular War setting a "diffuse pretext for some journeys and adventures" with "the usual patriotic proclamations" thrown in to win applause from the audience.[17] At the very least, this ignores the fact that setting zarzuelas during the Napo-leonic invasion was not a traditional practice, but one that only developed in the mid-1880s in the wake of the success of *Cádiz.* True, these later works are much closer to the *El barberillo* model than they are to *Pan y toros* since the primary interests of the authors are dramatic, not historical. However, one key component of the historical setting in these works informs us what exactly the authors were up to. *La viejecita* and *El tambor de granaderos* are set in the moment of the Spanish victory over Bonaparte and the expulsion of the for-eign (French) conquerors from Spain.

La viejecita (The Little Old Lady) seems to treat its historical backdrop as the lightest gloss on the plot. The piece itself is a musical adaptation of the classic British farce *Charley's Aunt*—although not billed as such, probably to avoid paying royalties—in which a young man dresses up as an elderly lady in order to further his love affair with a young woman. This being Spain and not Britain, the sexual overtones of the work come not from the transvestitism di-rectly in the plot, but from the fact that the young man is a trouser role played by a woman—which no doubt allowed for a rather fetching hussar's uniform in the opening scenes. The work is set very shortly after the French have been expelled from Madrid in September 1812, and the action of the plot is built around a ball that is being thrown in honor of the English for their assistance in driving out the invaders. The libretto uses English characters to make an explicit statement about the worth of Spain's soldiers. The English captain, Sir George, makes this speech to his Spanish comrades:

> In my country we are all valiant,
> as you are in this country.
> Courage is the same; only
> the manner differs.
> The English are cold-blooded.
> In Spain, you are hot-tempered.[18]

On the one hand, this effectively plays into certain stereotypes about "hot-blooded" Spaniards and "frigid" Englishmen. On the other hand, it effectively equates the guerrilla-style warfare that the Spanish used during the Peninsular War with the more organized standing army used by the English. As a result, this enhances the standing of the general uprising against the French invaders into something more coherent and more unified. The Spanish are not simply waging guerrilla warfare, but fighting an organized battle recognized as such by a representative English soldier. In other words, a national rising. It may be worth noting that Sir George's full name is Sir Jorge Dover, while the protagonist's full name is Carlos España. These ultrageneric first names with geographically specific last names have the effect of turning the characters into stand-ins for their entire countries.

This nationalist reading is further enhanced by the opening chorus. As such choruses are wont to do, this one provides us with the setting. The choristers announce they are happy that the French have been driven from Madrid while Carlos, the lead, indulges in mockery of Joseph Bonaparte. His joke, which puns upon the Spanish nickname for *El Rey José*—"Pepe Botellas"—leads to what in any other work might be a straightforward drinking chorus. Carlos quickly turns this around, however. He announces:

> Fire is the wine
> of the Spanish soul;
> fire is the air
> and fire is the sun;
> fire is running
> in my veins
> for loving and drinking
> and fighting and winning.[19]

The chorus enthusiastically takes up this theme, concluding its song with the announcement that "to fight is to live"—a fairly ominous announcement, given that this is supposed to be a celebration of victory. Indeed, this slightly dark tone that the opening chorus sets up is borne out by the end of the work. After the farcical encounters at the ball have been straightened out, an official enters to announce that the soldiers will have to depart to the front before daybreak. The work ends not with Carlos and his love Luisa in an embrace, but with Carlos's promise, "Do not fear, I will return."[20] The marqués de Aguilar has already announced that he will only award Luisa's hand to Carlos if he can prove himself in battle. Thus *La viejecita* ends on an oddly ambiguous note, and one that is hardly an exponent of facile patriotism. The lovers are not united but are parted by the final curtain, and the specter of war hangs over the entire cast.

This somewhat dark conclusion may not be surprising given that *La viejecita* premiered at the Teatro de la Zarzuela on 30 April 1897, during the two-year period of high tension before the outbreak of war with the United States. But the tone was leavened by all the farce and Fernández Caballero's elegant music. The magazine *Blanco y Negro* went so far as to state that "the most Spanish of our composers has created exquisite musical numbers for a very Spanish theme"; however, reviews stressing the work's nationalism were the exception to the rule.[21] The score does not indulge in those dance forms typical of the género chico. The only exception to this rule is a schottische in the second scene, which is used to characterize a group of English dragoons. Most of the other reviews tended to focus upon the beauty of the score rather than its supposed "Spanishness." *La viejecita* was not received as an exemplar of patriotism by the majority of the critics. This is a judgment that developed later, perhaps in response to the events of 1898 or under the influence of José Echegaray and Fernández Caballero's *Gigantes y cabezudos* from the following year, which was a much more critical view of Spanish patriotism, as we shall see.

La viejecita may also suffer by association with Ruperto Chapí's *El tambor de granaderos* (The Drummer of the Grenadier Guards), which was one of the most successful stage works of the 1894–1895 season. Like *La viejecita*, *El tambor* was also set against the French expulsion from Spain. If *La viejecita*'s patriotism is a subtle part of its dramatic and musical makeup, the same cannot be said of *El tambor,* which wears its patriotism on its sleeve. The ostensible plot is a dramatic cliché—young love threatened by the attempt of the ingénue's guardian to place her in a convent. This story is set in relief against the French occupation of Madrid, and it is the problems of this wartime occupation that are of primary concern during the opening of the play. The opening chorus features not the standard happy citizenry in celebration, but a group of beggars waiting for a charitable distribution of "some miserable soup" from the local clergy.[22] Although the love conflict is indirectly introduced in dialogue after this, before we actually meet the characters of Gaspar and Luz another scene refers to the problems of occupation. An army colonel confronts the local clergyman (a loveably venal soul in the way only fictional priests can be) who has been helping soldiers desert from the army. This scene sets up dueling definitions of national identity that will drive the dramatic action. The colonel declares that "true Spaniards are those who obey their king" and that since the Spanish crown has been ceded to Joseph Bonaparte, only those who swear allegiance to the French monarch are true Spaniards. This stands in stark contrast to El Lego, the lay priest who has been helping soldiers desert—and whose definition of "Spanish" rests on a different foundation from the question of who the monarch is.[23]

This distinction between ideas of nationalism becomes even clearer during— of all things—the love duet in the following scene. Gaspar and Luz declare their undying devotion for each other, sotto voce because Luz's uncle and guardian, Don Pedro, is nearby reading a newspaper. Chapí and Sánchez Pastor interpolate Don Pedro's reading of this paper and his commentary on the items between each verse of the love duet. Don Pedro has sided with the French, and vociferously approves of "el rey José" and the occupation. As he says after having read that Queen María Luisa lunched with Napoleon the previous day and later heard mass:

> Whenever they want to, our monarchs
> see the Emperor;
> later they enforce the laws
> against he who attacks King Joseph.[24]

Although Don Pedro is not thinking in the strictly nationalistic terms that arose in the scene between the colonel and El Lego, he is thinking in similar terms of allegiance and obedience. What is important to the colonel and Don Pedro is obedience to the new order that rules in Madrid. Their focus is on the dynastic allegiance characteristic of absolutism. There is a king and that is sufficient to determine loyalty and allegiance. This is in distinct contrast to El Lego, Gaspar, and Luz. These characters place a higher allegiance on something less tangible than a reigning monarch. For Gaspar and Luz, this is the idea of romantic love: their duet features them pledging their undying love for each other as Gaspar promises to rescue Luz from the awful fate of becoming a nun. Just as El Lego "rescues" soldiers who do not want to serve Bonaparte by aiding their desertion from the army, Gaspar promises to rescue Luz from a fate worse than death.

Sánchez Pastor sets up a scenario in which the three traditional pillars of Spanish governance—the crown, the church, and the army—have been corrupted. The crown has been corrupted by the nature of the man who rules Spain, a foreigner and a conqueror. The army has been corrupted by its allegiance to this crown, corrupted to the point that individual soldiers are no longer willing to remain loyal to their oaths of service. The church has been corrupted by its willingness to imprison an innocent girl against her wishes at the request of her Francophile guardian. In each case, the cause of the corruption is contact with the foreign occupying power. Having set up this problem, the remainder of *El tambor de granaderos* will set about the problem of purifying and regenerating the Spanish state. Luz is saved from the convent (after a mock musical exorcism, something unique in the annals of operetta), while the crown and the army are saved by the deus ex machina of the battle of Bailen, which forces the French to flee from Madrid. The final scene also links the love of Gaspar and Luz with the abstract vision of the nation originally espoused by El Lego, for as Luz exults that Gaspar has been freed from prison, he exults in the fact that this has happened "at the same time as the country [has been freed]!"[25] This vision of the Spanish nation is most clearly set out in the finale to the first scene of the play, in which the links between romance and nationalism come to a head and which defines the truly Spanish nationalism of *El tambor de granaderos*.

In this finale, the soldiers of the Madrid garrison are supposed to swear allegiance to José Bonaparte. The first sign that this is not going to be a completely festive occasion occurs about a third of the way through the number. The chorus, which to this point has been acting much as choruses are accustomed to do—that is to say, making remarks about how cheerful everything is—hears the strains of the Royal March as the French officials enter and immediately sing "Poor soldiers / who swear without faith!" The upshot is clear: the Spanish soldiers are swearing fealty to a monarch that they feel no loyalty toward. Luz, observing the scene, casts it in immediately personal terms. She knows that Gaspar's upright nature will not allow him to swear a false oath, and she fears that "for my love alone / he suffers this torture."[26] As in the love duet, the personal becomes political, and Luz fears that Gaspar's concern over her future will cause him to be untrue to his country.

As it turns out, she need not have feared. As Gaspar approaches the regimental flag, Luz sneaks in the opportunity to give him a kiss. This apparently gives him the courage to reject swearing the oath to Napoleon:

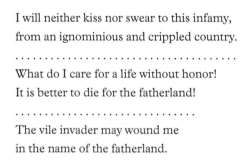

I will neither kiss nor swear to this infamy,
from an ignominious and crippled country.
. . . .
What do I care for a life without honor!
It is better to die for the fatherland!
. . . .
The vile invader may wound me
in the name of the fatherland.

The chorus instantly approves of Gaspar's stance, proclaiming "Very well done! . . . Long live the boy / who prefers to be faithful to the fatherland!" even as he is carted off to prison.[27] The chorus and Gaspar, much like El Lego in his earlier confrontation, swear their allegiance (through their actions, if not their words) to a much more abstract concept than Bonaparte. Their overarching loyalty is to the patria, their homeland. Gaspar becomes almost obsessive about his loyalty to the patria, referring to the word repeatedly in the finale. As might be expected of a soldier, his ideas of death and battle are intimately associated with his country; nor is his juxtaposition of a false country—one ruled by Bonaparte and the French—with a true country a real surprise.

El tambor de granaderos came in for heavy fire from the critics when it opened on 16 November 1894. *El Heraldo de Madrid* claimed that had any other composer but Chapí set the libretto to music, the work would have "died at birth." The reviewer for *La Correspondencia de España* even went so far as to term the libretto "literary anarchism" that strained for laughter. Furthermore, the plot was described as "an episode from the year 1808 that entertains one little and interests one less, despite its striking the relevant patriotic note." *La Época* cattily attributed the success of the show to the tight cut of the uniform worn by Isabel Brú, who played Gaspar—as in *La viejecita,* the leading male is a trouser role. The only explanation that occurred to the critics for the work's success on opening night was Chapí's score. And the high point of that score, singled out almost unanimously by the critics, was Gaspar's refusal to swear the oath. Much of this scene was set to a military march that Chapí was shrewd enough to open and close the overture with as well, which doubtless helped to build up an enthusiastic response to the music. The only paper not to ascribe the full reaction of the audience to the music was *El Liberal,* which judged that the audience reaction was driven by their enjoyment of "the adventures that happen to the drummer boy, who with noble strain refuses to swear to the flags of the intrusive monarch."[28] Clearly, the one thing everybody liked about *El tambor de granaderos* was Gaspar's rejection of the French. Both the audience and the critics recognized this was the crux of the work, regardless of whether they were swept along by Chapí's stirring martial music or by the high drama of the situation. In either case, the audience was reacting to an idealized moment in Spanish history, when at least one person was willing to reject a foreign invader for the higher cause of the patria.

But what exactly were men like Chapí, Fernández-Caballero, Chueca, Sánchez Pastor, Burgos, and Echegaray trying to do by adapting history into the género chico format? On the surface the format of the género chico is hardly suitable to the broad and sweeping canvas of history, since it relies on simple dance music and has minimal character and plot development. Historical themes have always found a comfortable home on the lyric stage, but generally only as the backdrop for musical romance. But by reducing traditional plot elements like historical intrigue and romantic love to incidentals, the género chico developed the role of the Spanish people into protagonists of history, to the sole force that determined the destiny of Spain. This was clearly a response to the problems of the Restoration régime, which had stymied the traditional role of the Spanish people in favor of political stability. The historical zarzuelas of the género chico suggest that the only response to such political corruption is to remove the politicians and the elites from power. All political movement should come only from the Spanish people, who would act as a united whole without class distinctions. This was not merely a stage vision, since it was reflected in the ideas of a wider selection of the Spanish intelligentsia. In the absence of an agenda from the state, popular culture was again developing ideas crucial to Spanish national identity.

How influential were the historical zarzuelas in their attempts to shape Spanish national identity? The answer to that question can be found in the role that music played in the run-up to the Spanish-American War of 1898.[29] As the press and the government attempted to whip the Spanish people into a patriotic frenzy to build support for conflict with the United States—a frenzy that the Spanish people were reluctant to take part in—there was an attempt to use the popularity of *Cádiz* as a rallying mechanism. There was an effort in the press to turn the most popular musical number from the zarzuela, the orchestral march that Chueca and Valverde had used to introduce the Constitution of 1812, into a new national anthem. In a country where the institution of nationalism was so weak that the state could not even promote a unifying national anthem, popular culture seemed to fill a vacuum. The fact that there was a vacuum to fill does not merely indicate how weak the Spanish state was; it foreshadows the disaster of 1898 that would set the stage for the crises of the Spanish state in the twentieth century.

The orchestral march from *Cádiz* received new life in 1896 when the librettists Celso Lucio and Enrique García Álvarez teamed up with composers Ramón Estellés and Quinito Valverde to pen *La marcha de Cádiz.* The motor of this farce is the prevalence of community bands in Spanish villages. The governor of Castile is about to make a visit to the small town in which this zarzuela takes place, and he asks to be received by the community band playing the March from *Cádiz.* Unfortunately, local officials had pocketed the money earmarked for the local band. In a desperate attempt to hide their embezzlement from exposure, they decide to shanghai Pérez, a visiting clarinetist from Madrid, into organizing a makeshift band to welcome the governor. This being a farce, they mistake Atilano (who has come to the village to elope with the mayor's daughter) for Pérez. Atilano, who cannot read music, is put in the awkward position of training the musicians and playing clarinet with them.

If *La marcha de Cádiz* is an accurate reflection of musical and political customs in rural Spain, it is evidence of the spread of zarzuela music outside Madrid. The four musicians hired to make up the municipal band clearly have fairly broad musical tastes—"we play more than just Wagner / Rossini and Mozart" they boast.[30] However, in spite of this fairly advanced taste in music, there is the implicit assumption that it is Chueca's march that is most appropriate to welcome a visiting dignitary. Even more astonishing is the claim made for the piece at the fall of the curtain. As the mayor hustles Atilano off to jail, his daughter Clarita turns to the audience and asks for applause in these terms:

> The march has now finished;
> if it didn't seem bad to you,
> applaud, I beg you,
> for the national hymn.[31]

The popularity of Chueca's march is so sweeping that it manages to displace the national anthem—not only on the stage, but for the audience as well. Furthermore, the applause of the piece is solicited not for the dramatic characteristics of *La marcha de Cádiz* or the performances of the actors, but rather for the nationalist characteristics of the music.

Part of the reason that Chueca's march could be referred to as the "national hymn" stemmed from the fact that just exactly which piece of music was considered the national anthem was disputed throughout the nineteenth century in Spain. Hard-core royalists tended to respond to the "Marcha granadera," which became known as the Royal March in the early nineteenth century, while liberals advocated the "Himno de Riego," which had been written to celebrate the accomplishments of General Rafael de Riego, whose defiance of King Ferdinand VII in 1820 had ushered in an abortive three-year experiment in liberal constitutionalism. Then there was the revolutionary Left, which preferred the "Internationale" or the "Marseillaise." Unlike other European countries, Spain failed to adopt an official national anthem during the nineteenth century, so that by the time of the Restoration there was no official musical symbol of national unity. Combined with the reluctance of the Restoration régime to seriously undertake any nation-building initiatives, this failure left a large symbolic gap. Chueca's march seemed poised to fill that gap partially due to its patriotic sound—as a march, it shares the common tempo and rhythmic feel of many national anthems—and partially due to its popularity. Success in the theater was one potential sign that the "*Cádiz* March" might overcome the partisan factionalism that surrounded the Royal March and the "Himno de Riego."[32]

La marcha de Cádiz premiered at the Teatro Eslava on 11 October 1896 and was an immediate popular hit. It was presumably this success that prompted the newspaper *El Liberal* two months later to publish a new version of the "*Cádiz* March," this one with a lyric by Leopoldo Cano that also calls the piece the "Himno Nacional." The new lyrics are both patriotic and martial, calling the men of Spain sons of El Cid and declaring that "the soldier of my country will climb up a mountain to the skies and will descend to hell if he must."[33] The tone seems to have been inspired by a similar piece in that paper the previous week, which had published a selection of *villancicos*—Christmas carols—with a war theme. The majority of these also sounded a virile and patriotic note, although a few of these carols have a decidedly darker tone that specifically attacks the United States. Felipe Pérez y González (the librettist for Chueca's *La Gran Vía*) was particularly virulent:

> The pigs of Chicago
> say they have taken it badly
> that so many compare them
> with Sherman, Morgan, and Call.
> This is because pigs provide
> very good chops and good ham
> and those others only
> provide tongue . . . of a scorpion.[34]

Goodwill toward men had apparently been suspended for this particular holiday season. It is also worth noting that the Spanish press had a penchant for comparing the United States and its citizens to pigs, so this passage has a nasty double meaning: Pérez y Gonzalez is not just talking about the denizens of the Chicago stockyards here, but is making a reference to the American people at the same time.

These villancicos and *La marcha de Cádiz* were part of a rising tide of patriotic fervor that had begun when news of the Cuban revolt reached the Iberian Peninsula in early 1896. Chueca and Valverde's *Cádiz* had been successfully revived at the Teatro Apolo, and in late February the queen, along with her daughter and son-in-law, attended a performance for the specific purpose of hearing the famous "*Cádiz* March." This event prompted one anonymous commentator to suggest that the queen "in a certain manner had just awarded Chueca the Cross of Military Merit."[35] This particular revival of *Cádiz* had led the conservative daily *La Época* to begin agitating for the march to become the new national anthem.[36] The ever-patriotic Antonio Peña y Goñi actually went so far as to call the "Himno de Riego" "leftovers [*ropa vieja*] from the era of military coups."[37] On the other hand, Peña y Goñi mocked the attempts to alter Chueca's original intent by adding subpar poetry, in particular the attempts of *El Imparcial* to hold a contest that would set words to Chueca's march. Peña y Goñi noted that the paper had only published one of the entries. (The paper seems to have been so embarrassed by the quality of the entries that the contest was quietly forgotten and no prize ever awarded.)[38] Peña y Goñi agitated for both a new national anthem and a new flag, implicitly citing Spain's degeneration, but setting amateurish words to already established music was hardly the way to accomplish this.

Nevertheless, the "*Cádiz* March" became even more popular in the wake of *La marcha de Cádiz*. Audiences began demanding it at band concerts and other public performances, as happened at a performance in the Teatro de la Zarzuela in late November: the coronet band that was sharing a bill with a performance of Chueca's *El chaleco blanco* was not allowed to continue with its performance until it had played the March.[39] Traditional historiography on the 1898 crisis has suggested that such popular fervor helped to drive Spain into conflict with the United States, although more recent work has suggested that much of this popular groundswell was in fact created by the press; the populace as a whole was much more ambivalent about taking on "Sherman, Morgan, and Call."[40] The examination of zarzuela literature would seem to suggest that ambivalence was the order of the day. Patriotism was popular, but the sophisticated theatrical audiences of Madrid already knew that the government had a tendency to promise more than it could deliver.

It is no coincidence that a historical narrative which deemphasized the role of the Spanish government was highly popular in the 1890s in Spain. The corruption engendered by the turno pacífico was becoming increasingly plain—and worse, it was not promoting stability as the architects of the Restoration régime had hoped to do. With many people isolated from formal politics, anarchist activity was becoming more and more prevalent in Spain. Anarchists revolted in Jerez in 1892 and when the rising was violently suppressed, other anarchists bombed the Teatre del Liceu in Barcelona (ironically, during a performance of Rossini's *William Tell* with its ringing calls for freedom). Prime Minister Antonio Cánovas del Castillo, the main architect of the Restoration régime and the turno, was assassinated by an anarchist in 1897. Colonial conflicts also had the country sliding toward chaos. In 1895 a revolt against the Spanish government had broken out in Cuba. By the following year, the revolt had spread to the Philippines. Both of these revolts brought Spain into conflict with the United States, which supported the rebels as "freedom fighters" while hoping to pick up some colonial holdings of its own. Inexorably, the Restoration government led Spain into a war it could not hope to win. The Disaster of 1898 proved the stage vision was right: Spain had been corrupted by its political system.

In the vacuum created by the weakness of the Spanish state, it fell to commercial musical theater to create a unifying historical vision of the Spanish nation. The timing of this effort would turn out to be critical: the number of historical zarzuelas would increase in the 1890s as Spain was beginning to move toward a confrontation with the United States. If Spain were to enter into armed conflict, it would be necessary to mobilize the population behind the effort—and nationalism would be critical in binding the country together in order to undertake a war. This would be especially critical in a situation where the population was dubious about the ability of a weak and corrupt government to succeed in such an undertaking. The attempt failed. Spain was not merely defeated in the Spanish-American War, it was humiliated. In Spain, the War would become known simply as *El Desastre,* or the Disaster. In the wake of such a humiliation, the liberal patriotism of *Cádiz, Trafalgar, El tambor de granaderos,* and *La viejecita* would fall out of favor. But the genius of nationalism in a popular medium like zarzuela is that its message is mutable and can shift to take account of popular trends and swings in public opinion. The self-sufficient message of *Cádiz* and the idea that the Spanish people were at the core of the idea of the nation had not worked in 1898. In the early years of the twentieth century, the nationalist message of zarzuela would shift once again. If self-reliance could not win a war, the outside ideas would be needed to fix Spain's problems. Zarzuela would show Spaniards how to become more European and more modern without losing their core national identity.

4

Regenerationism, Viennese Operetta, and Spanish Nationalism

I n the history of light musical theater, one of the most genuinely subversive and disturbing works ever performed might well be *Gigantes y cabezudos* (Giants and Fat-Headed Dwarfs), the hit of the 1898–1899 season at the Teatro de la Zarzuela. The work is an operetta that takes a critical look at the aftermath of a misguided war. Set in Zaragoza, the plot revolves around the interference by the local police sergeant in the love life of Pilar and Jesús. The sergeant attempts to convince each of the lovers that the other has married while Jesús was fighting against the Americans in Cuba so that the sergeant may wed Pilar. While the unvarnished portrait of a corrupt official would be unusual enough for an operetta, the work is most notable for its realistic portrayal of the repercussions of the crisis of 1898 onstage. *Gigantes y cabezudos* is both a satirical diagnosis and a clear articulation of Spain's problems in the aftermath of the War of 1898; it also manages to encompass the regenerationist solutions that could heal the country.

The zarzuela opens with a scene of tumult and turmoil: nothing short of a riot (accompanied by music, of course) is in progress. The women of Zaragoza have just been informed of the latest increase in food taxes and are furious. Such a scene had been duplicated many times over—sans music—in towns across Spain in the months before the premiere, and would continue well into the next year. The women sum up their contempt for the Spanish government in a couplet at the end of the opening chorus: "the marketplace has voted / and it has voted no."[1] This riot, like its counterparts in real life, featured the unrepresented in Spanish political life making their voices heard in the public sphere, replacing the nonrepresentative "voting" of the Restoration system with a "vote" that was more meaningful in practical terms.[2] The opening scene of the zarzuela ends with the women attacking the municipal officers who turn up to enforce the new tax policy and a song that goes even further in its rejection of authority. The stage directions indicate that the chorus comes to the proscenium and sings the following chorus directly to the audience:

> Though we are weak we can be what men can't,
> and when we look furious they are frightened
> and they will cede us the country
> . . . .
> although the mayor may bring a cannon here,
> we will not be moved if we are unified.[3]

Although it would be going too far to read this as a call for the audiences to revolt against the Restoration régime, it is by far one of the most confrontational passages in zarzuela literature. And as if to reinforce the points made by this fictional riot, the scene closes with the couplet that reaffirms the rights of Spanish citizens to participate in their own government—"the marketplace has voted no."

Manuel Fernández Caballero uses his music to further this point. He makes extensive use of the jota, a traditional folk dance, in constructing his score. The score itself consists of six separate numbers, four of which are jotas. Since these four numbers are also the most complex numbers in the score (each except the last is broken down into two or three separately numbered sections), close to three-quarters of the music in the work is inspired by the jota. (As the reviewer for *La Época* laconically noted, "there is a plethora of jota here.")[4] More importantly, three of these four jotas are the numbers that transmit the political message of the zarzuela. The first jota is the opening scene that features the fight among the vendors and concludes with the chorus "the marketplace has voted. . . ." The second jota is a number in which the female vendors fantasize about how life would be if women ran the government—which concludes with the riot against the tax collectors. The third jota is less politically charged, but features a procession of gigantes that celebrates Aragón, the area of Spain in which the musical form originated. The final number, a religious procession (marked "Salve" in the score), is a straightforward choral piece—but even here Fernández Caballero cannot resist mixing in "the happy sounds of the jota."[5] While it had begun life as a regional folk music idiom, by 1898 the jota had become one of the most self-reflexively "Spanish" forms in the musical vocabulary of the género chico. In *Gigantes y cabezudos,* Fernández Caballero uses the jota to construct a musical vision of Spanish society that pits the popular classes against the government.

While *Gigantes y cabezudos* has a "ripped-from-today's-headlines" quality about it, the work unites a satirical vision of Spain's problems with a potential solution to those problems—lessons that had been learned from the historical works of the género chico. The corruption of the Restoration régime is evident in the character of the sergeant and his abuse of political power for personal gain. But the work also suggests the power of the people to fix such corruption when the women proudly proclaim that corruption cannot remain if the Spanish people are united. Fernández Caballero's music supports this idea. By composing virtually the entire score in the form of a jota, he suggests the unity and strength of the Spanish people. The jota, after all, is folk music—the music of the pueblo—and its message will eventually override the corruption of the régime. It is suggestive that the sergeant, alone of all the main characters, does not sing during the course of the work. Musically, he is not part of the pueblo; he is isolated from the Spanish people and therefore not a true member of the Spanish nation. As with the historical zarzuelas discussed in the previous chapter, the Spanish people find themselves resisting a corrupt government.

Gigantes y cabezudos is set against the highly dramatic backdrop of the defeat of Spain at the hands of the United States in the War of 1898. The collapse of the Spanish Army and the exposure of the corruption of the political system that followed was so traumatic that it was simply referred to as *El Desastre*—"The Disaster"—in Spain. Losing the war was only the beginning of Spain's problems. During the first two decades of the twentieth century, the country was assailed by a crisis of self-confidence engendered by the military defeat and by the severe economic dislocations of World War I. The years from 1898 to 1909 saw increasing social unrest as the working classes pressed for entry into the Restoration political system, which had been designed specifically to keep them out. This tension climaxed in 1909 with what became known as "The Tragic Week," when working-class groups and trade unions in Barcelona, in response to a military expedition to Morocco, called a general strike that resulted in an uprising against the government. The tragedy of the week was the violent official response, which left scores of people dead across the city. Social tensions were intensified by rapid inflation after 1914. The influx of money thanks to World War I and subsequent inflation exacerbated the sense of social crisis, especially when rising food prices prompted a nationwide general strike in 1917. The Restoration settlement was rapidly devolving into a conflict between the popular classes who wanted political representation, and the elites that preferred stability to what they perceived as the inherent threat of mass politics.[6]

As social unrest threatened to envelop the country, a regenerationist movement began to accelerate within Spain. Calls for political and social reform can be traced back to the activists in the *arbitrista* movement of the seventeenth century who were seeking to rectify what they regarded as Spain's decline. Intellectuals in the late nineteenth century were still decrying the corruption of the government and the disconnect between Spain's elites and el pueblo—the idealized version of the Spanish people. This disconnect had been exacerbated by the turno pacífico, which demobilized the working class to keep the elites in power. The disaster of 1898 had laid bare the corruption of the political system and the rottenness of Spanish society. As a result, intellectuals began looking for ways to fix things and regenerate Spain into something grand and glorious. While the state might have been weak and corrupt, intellectuals trusted in the inherent integrity of the Spanish nation. The regenerationist movement refutes the idea that Spanish nationalism was weak in the early twentieth century—regenerationism, by necessity, could only have developed due to a powerful feeling of national identity.

The regenerationists of the early twentieth century are often collectively referred to as the "Generation of '98" in order to emphasize the extent to which the defeat in the Spanish-American War influenced their thinking. These thinkers turned toward Europe to counter Spain's decline. Spain represented the past; its customs and traditions had landed the country in trouble. Europe was modern and represented the future; it could provide the solutions that would take a moribund country into the twentieth century. This idea gained added force in the wake of industrialization, which had changed the social and economic landscape of Europe. It did not escape the notice of educated Spaniards that their country in many ways had remained stuck in 1800 while the economies, the societies, and the political systems of the rest of the continent had advanced dramatically.[7]

The Spanish government undertook a number of initiatives in the first two decades of the twentieth century to try to reform Spanish culture by making it more European. Government offices and ministries were supposed to open for business promptly at 9.00 A.M. rather than the more lax 10.00 or 11.00 A.M. openings that had become customary. To aid with this new efficiency, in 1907 Prime Minister Antonio Maura pushed through a law that forbade theaters from operating after 12.30 A.M. This would force audiences home to get a good night's sleep, better preparing them for being up and around early the next morning. At the same time, theatrical composers and librettists used the new atmosphere of regeneration to enact copyright reforms that protected their interests from the greed of musical copyists and archivists, who had previously swallowed up most of the profits that should be due to authors from their theatrical ventures. By setting up the Sociedad de Autores Españoles, zarzuela composers and librettists created a fairer way of distributing author royalties, thereby taking power away from the corrupt musical archivists— a theatrical parallel to what the regenerationists hoped to accomplish in the formal political sphere.[8]

In addition to the institutional reforms being carried out in the Spanish theaters, there were musical attempts at regeneration during this same period. If anything, the musical ideas behind regeneration had deeper roots than the Disaster of 1898. Zarzuela once again drew on the ideas of Unamuno and the vitality of the Spanish people that undergirded the género chico in the 1890s. Regeneration called for power to be taken away from the political elites who had so mismanaged Spain's affairs under the Restoration in order to give it to the Spanish people. As we have seen, the género chico had already developed the idea that a significant portion of the Spanish people was its growing urban population—which was characterized onstage by European dance music. Although the discourse around the zarzuelas had categorized the waltzes, polkas, mazurkas, and schottisches as quintessentially "Spanish," their foreign origin could not be completely denied. The collision of these two tropes—the urban masses as integral parts of Spain and their characterization through European dance music—would pick up greater force in the early twentieth century when European dance music would once again invade the Teatro de la Zarzuela. European music would be deemed to have the power to fix Spain's problems and would again become a marker of Spanish national identity.

The figure who brought European music to the forefront of Spanish consciousness a second time was Hanna Glawari, known to most musical theater buffs as *The Merry Widow*. This operetta, which premiered in Vienna on 30 December 1905, was arguably the most popular international hit in the two decades before the First World War—the *My Fair Lady* or the *Phantom of the Opera* of its day. The operetta traveled throughout Germany and Central Europe in 1906 and made its way to London, New York, and Buenos Aires by 1907. The Latin countries of Europe waited until 1909 to succumb to its charm. The Madrid premiere was 8 February, close to three months before the Paris premiere on 28 April, reversing the normal trajectory of European musical premieres. Even today, it is easy to hear why fin-de-siècle Europe succumbed to the charm of Franz Léhar's lush and romantic music, which includes such evergreens as the "Vilja *Leid*" and "Da geh'ich zu Maxim," better known as "The Merry Widow Waltz." The popularity of the work inspired hat and corset designers. The work would prove to be so durable that it would be filmed four times, twice in the silent era and twice with sound—most memorably in 1934 with Jeanette MacDonald as the widow and Maurice Chevalier as her suitor. In the movie versions, the plot tended to be radically altered from Viktor Léon and Leo Stein's original libretto, proving it was the music that made *The Merry Widow* immortal.

The music of *The Merry Widow* ushered in a completely new era in the history of musical theater, what operetta historian Charles Traubner has termed the "Silver Age" of operetta.[9] "Golden Age" works from the 1850s through the 1880s—those by Offenbach, Gilbert and Sullivan, Suppé, and their contemporaries—were driven by satire. They were comedies with music, and the humor was the primary dramatic concern. The dramatic motor of Silver Age works, by contrast, is romantic sentiment. (To understand the difference, consider the classic Gilbert and Sullivan Savoy Operas: the least interesting characters are almost always the romantic leads.) Although humor is not absent in Silver Age operetta, it would be increasingly relegated to the secondary characters. The move toward sentimental romance prompted an analogous shift in operetta music. The music of Léhar and his contemporaries is generally more lush and melodic than that of previous works. Rather than music written to fit the constraints of actors who were not primarily vocalists, Silver Age operetta requires trained, legitimate voices to put its music across.

The music of Silver Age operetta was critical to reforming Spanish theater and society. A major problem with the género chico at the turn of the century was its reliance on simple dance music in its scores. Critics were intensely concerned that the often repetitive emphasis on jotas, seguidillas, and polkas had lowered the quality of Spanish music. Certainly, there was none of the complex and quasi-operatic music that had been the hallmark of zarzuela grande scores from the 1850s to 1880s that the género chico had supplanted. By the turn of the twentieth century, debates were raging in theatrical circles over the supposed decline of the género chico. In a piece published on New Year's Day 1901, the critic Caramanchel characterized the género chico as evidence of Spain's "present national degradation": "The género chico was a formula born logically in order to summarize our smallness and an appropriate mirror in which our decadence is reflected and in which we can contemplate it."[10] Critics like Caramanchel pointed out that the majority of legitimate dramas in Spain were foreign imports—Ibsen, for example, was then currently in vogue in Madrid theaters. Spain could only excel in a "little genre" of theater; bigger works of social import were beyond the capabilities of Spain's authors.

Supporters of Spanish theater could sound defensive when discussing the género chico. While trying to defend the genre a few years later in the pages of *El Heraldo de Madrid,* the critic Lara pointed out that not everybody wanted to attend advanced works by Ibsen or Wagner. This left the genre with an important role: "The género chico teaches our popular classes to sing melodies other than the melancholy and weepy ones inherited from the Moors," but even so, "the mass theater audience [*público*] will only become interested in those works which remain forever in their infancy."[11] Given that Spanish theater had a mission to educate its audience, how was it to get them out of childhood? Silver Age operetta would be a return to the melodic and complex scores that the género chico had abandoned. Such scores required training to execute. Operetta melodies provided a path around the overreliance on dance music that had come to seem trite and commonplace in Spanish theaters. To be sure, the music was still popular music, but its reliance on melody rather than rhythm was a distinctly fresh idea in Spain—one that critics would increasingly associate with artistic ideals rather than mere profit. *The Merry Widow* started this trend, and it is appropriate that an operetta that changed the course of musical theater history would also be the springboard for change and regeneration in Spain.

The arrival of *The Merry Widow* in Madrid was originally viewed by critics as simply the importation of another foreign hit in the vein of Franz von Suppé's *Boccaccio* in the 1880s or French composer Edmond Audran's farce *Miss Helyet* in the 1890s. Even Gilbert and Sullivan, whose works had never fared well on the continent outside Germany, found a welcoming home for *H.M.S. Pinafore* at the Teatro de la Zarzuela in 1885.[12] The first Madrid production of *The Merry Widow* received mixed reviews. The critics were enthusiastic about Léhar's music, the performers, and the luxurious production (which cost in excess of 70,000 pounds sterling, according to *ABC*), but the libretto received a critical drubbing. *El Heraldo de Madrid* went so far as to call the script "stupid." In *ABC*, Floridor noted a sense of something frivolous and decadent about the work: "It does not lack—we are the midst of operetta— cuckolded spouses, good humored people, amorous traps in the pavilion of a garden, gallants, little adventures and other side-arms that decorate the fundamental action." Especially noteworthy is his use of the phrase "side-arms" to denote what seem to be deviations from the main plot of the work. Here the term operetta is used to denote frivolity and a lack of linear construction in the plot. Spanish zarzuelas tended to have one single plot line, and supporting characters did not have their own independent subplots as they did in *The Merry Widow*. Floridor uses the term *operetta* to denote theatrical decadence—foreign and exotic. But it was this sense of foreignness about operetta that would allow it to become a force for regeneration. And buried in the critical reception was the idea that this particular European operetta was linked with Spain: a number of the Madrid critics thought the plot had been lifted from the seventeenth-century Spanish drama *El desdén con el desdén.*[13]

European operetta initially engendered a mixed reaction when it arrived in Spain, especially from Spanish composers. Amadeo Vives (who within a few years would become one of the masters of Spanish-style operetta) groused about *The Merry Widow* and its popularity. In an essay that probably dates from about 1910 entitled "Hora de angustia o *La viuda alegre*" (The Hour of Anguish, or The Merry Widow), Vives sets out to have a serious conversation about Spanish opera and Wagner with a friend.[14] Unfortunately, Vives is driven to distraction because no matter where he and his friend go, café orchestras are playing selections from *The Merry Widow*. The essay concludes with an amusingly telling vignette. Vives encounters another friend, a pawnbroker, who wants to lend Léhar some music scores at 25 percent interest. The humor lies in the fact that Vives's friend does not realize that Léhar is not a resident of Madrid (nor, for that matter, is the Emperor Franz Josef, to whom Vives ultimately refers his friend). The popularity of *The Merry Widow* overrode any basic questions of whether or not the composer was Spanish. It was this instant familiarity of Viennese operetta music that would prove to be the key to integrating it into Spanish theater.

Whatever the reservations about *The Merry Widow,* critical evaluations of this new style of European operetta underwent a rapid reversal with the premiere of the next Léhar work to appear in Madrid, *The Count of Luxembourg.* The libretto of *The Count* indulges in a plot mechanism bizarrely outré even by musical theater standards: the central lovers are not aware that they are, in fact, already married. (It was a wedding of convenience, and a screen separated them during the ceremony. Only later do they meet and fall in love.) This plot, oddly, does not seem to have bothered the Madrid critics. Instead, they were completely bowled over by Léhar's music. *El Heraldo de Madrid* went so far as to compare Léhar to Mozart and Beethoven. José Juan Cádenas, writing for *ABC,* went even further. The day of the premiere, he called the work "almost an opera" and humorously declared he would not be surprised to hear of the company of the Teatro Eslava, who staged the premiere, mounting a Requiem Mass in the days to come.[15]

Cádenas's review seems to have been the piece that introduced the notion that Viennese operetta could save the flagging fortunes of the Spanish lyric stage. Financial problems had led the Teatro Eslava to begin staging cabaret performances in the previous decade, something that was generally disdained by the community of zarzuela authors and composers. In staging *The Count of Luxembourg,* Cádenas noted, "It isn't that the Eslava is regenerating, it is that they have modified and are cultivating a genre that exists everywhere and there is no reason why we should not know it here. What is happening in the theater is what is happening in books and newspapers: everything can be said, on the condition it is well said."[16] Although rejecting the idea that this particular work was somehow a regenerating force, he still manages to talk about the piece with all the essential terms of regeneration: it is something that is unknown in Spain but ought to be, because it can raise the overall quality of Spanish life. It is well done, and that should be the only criterion for its production. A large portion of Cádenas's piece—which was more advance publicity for Léhar's work rather than an actual review—was devoted to detailing the triumphal reception of *The Count of Luxembourg* across Europe and America, stating that it was about time the work should come to Madrid. Admittedly, Cádenas was hardly unbiased in the matter as he was the translator and adaptor of the original German script.

Cádenas also makes clear exactly why *The Count of Luxembourg* was needed in Madrid. He posed the question of whether the actors who would perform in the work would be up to the task of interpreting such a sophisticated piece of stagecraft: "Our artists, in general, lack flexibility. . . . They are typecast [*achulapados*] and stultified. . . . Authors have been dedicated, for the last twenty years, to present on stage wiseacres [*chulos*] and hicks, and naturally, the repertory has made the artists. . . ."[17] The fundamental weakness of the teatro por horas system as practiced in Madrid in the 1890s was the formulaic quality of most of the works. Since only certain types of shows were popular and made money, only those types were written. As a result, actors and actresses only perfected their stagecraft (such as it was, Cádenas hints) in performing those types of works. In reviewing the performers who would star in the Léhar operetta, Cádenas focused on their musical qualifications, noting that one actress had gained the personal approval of Maestro Léhar himself. In addition, Cádenas had only praise for Vicente Lleó, who would conduct the orchestra and arranged the music for the Madrid production. He called Lleó a true artist who had lost as many fortunes as he had made in the theater—in contrast to the theatrical impresarios whose only concern was profit. Cádenas saw in the entire production of *The Count of Luxembourg* a way to redeem the purely economic component of Spanish theater and infuse it with a more artistic product.

Cádenas was prescient in picking out Lleó as one of the driving forces behind the lure of Viennese operetta. Not only was the Valencian-born composer soon to become one of the foremost adapters of foreign operettas for the Spanish stage, he was also one of the first to try creating a European-style work in Spain. Lleó's *La corte de Faraón* (The Pharaoh's Court), with a libretto by Guillermo Perrín and Miguel de Palacios, manages to join the parodic tradition of the género chico, the racy humor of cabaret songs, operatic pastiche, and Viennese waltzes, into an enticing package that was equally influential as *The Merry Widow* or *The Count of Luxembourg* in bringing continental Europe to Madrid. The plot is a parody of the story of Joseph and Potiphar's wife as recounted in chapter 39 of the book of Genesis. In the Perrín-Palacios version, Potiphar's wife—here named Lota—is a sexually frustrated virgin whose husband cannot consummate their marriage because of a battle wound. In fact, although not explicit, the text suggests that Potiphar may even have been castrated. His servant Selha notes that "He had such a grave wound . . .

/ after the operation . . . / he'll marry that girl?"[18] Bawdy humor is the order of the day, accentuated by Joseph's increasingly frantic protestations that he is "chaste Joseph," and the work climaxes in a scene omitted from the Bible where Lota and the Queen of Egypt attempt to seduce Joseph simultaneously.

Literary parodies were a common subgenre of the género chico, although they usually tended to parody popular stage hits of the day. These had a rather short shelf life, and only *La corte de Faraón* has entered the zarzuela canon, primarily due to the enduring popularity of the parodied text. Lleó incorporated parodic elements into the music as well. Much of the first scene of *Faraón* is a send-up of Verdi's *Aïda,* specifically the Act II triumphal sequence. If Lleó's use of trumpet fanfares and rising string figures failed to tip off audiences to the nature of the parody, the chorus singing "Ritorna vincitor!" surely must have. However, most of the critics chose to ignore this aspect of the music and focus on other numbers. Most commented heavily on the "Canción babilónica" (Babylonian Song) from the third scene. These couplets, sung by a secondary character, are essentially a comic diversion, and their risqué humor betrays the influence of cabaret songs in Lleó's work. Cabaret singers quickly separated the "Canción babilónica" from its dramatic context, and it became a staple of Spanish cabaret performances. As *La Época* had predicted of the song, "we will hear it soon everywhere."[19]

However, it was not just opera and Spanish song traditions that Lleó melded into his score. *La corte de Faraón* also has two waltzes that betray Léhar's influence. The first is sung by three widows giving marital advice to Lota (No. 3 in the vocal score).[20] The element of parody rears its head again: the idea of widows giving sex tips was doubtless inspired by *The Merry Widow* itself. Singing a waltz tune, the three widows advise Lota to submit herself to her husband. To modern ears, there is a certain amount of double entendre in the lyrics, though it is impossible to determine how much of this was intended by Perrín and Palacios. On the other hand, there are few alternate interpretations for lyrics like this:

> It is very hard
> and bothersome, I assure you,
> . . . .
> the right a husband has
> over his wife.[21]

The second waltz in Lleó's score, the "Vals del juicio" (Justice Waltz, No. 6 in the vocal score), features the attempted seduction of Joseph by both the Queen of Egypt and Lota. Although it is unclear if Lleó and his librettists were attempting to suggest a biblical ménage à trois, we can see a pattern emerging. Lleó uses the Viennese waltz as a way of reinforcing the sexual element in *La corte de Faraón*. It unites the tradition of bawdy humor of cabaret and the género chico with the new musical strains of Silver Age operetta. It is probably this, as much as anything, that helped to pave the way for Léhar's operettas in Madrid and explains why the reception of *The Count of Luxembourg* was even more rapturous than that of *The Merry Widow*. Still, Lleó had not fully integrated the new elements from Vienna into the Spanish theatrical tradition.

That would be left for the other main adaptor of European operettas, Pablo Luna. Born in Zaragoza province, he studied music at a provincial conservatory and then gained practical experience playing in a theater orchestra. He had moved to Madrid in 1905 and scored a minor hit in 1908 with *Musetta*—another adaptation of Henri Murger's *Scènes de la vie de bohème,* which had earlier inspired Giacomo Puccini's opera *La bohème* in 1896 and Amadeo Vives's zarzuela *Bohemios* in 1904.[22] The work that cemented both Luna's fame and the vogue for operetta *à la española* was *Molinos de viento* (Windmills), a semitragic love triangle set in a fairy-tale version of Holland with more wooden shoes and tulips than Vermeer ever dreamed of. Capitán Alberto, a prince from one of those imaginary Central European countries that form a large part of the geography of operetta, has washed ashore on the Dutch coast. He promptly falls in love with his nurse, the beautiful Margarita, who is in turn loved by Romo. The plot is a variation on *Cyrano de Bergerac.* Romo has never had the courage to declare his love, so he gets Alberto to teach him how to sing in order to win Margarita. The play ends with Alberto sailing away, Margarita pining for him, and Romo's realization that Margarita will never love him.

The real attraction of the work was the music. The critics viewed the score as fresh and original, although it alternates between music in a 2/4 march time and music in a 3/4 waltz time in the time-honored manner of the género chico.[23] The waltzes in particular attracted the attention of the audience, especially as Luna had orchestrated them with a Viennese gloss. There was more emphasis on the strings and less on the percussion than in a typical Spanish waltz orchestration of the 1890s. Luna's strings enhanced the lyricism of the waltz rather than the functional dance-music approach to the form favored by earlier Spanish composers. The review in *ABC* decreed that Luna had written "numbers worthy of being signed by Léhar, [Leo] Fall, [Oscar] Strauss and other princes of operetta."[24] *Molinos de viento* also doubtless benefited from the proximity of *The Count of Luxembourg,* which had opened shortly before the premiere of Luna's work and at the same theater where the Dutch treat would play. The timing of the premieres of these works is significant. *Molinos de viento* was the first major zarzuela to receive its premiere production outside Madrid, having opened at the Teatro Cervantes in Seville on 2 October 1910, two weeks before *The Count of Luxembourg* opened in Madrid. Luna was forming part of a trend and not riding the coattails of one. The combined success of *Molinos de viento, La corte de Faraón,* and *The Count of Luxembourg* helped to save the Teatro Eslava from financial disaster, just as they were poised to save Spanish theater from artistic ruin. The three works shared the evening bills at the Eslava for well over a year, usually with the Léhar work playing the early evening "vermouth" sections and the Spanish works alternating the late evening spots.

La Correspondencia de España suggested exactly why *Molinos de viento* was so important: it was, the reviewer claimed, "an operetta with the cut of classic Spanish zarzuela."[25] Luna's work had merged Viennese operetta with traditional zarzuela to form something that was fresh and new. Even if the plot sounds hackneyed today, it was viewed by the critics in 1910 as suitably theatrical and entertaining. And the Viennese gloss that so enraptured the critics does add a certain refinement to what might otherwise be a merely workmanlike score. *Molinos de viento* pointed the way toward more sophisticated scores and plots that were less reliant on género chico stereotypes and musical tropes. The following year, a review of Amadeo Vives's *La Generala* (The General's Wife) suggested that Viennese operetta had actually advanced the stature of Spanish stagecraft: "Score and book are wrapped in the aristocratic prestige of Art."[26] Nobody had ever suggested that the género chico was art with a capital "A." Operetta seemed to have rescued Spanish theater from the crudely capitalist machinations of the género chico and restored artistic prestige to the theater. European operetta music had revitalized Spanish theater, giving it artistic pretentions. But was operetta merely an exotic import that remained foreign, or had Spanish composers made it nationalist in the way that they had naturalized the waltzes and mazurkas of the 1880s and 1890s?

To determine what European operetta actually meant to Spanish theater, we must move forward to 1918 and the premiere of *El niño judío* (The Jewish Boy), which chronicles the misadventures of three Spaniards traveling through the exotic Middle East: "It is one of those fantastic trips that seems to have been written by the enemies of the Cook Agency," as one reviewer put it.[27] The ostensible plot—a search by Samuel, the Jewish boy of the title, for his rich father so he can marry Concha—is a mere thread on which to hang a series of exotic tableaus and Pablo Luna's vaguely orientalist score. The music was praised by the critics, while the libretto was felt to be amusing, if episodic (*ABC* termed it "extremely funny" as well as "arbitrary and incoherent").[28] Every review singled out Concha's "Canción española" from the second act as the highlight of the work, which created such a stir that at least one review focused entirely on this one song.[29]

Part of the attraction of this song is the fact that musically it is unlike anything else in Luna's score. The other numbers in *El niño judío* are a professional mix of operetta melodies (such as Manacor's song from Act I—a Viennese waltz) and orientalist exotica (stereotypically Indian dances and so forth), but the "Canción española" sounded quintessentially Spanish to its first audiences. "Miss Leonís decides to sing, accompanied by the guitar, a little number that ably mixes original airs from Andalucia and Madrid," summed up the reviewer for *El Sol,* noting "the association of granadinas and of seguidillas was realized quite well by the singer, and the audience acclaimed her unanimously. . . . The song was repeated three times, and the entire work was held up by this solid foundation."[30] The "Canción española" is easily the most inspired number in the score, and the critic scarcely exaggerates in declaring that the song saved *El niño judío* from oblivion. (It has been a frequent favorite of Spanish singers like Victoria de los Ángeles in recitals.) But the "Canción española" displays a very self-conscious sense of Spanish identity. The scene, with a beautiful young woman accompanying herself on a guitar while singing Gypsy melodies, is the sort of thing that almost automatically comes to mind when one tries to think of Spanish clichés. The central portion of the song, which features stereotypical references to "black eyes," flowers, and Gypsy shawls, makes one wonder if the librettists were actually trying to parody the genre of "Spanish song." If they were, it would seem the humor went right over the heads of the critics.

The "Canción española" sums up an entire decade's worth of zarzuela scores and the aspirations for incorporating European operetta into the zarzuela canon. The specifically Spanish dance forms of the granadinas and the seguidillas that make up the musical fabric of the number become just two more dance forms in a score full of exotic music. Even more importantly, consider the import of the words that open the song:

> I am Spanish, from Spain I come.
> In my eyes I bring the light of her skies
> and in my body, the grace of her womanhood.
> I am Spanish, from Spain I come
> and my brown face proclaims
> that I was born in Spain, to where I am returning.[31]

It is a most emphatic declaration of the singer—and the song's—Spanish identity. But in the middle of a cosmopolitan score built heavily on a base of Viennese operetta, such assertions of *españolismo* take on a slightly different tinge. It is a forthright musical assertion that while the specific song may be specifically Spanish, the wider context—the score as a whole—is Spanish as well. Consider especially the import of the last line: operetta came to Spain and became Spanish. What started out as foreign became part of the necessary musical fabric of Spanish identity.

The move toward operetta was prompted by a generational shift among theatrical composers. Lleó, Luna, and Vives had been too young to contribute to the género chico during its heyday in the 1890s. The musical career trajectory and training of these up-and-coming composers was vastly different from that of their older counterparts. They possessed the technical capability and musical sophistication to rescue Spanish theater from the moribund tropes of the género chico and rejuvenate zarzuela music. For most nineteenth-century zarzuela composers, music was not their original vocation and formal training played a minor role in the development of their musical style. Francisco Asenjo Barbieri may serve as a model. He originally intended to study medicine and only later switched to music, acquiring his musical style while serving as a member of a military band. Similarly, Ruperto Chapí's formative musical experiences were in community and military bands. His studies under Emilio Arrieta at the Escuela Nacional de Música seem only to have given him the necessary technique to put down the music he was already hearing in his head. Those who composed strictly for the género chico, like Federico Chueca, often had no formal training at all. Their entire musical training consisted of playing in cafés and theater pit orchestras.[32]

The zarzuela composers who launched their careers in the 1890s and early 1900s had a different trajectory. The expansion of the economy and the growth of the bourgeoisie meant that more families could allow their children to pursue a career in music rather than a profession like law, medicine, or engineering, which had been the traditional way in which families cemented and enhanced their socioeconomic status. Amadeo Vives knew early on in his life that he wanted a career in music, which was launched when he joined the children's choir at the Teatre del Liceu, where he sang in the first Barcelona production of Boito's *Mefistofele*. Vives was one of the few of the newer generation who did not have conservatory training, but he gained practical experience as the music master of a convent. He was also one of the founders of the Orfeo Catalá, the choral society that was part of the wider renaissance of Catalan music and culture.[33] José Serrano came by his musical inclinations through his family. His father had originally trained as an opera singer in Italy and was conductor of the municipal band in Sueca, near Valencia. Serrano mastered the piano, guitar, and violin by age ten, and he later studied at music conservatories in Valencia and Madrid.[34] When some of his early music was shown to Tomás Bretón in 1895, that prickly composer gave it the supreme accolade: it was not "vulgar."[35]

Bretón's tart comment provides insight into a fundamentally important difference between nineteenth-century zarzuela composers and the new generation that came to prominence after 1900. Men like Barbieri or Chueca were not unsophisticated composers, but they did lack the spit-shine polish of conservatory graduates. The music of nineteenth-century Spanish theatrical composers can seem unsophisticated—and in the case of many composers who never rose to the heights of either Barbieri or Chueca, crude. The orchestrations may seem trite, the choral arrangements unimaginative, and the repetitious use of a few dance forms monotonous. Such rough and ready compositional techniques should not be an indictment of the composers themselves, but rather of Spain's meager infrastructure for musical training in the mid-nineteenth century and of theatrical economics that demanded scores be composed rapidly with an eye toward popular acceptance.

The growth of the Spanish economy in the late nineteenth century also propelled musical education in the country, which allowed budding composers like Vives and Serrano to receive systematized musical training and support, unlike their predecessors. Serrano, for example, was awarded a pension of 3,000 reales from the Ministerio de Fomento when he enrolled at the Conservatorio de Madrid in 1895, thanks to his two very powerful patrons, composers Jesus de Monasterio and Emilio Serrano (no relation).[36] This was luxurious compared to the conservatory career of Bretón, one of the only composers of the earlier generation with formal musical training, who paid for his studies and supported himself by playing violin in a Salamanca theater pit orchestra.[37] Younger composers also tended to have broader musical tastes thanks to their exposure to the latest trends in European music. Composers like Bretón and Chapí studied abroad in musically provincial Rome—a center only for theater music—but after 1900 composers looking for foreign polish turned to Paris. The City of Light was arguably the center of the musical world in the first decades of the twentieth century, and it attracted two of Spain's major compositional talents at that time, Manuel de Falla and José María Usandizaga. Newer Spanish composers had greater technical skill and mastery of their craft than their predecessors and were thus in a much better position to appreciate—and assimilate—new music and techniques from north of the Pyrenees. As composers, they had a broader, more European mindset; this would be crucial to regenerating the moribund Spanish lyric theater.

The development of a new generation of European-influenced composers would have gone for naught had it not been for the simultaneous development of institutions that disseminated concert music. These structural developments would allow Spain to better assimilate the regenerating force of European music and further educate fledgling composers. The first full-time, professional orchestra in Spain, the Orquesta Sinfónica de Madrid, was founded in 1903. Two years later, Enrique Fernández Arbós became the orchestra's musical director and made it a force to be reckoned with in Spain's musical life. Fernández Arbós made it a crucial part of the orchestra's mission to present new works by Spanish composers. In the years between the orchestra's founding and the Civil War, Madrid audiences would have the chance to hear new works by Manuel de Falla, Conrado del Campo, Joaquín Turina, Ernesto Halffter, Óscar Esplá, and dozens of other young Spaniards. The early years of the twentieth century saw the foundation of philharmonic societies in a number of cities, as well as the founding of two more professional orchestras, the Orquesta Sinfónica de Barcelona in 1910 and the Orquesta Filarmónica de Madrid in 1915. There was also something of a renaissance in choral music (especially prominent in the Basque Country and Catalonia) and the development of several string quartets that helped to create a foundation for the performance of chamber music in Spain.[38]

Such developments would be crucial, because one of the most obvious problems of Spanish theater at the turn of the century was the fact that the most popular theatrical composers of the 1880s and 1890s were no longer writing for the theater. The three composers who had dominated the género chico died within four years of each other. Manuel Fernández Caballero passed away in 1906 and Federico Chueca died in 1908. Even before their deaths, these two composers had ceased to be active forces in the Spanish theater. Fernández Caballero suffered from cataract problems and had been virtually blind ever since the composition of *El dúo de la Africana* in 1893. He hired younger composers to transcribe his music, and in some cases he seems to have appropriated their compositions as his own. He did this with José Serrano, who transcribed *Gigantes y cabezudos* and wrote music for Fernández Caballero that the older composer "accidentally" claimed as his own.[39] Chueca had also been suffering from ill health, and had not had a major hit since *El bateo* in 1901.

But the death of Ruperto Chapí in 1909 was a blow not only to zarzuela but to Spanish musical life in general. Chapí was not only the last of the old-school género chico composers, he was arguably the most eminent and respected Spanish composer of the day. (Tomás Bretón could perhaps challenge that title, but Bretón only ever managed to compose one popular stage success— *La verbena de la paloma*—while Chapí managed to turn out hits in vast quantities.) Newspaper reports of Chapí's death rivaled, in both the quantity of the reporting and the quality of the panegyrics, the honors due to royalty. The entire front page of *El Heraldo de Madrid* was devoted to the death of the composer (including, dead center under the headline, a photograph of the corpse), while *ABC* placed a portrait of the composer on the cover and spread their reporting of the death across three pages.[40] All the news coverage was devoted to the enormous contributions of Chapí to Spanish musical life, not only as a zarzuela composer, but as a conductor and a composer of concert music as well. The tragedy of Chapí's death was only heightened by the fact that it had occurred a mere month after the triumphal premiere of *Margarita la Tornera*, his last and most successful attempt at opera composition. There was a distinct sense that the death of Chapí was the end of an era in Spanish music—a sense strengthened in hindsight, since *Margarita la Tornera* premiered exactly two weeks after *The Merry Widow*.

The Merry Widow and her Spanish progeny had come along at a crucial moment in Spain's theatrical history. The first two decades of the twentieth century were a period of intense change in Spanish theatrical circles. Audiences were dwindling due to competition from new forms of entertainment like cabaret and cinema. The deaths of significant composers like Fernández Caballero, Chueca, and Chapí further reinforced the idea that the glorious days of the género chico were at an end—a notion reinforced by the explicit link between zarzuela and the Spanish nation. As the latter had taken a drubbing in 1898, the former suffered by association. The idea that both theater and nation were in decline was so strong that beginning in December 1908, *El Heraldo de Madrid* ran a series of retrospective pieces on the premieres of some of the major works of the zarzuela repertory. This series, "Estrenos de antaño" (Premieres of Yesteryear), gave the historical background to the works, provided cast lists, reprinted lyrics, and published photographs of the composers, librettists, and actors. The series highlighted classic zarzuelas like *Jugar con fuego* and *Pan y toros* and also featured important género chico works like *La Gran Vía* and *Cádiz*. The overall tone was one of nostalgia, implying that the glory days of zarzuela were a vanished epoch in history just as Spain's glory had evaporated in 1898.[41] This sense of loss was only reinforced by a fire at the Teatro de la Zarzuela on 8 November 1909.

The history of the Teatro de la Zarzuela reflected the history of zarzuela in Spain. Built to house the genre as it was reborn in the 1850s, its fortunes suffered along with the depoliticization of zarzuela in the 1880s, and in the 1890s it became a género chico house with great success. The decline in the género chico after 1900 forced the impresarios to revamp the house again. It hosted cabaret performances, films, and even—at one low point that might have sent Barbieri spinning in his grave—wrestling matches.[42] In any event, the 1909 fire (whose origin was never determined) gutted the interior of the theater, destroying numerous sets, costumes, and musical instruments in the process. More importantly, it seemed to have destroyed a symbol of the

Spanish nation. As *El Liberal* stated: "For what it was and what it signified in the history of Spanish lyric art, the coliseum that was devoured by flames in only a few short hours could be described as a most fateful omen of national catastrophe. . . . Yesterday's fire has not destroyed 'just another theatre.' Within a few minutes, the flames had devoured the temple where the national lyric art, Spanish Zarzuela, was born and lived."[43] The fire was, in essence, the final blow to what had been a slow and painful decline in the quality and very nature of Spanish lyric art. All the reports on the fire explicitly conveyed the feeling that the theater was a stand-in for Spain itself. Both the nation and its lyric representation were in decline, and the destruction of the home of modern zarzuela confirmed this.

The Teatro de la Zarzuela fire gutted the showcase for Spanish lyric theater exactly nine months after the premiere of *The Merry Widow*. If there was ever a symbol of the need to bring new vitality to the Spanish theater, the fire was it. The Teatro de la Zarzuela would be reopened in 1913 and Viennese operetta–inspired zarzuelas would entertain Spanish audiences there for close to a decade. Yet musical regeneration from Europe would prove to be somewhat elusive. The operetta form would not completely dominate Spanish stages in the way that the género chico had ruled the roost in the 1890s. Furthermore, the success of operetta was fleeting: following the premiere of *La canción del olvido* in 1918, there would be a six-year hiatus in which no new zarzuela achieved hit status. The theatrical scene of the 1920s would look very different, as we shall see. While operetta gave a boost to Spanish box offices after 1909, it never quite became fully grounded in the theatrical vocabulary of Spanish authors, composers, or audiences.

Why this is the case might lie in the subjects that Spanish operettas chose to portray. While works like *La corte de Faraón, Molinos de viento, La Generala,* or *El niño judío* were exceedingly popular, they were not set in Spain. Only *El niño judío* featured Spanish characters (as well as an opening scene set in Madrid), but aside from the "Canción española" there is nothing intrinsically Spanish about the piece. For all the proclamations of the critics that operetta was a regenerating force and that operetta could be quintessentially Spanish, that logic seems to have rested on the fact that European dance forms had been integrated into the género chico in the 1880s. What this logic ignored was the fact that those songs were sung by the types of people a Spanish audience would encounter in the streets everyday, not Dutch peasants or Central European aristocrats. Regeneration relied upon the idea that the people of Spain could solve the problems brought about by the corruption and ineptitude of the Spanish government—or to use the terms that José Ortega y Gasset would increasingly use to frame discussions of regeneration, that "vital Spain" would come to supplant "official Spain."[44] Musical regeneration could not function if that music did not issue forth from the lips of Spaniards.

The problems with musical regeneration reflect the problems facing the advocates of social and political regeneration in Spain during that time period. The turno pacífico placed political discourse in Spain in a stranglehold: while discussions of regeneration and reform could be held openly in the press, the cafés, and the *ateneos,* concrete political action could only come through a government that was doing its best to ignore "vital Spain." For all the vibrancy of popular political movements like Republicanism in the early years of the twentieth century, which managed to elect local officials across Spain and play a dominant role in the regional politics of Catalonia, those political movements were still excluded from the Cortes and national political institutions. This meant there way no real way to move a reform movement forward against the entrenched turno parties.[45]

The turno parties did not completely ignore the calls for or the need for regeneration. The government took steps—if hesitant ones—toward reform in the first few decades of the century. Most notable in this regard was the Conservative Party under the stewardship of Antonio Maura, who was the political heir to Antonio Cánovas del Castillo. Maura clearly recognized the need to change the way things were done in Spain, but he was also loathe to open up the system to new and potentially destabilizing forces. During his second term as prime minister between 1907 and 1909, Maura instituted a policy of what might be referred to as top-down regeneration: the government did undertake a series of reforms, but not reforms that had been demanded by the populace.[46] In the theatrical realm, Maura and his minister of the interior, Juan de la Cierva, instituted the unpopular curfew that closed all performances by 12.30 A.M. to force Spaniards to be up and about in the morning on a European schedule. Not to be outdone, in 1911 the Liberals instituted a 15 percent tax on theatrical tickets designed to offset food and alcohol taxes. None of these attempts at reform came from the populace, who had delighted in late-night theatrical performances and cheap ticket prices.[47] Regeneration from official Spain did not have the ability to fix Spanish society because it failed to solve the problems that Spanish society actually had. It was merely an attempt to use the language of reform to uphold the status quo.

The ultimate symbol of the failure of state-sponsored regeneration was the Tragic Week of 1909, which would help to topple Maura from his post as prime minister. The fact that crowds in Barcelona took to rioting to protest an unpopular war demonstrated that official Spain had failed to learn the lesson that Manuel Fernández Caballero had tried to teach in *Gigantes y cabezudos.* Political regeneration failed because it was not rooted in the problems articulated by the Spanish people. In the same way, musical regeneration also failed: for all that critics might insist that *The Merry Widow* grew out of *El desdén con el desdén,* theatrical audiences could sense that it was an adaptation of *L'attaché d'ambassade.* Musical regeneration was not organic to the Spanish theater, but a way for impresarios to continue to make money. Audiences might accept and delight in Viennese waltzes, but the failure of the form to generate new works after 1918 indicates the fragility of audience identification with the trope that operetta could be a marker of Spanish identity. But it was also an indication of the varying ways in which Spanish identity could be portrayed through zarzuelas. Even as Viennese-style regenerationism was becoming popular on Spanish stages, other works were turning inward and looking toward the countryside for answers to Spain's problems. Those who distrusted reform and regeneration could take comfort in a traditional image of life in rural Spain that promised an essentialist vision of an unchanged nation. The War of 1898 had fragmented Spain's sense of self. It would also fragment the vision of the nation staged in the country's theaters.

5

The Romance of Rural Spain and the Failure of the Restoration Settlement

Late in her career, the Spanish soprano Victoria de los Ángeles would often end her recitals with an exciting encore: "La tarántula é un bicho mu malo" from *La tempranica*, a zarzuela by Gerónimo Giménez. Although she doubtless picked the song for its applause-garnering qualities (fast tempo, rapid-fire lyrics, short duration), it also tapped into a deep vein of Spanish sentiment. While audiences outside of Spain would have failed to appreciate the subtext of Giménez's song, it could not have escaped de los Ángeles, whose career always remained rooted in the music of her native country. *La tempranica* tells the story of the Gypsy María, who lives in the mountains outside Granada and pines for the wealthy Don Luis even while engaged to the steadfast Miguel. Eventually María finds out that Don Luis is married, and she vows to make her future marriage to Miguel a success. (Manuel de Falla would use an extremely similar plot and setting, albeit with a tragic ending, a few years later in his seminal opera *La vida breve*—one of the works that catapulted de los Ángeles to international recognition in the early 1950s.)[1] "La tarántula é un bicho mu malo" is sung in the first scene by María's brother Grabié (a soprano trouser role) and likens falling in love to being bitten by a tarantula.

The score of *La tempranica* is filled with Spanish folk music. Giménez employs flamenco, tangos, and a *zapateado* ("La tarántula") to tell most of his story. Then, when the setting moves to the city of Granada in the final scene, this folk music is upended by a waltz, reflecting the prevalence of urban dance music discussed in Chapter 2. But *La tempranica*, with its Gypsies singing traditional Andalusian folk music around campfires, sounds much more stereotypically "Spanish" than the urban delights of *La verbena de la paloma* or *Agua, azucarillos, y aguardiente*. This idealized Spain of charming villages, cheerful peasants, and flamenco-style folk music was being supplanted—to the extent that it had ever existed—by the urbanization and industrialization of the country in the late nineteenth century. Nevertheless, there was a heavy sentimental attachment to rural Spain among the zarzuela composers and writers of the género chico. Side-by-side with the sophisticated urban comedies and their up-to-date dance music, Spanish theaters staged sentimental romances set in the countryside among peasants who went off to work every morning singing a chorus. This elegiac subtext may well have struck a deep chord with Victoria de los Ángeles when she sang "La tarántula," since Spain was undergoing a similar round of modernization at the height of her international fame between the 1950s and the 1970s.

Understanding the role that rural Spain played in the development of a modern national identity has been complicated by the concurrent development of Spanish regionalism. During the nineteenth century, at the exact same time that European countries were developing the policies and ideas that put the "nation" in nation-state, vibrant non-statist nationalisms were developing in the peripheral regions of Spain, especially Catalonia and the Basque Country. Not coincidentally, these regions tended to be the most industrialized and urbanized in Spain; the development of regional nationalisms was tied to the feelings of the Catalan and Basque bourgeoisie that the material fruits of their (workers') labor was being siphoned off to support a government in Madrid that had little interest in industrializing the country.[2] These regional nationalisms took even greater root in the twentieth century under the Second Republic, which promised the Catalans and the Basques greater political autonomy. The subsequent backlash under the Franco régime, which attempted to quash regional identities by outlawing the Catalan and Basque languages, only reinforced the idea that regionalism could oppose a corrupt government in Madrid. Regionalism was formally enshrined as a democratic principle in the 1978 constitution, which used the historic claims to regional identity to construct a federalist system that granted autonomy to Spain's regional governments at a level not seen since the unification of the crowns of Castile and Aragón by the marriage of Ferdinand and Isabella in 1469.

Traditionally, regional identities have been seen as detrimental to the nationalist project in Spain. The weakness of the central government and its failure to develop a coherent state-run nationalist project in conjunction with the development of regional nationalisms has led many scholars to assume that Spain had a particularly weak sense of nationalism. Recent historiography has added nuance to this view. If one accepts that a national identity is not monolithic and that people are capable of functioning within a set of multiple identities, then regionalism does not have to be antithetical to nationalism. Rarely did even the most ardent of Basque or Catalan nationalists in the late nineteenth and early twentieth centuries speak of separation from the Spanish state; their argument was that their unique regional identities entitled them to greater political representation at the level of the national government. In this sense, regional nationalisms have virtually the same agenda as traditional nation-state nationalism in Spain: the integration of a population into the nationwide political system. Regionalisms also tended to focus on the cultural aspects of nationalism, using language, art, music, and literature to build up regional conceptions of nationalism. In this way, Spain's regional nationalisms are a counterpart to the more informal, populist ideal of nationalism discussed previously and of which zarzuela was also an integral part.[3]

Music played a significant role in integrating regional nationalisms into a more traditional state nationalism. Much of what we think of as "Spanish" music is folk music, but from traditions far wider than those of the Basque Country and Catalonia. Most people from outside Spain associate Spanish music with Andalucian folk music, such as the flamenco, the malagueña, and the habanera (imported from colonial Cuba). The percussiveness of castanets and hand-clapping, the minor-key harmonics, and the vocal melisma that are part of the flamenco world rapidly came to represent Spain musically. For example, consider how Georges Bizet managed to use such musical ideas to evoke the country in *Carmen*—an even more astonishing achievement when one considers that Bizet never got any closer to Spain than the library of the Conservatoire de Paris. In contrast, Spanish composers were far more egalitarian in adopting the wealth of Spain's folk tradition into their compositions, looking to regions other than Andalucía for inspiration. The best example of this is the piano music of Isaac Albéniz: the *Suite española* (1886–1888) and *Iberia* (1905–1908) both present a vision of Spain through a compilation of regional folk styles that ranges from Navarre to Seville.[4]

Understanding how regionalism and the use of folk music functioned in Spanish musical theater requires a different framework from the traditional lens of Basque and Catalan nationalism. Spanish composers tended to use folk music from Andalucía, Castille, and Aragón—regions that were not pushing for greater autonomy from the Spanish government. The point of using folk styles in music was not to create a sense of specific regionalism; it was instead to create a general sense that the various parts of rural Spain were components of a homogenous whole. The regions of rural Spain were to be interchangeable to encourage the identification of rural Spain as part of a national culture.[5] An examination of Albéniz's piano suites bears this out. While each individual piano piece is given a regional title, Albéniz treats these markers lightly, mixing together folk styles from various regions to form completely original music. Walter Aaron Clark, perhaps the keenest analyst of Albéniz's music, points out that while Albéniz's piano works sound quintessentially Spanish, they do so by building up a complex mixture of flamenco, *cante jondo,* Gypsy music, and French Impressionism—and that flamenco itself is a syncretic form with elements from Islamic, Jewish, Gypsy, and Latin American music.[6] Such homogenization and syncretism is congruent with traditional literature on nationalism, which suggests that the process was a way of creating unity in rapidly urbanizing societies. As cities drew in industrial workers from across the country, some method had to be employed to give the proletariat something in common and allow employers to effectively communicate with employees who might speak different dialects.[7]

But musical nationalism was more than simple nostalgia for an evaporating way of life. Even as the country was slowly urbanizing in the late nineteenth century, the Spanish political system remained rooted in rural Spain. As discussed in Chapter 1, the entire premise behind the Restoration government was to promote political quietism and avoid the consequences of popular political mobilization, which is why Antonio Cánovas del Castillo set up the turno pacífico. There was one major flaw with this system (aside from the fact that it manipulated the electoral system, naturally), and that was its reliance upon a heavily rural population to maintain the necessary political control. Spain's growing cities lacked the caciques and other forms of social control necessary to ensure that the masses voted the "correct" way. The result was a political system that was unresponsive to the political demands of the lower-class urban population. If Spain had remained the rural society it had been during the first half of the nineteenth century, the turno might well have worked. As it was, the system that Cánovas devised was outmoded even as it was being implemented. To further heighten the problems, the political movements toward which these new urban classes leaned—specifically Republicanism and Socialism—were not represented in the turno pacífico and thus had little formal political influence. As a result, mass political mobilization in Spain frequently took on an informal tinge in which meaningful political participation by the new urban working class took place not at the voting urns, but in workingmen's clubs and casinos as well as in the streets themselves.[8]

The portrayal of rural Spain in the zarzuelas of the género chico was an integral part of the Restoration political system. It was an attempt to reify the *caciquismo* at the heart of the turno. The género chico placed onstage an idealized rural life, with happy peasants and benevolent landlords, leading toward the stability that was on the surface of Cánovas's political system. Rural and regional zarzuelas were a reaction against the urbanization that was rapidly changing Spanish society in the late nineteenth and early twentieth century, a conservative vision of peace and tranquility that probably never existed in actuality. At a time when Republican politicians were mobilizing Spanish workers in street protests, Gypsies singing songs about love in the countryside represented the apolitical society that Restoration politicians had created the turno to propagate. The irony was that these pictures existed side by side with the urban reality of the género chico. The Spanish stage could contain multitudes, but Spanish political life could not.

Depictions of rural life became more prevalent in the years following the disaster of the Spanish-American War. The date is certainly not a coincidence. Spain's defeat in the Spanish-American War of 1898 had done significant damage to turno pacífico. The argument for suppressing popular political participation was that it would bring stability and better government to Spain, but the stable government had done nothing to prepare Spain for a disastrous war. With the failure of the traditional Liberal and Conservative Parties, the new working-class movements in the cities—areas uncontrolled by the system of caciquismo that underpinned the turno—became even more clamorous in their demands to enter the closed political system. As urban spaces and urban politics became even more contested, what would be more natural than for zarzuela composers and librettists to turn to a romanticized rural past—one that had provided, no matter how ephemerally, peace and stability at the end of the nineteenth century? Spain might have modernized and urbanized, but these trends were threatening to destabilize the country. Rural Spain would have to be reintegrated into the modern nation if Spain as a whole were to survive. Thus, depictions of rural life and the sounds of rural music would soon come into Spanish theaters, to join the depiction of urban nationalism that had become prominent in the previous two decades. The dual successes of Federico Chueca's *La alegría de la huerta* and Gerónimo Giménez's *La tempranica* in 1900 were the beginning of a trend toward more rural and regional zarzuelas on the Spanish stage.

While the first major zarzuela to use a regional setting was *Gigantes y cabezudos* (discussed in Chapter 4), the work that announced the arrival of rural zarzuelas on the Madrid stage was *La alegría de la huerta* (The Pride of the Orchard), which moved the dramatic action south to Murcia. The name of the composer for this initial excursion into the countryside would have been a surprise to most audience members: Federico Chueca, who had more or less invented the urban género chico with *La canción de la Lola*. Perhaps it was Chueca's pronounced *madrileñismo* that allowed him to take theatergoers into such unfamiliar terrain. But Chueca tempered the move by constructing the score mostly out of music familiar to audiences of his Madrid-based works. The main subplot of the work features a local musician, Heriberto, who has composed a pasodoble (also marked pasa calle in the score) that would not have sounded out of place in *La Gran Vía* or *Agua, azucarillos, y aguardiente*, nor would the duets between the lovers Alegrías and Carola have sounded out of place in Chueca's other works. But Chueca frames his score with two distinctly nonurban pieces of music. *La alegría* opens with a chorus of Gypsies singing distinctive flamenco music (Chueca indicates a *zambra* in the score) followed by a solo song for one of the female Gypsies. And he concludes the work with its most famous piece, the jota "¡Huertanica de mi vida!"[9] Chueca had frequently used the jota in his Madrid-based works—most notably in the "Jota de las Ratas" from *La Gran Vía*—as it was one of the most popular dance forms in Spanish music. Here, Chueca moves the jota from the city to the country and places it in the mouths of a Murcian chorus. This prefigures the use of the jota as generic regional marker in many later rural zarzuelas, just as the use of flamenco music would come to define Spain in many later works as well.

Politically, *La alegría de la huerta* also moves away from the depiction of urban life in Madrid. The work has one of the few oblique references to the system of caciquismo that undergirded the turno pacífico. The character of Heriberto is a local bandleader who dreams of moving to Madrid and leading the prestigious San Bernardino band. Although his actions and the onstage performance of his local band, which is used for comic relief throughout the zarzuela, make it clear that this is a pipe dream, Heriberto hopes to achieve his fantasy through Juan Francisco, son of the local parliamentary deputy. Heriberto plans to engineer the marriage of Juan Francisco to local beauty Carola and then dedicate his latest pasodoble to him, in the belief that Juan Francisco will proceed to use his father's political powers to get the mediocre musician appointed to the post. This system of patronage, while implausible in the play's narrative, was exactly how the system of caciquismo was supposed to work.[10]

Even more telling of the nonurban atmosphere is the opening of *La alegría*'s final scene, which features a group of local women leaving a church service at the Hermitage of Fuensanta. Astonishing as it may seem, the one aspect of Spanish life that is almost completely missing from urban zarzuelas is religion. But for the countryside, the librettists give us the full panoply of religious life. There are vendors selling religious trinkets outside the Hermitage, a blind beggar asking for alms, and a chorus of women who have enjoyed the service and will enjoy their lunch even more:

> And when I return
> from Fuensantica
> cleansed of sins
> at around about ten
> I have garbanzos
> so buttery
> that can be crushed
> with the mortar.[11]

This mildly satirical take on rural devotional life is reflected in many novels of the period, such as the episode in Chapter 9 of Benito Pérez Gáldos's *Doña Perfecta* in which the church organist uses music from Verdi's *La traviata* for the offertory—completely unaware of the inappropriateness of using operatic music depicting a Parisian prostitute to honor God.[12] Popular religious beliefs had always differed significantly from Catholic theology, although Spanish identity had come to revolve around the conception of an orthodox Catholic nation. After 1898 reformers regularly attacked the Catholic Church as part of the problems confronting Spain, and the satirical portrait in *La alegría de la huerta* gently punctures the idea that the country was intrinsically Catholic.[13] The work anticipates the regenerationist turn that zarzuela would take in the next decade. In this sense, it is dually reflective of the shifts taking place in Spanish national identity at the turn of the century.

But it would not be a comedy like *La alegría de la huerta* that would cement the vision of rural Spain on the zarzuela stage. That would be left to the serio-tragic *La tempranica* (The Temperamental Gypsy). Librettist Julián Romea was clearly inspired by the trend toward verismo in Italian opera—the musical equivalent of realism in literature, which had in turn been the framework for urban zarzuelas. Romea's libretto, which focuses on the interaction between the local gentry in Granada and a nearby enclave of Gypsies, presents a picturesque Spain in need of modernization. One of the minor characters is an Englishman, Mr. James, who has come to Granada in order to build a sugar refinery. The entire first scene of the work is built around the fact that Don Luis has taken Mr. James on a hunting expedition, and as the curtain rises the hunters have returned at nightfall to meet the colorful locals. Among the first of these is La Moronda, who will be fixing dinner for the hunters. The fare is simple (rice, ham, peppers), but she speaks of it as if presenting the menu for a grand feast. She climaxes her announcement by boasting that, "the King of Spain couldn't eat a better bacalao wrapped in ham," to which the character of Mariano drily replies, "That is a great truth. Kings do not eat bacalao." The picturesque poverty of the region is on display for the benefit of Mr. James. This becomes even clearer when Don Luis tells the assembled group of the adventure that embroiled him with María *La tempranica*. Acknowledging that he is "an aficionado of all that is popular and picturesque," Don Luis takes off (without telling his family or his wife) to explore the territory around Granada. He repays the hospitality of his Gypsy hosts by dallying with María and then abandoning her sobbing as she declares her passion for him. Perhaps because there are no women in the audience, the hunters ignore the rather tawdry nature of this narrative—Mr. James even goes so far as to declare it a "very Spanish" adventure.[14] While the first scene is meant to set up the basic dramatic framework of *La tempranica*, it is also an extended exercise in local color. As zarzuelas were wont to do, it depicts local customs—and as with the urban zarzuelas, it stakes a claim that these customs represent the nation.

A comparison of zarzuela with nineteenth-century Spanish novels might be useful at this point. Over the nineteenth century, Spanish authors had built a rich tradition of regional novels centered on the idea of *costumbrismo,* or the depiction of daily customs and manners. (This same idea was at the core of the sainete, one of the genres that were musicalized in the género chico.) Novels such as Juan Valera's *Pepita Jiménez* and Pedro Antonio de Alarcón's *El sombrero de tres picos* moved Spanish literature geographically away from Castile and to the periphery—in the case of both of these works, to Andalucía. (Not coincidentally, both of these novels were later adapted to the musical stage: *Pepita Jiménez* as an opera by Isaac Albéniz and *El sombrero de tres picos* as a ballet by Manuel de Falla.) Regional literature had an implicit claim that it represented the nation by depicting the patria chica, or the "little homeland." Roughly analogous to the idea of *Heimat* in Germany, the patria chica embodies the values of the Spanish people. This is usually attributed to the fact that the patria chica is located away from large urban centers (especially the artificial capital city of Madrid) and therefore maintains the natural virtue and innocence of the nation. Life in urban centers is corrupting and degrading, while life in the countryside helps the Spanish people to reconnect with their innate characters.[15] In this sense, regional and *costumbrista* literature comes to represent the nation, since it explores the best parts of the nation. Thus bacalao becomes representative of the Spanish people, uncorrupted by the foreign influences of Madrid.

La tempranica, like many works set in Andalucía, has Gypsies and Gypsy life at its core. On the surface, it might seem odd that Spanish composers would use Gypsies—who are the quintessential European "outsiders"—to portray the country's national identity. But just as Europeans had begun to equate the Gypsy with Spain, Spaniards themselves had begun to appropriate the Gypsy as part of their national culture. This process began in the late eighteenth century in reaction against French cultural influences that were playing a larger and larger role in Spanish culture, and the process accelerated in the nineteenth century as romanticism came to dominate European culture. The Gypsy was not only authentic "local color" but a representative uncontaminated by the modern influences of urbanization and industrialization.[16] It makes perfect sense that the Gypsies should come to inhabit the same role as the patria chica, since both played the same function in Spanish culture. It also makes sense that Spanish culture should emphasize that both the patria chica and the Gypsies come from Andalucía, since by the late nineteenth century Andalucía had come to represent the opposite of the increasingly industrial and urbanized northern half of Spain. The portrayal of Gypsy women in art, literature, and music was an integral part of this strategy to fashion southern Spain into a timeless representation of traditional Spanish culture. Andalucía was presented as a uniquely feminine representation of Spanish virtues. National identity came to be represented through stereotypes of Gypsy women: they inevitably fell in love with non-Gypsy males and came to tragic endings, thus representing the dangers of mixing outsiders into national cultures.[17]

La tempranica emphasizes the tension of using Andalucía and Gypsies as markers of national identity by using two devices to distinguish the Gypsies from the local "Spanish" characters.[18] The first is through pronunciation. The Gypsy characters have a distinctive accent, pronouncing "s" as "z"— "España" becomes "Ezpaña"—and clipping the endings off certain words. Romea was so concerned with the linguistic tics of his Gypsy characters that even though the pronunciation is clearly indicated in the script dialogue, he also included a note: "The artists charged with playing the roles of María and Grabié must take care to never pronounce the *ess,* and in all the words, *in absolutely all,* substitute them with a very soft zee. All the Gypsy personages ought to do the same." The locals from Granada, by contrast, speak standard unaccented Spanish. This might seem to mark off the Gypsies as a separate population distinct from the Spanish population, were it not for the second distinguishing factor: Giménez's music.

The score for *La tempranica* consists of a prelude and six musical numbers. Aside from the chorus, the only soloists are María (the titular Gypsy), her brother Grabié (a soprano trouser role), and Don Luis. But Giménez is careful to distinguish between the Gypsies and the Granadinos musically. María, Grabié, and the Gypsies sing Andalucian folk music, while the citizens of Granada sing music without folk origins. Consider the contrast between the first two musical numbers. The first sung music in the work is the opening chorus, as the hunters celebrate returning home as "the light of day is fleeing" (No. 1 in the vocal score). The chorus is a fairly generic 6/8 strophic song that could be dropped into any number of musical works without issue.[19] There is an extreme contrast with the next number, Grabié's "La tarantula é un bicho mu malo" ("The tarantula is a very evil beast"), the soprano showpiece mentioned in the opening of the chapter (No. 2 in the vocal score). This is an extremely rapid zapateado, a style of Andalucian flamenco normally marked by the percussive sounds of a woman's heels striking the floor. The number plays with the fact that Grabié is a trouser role—normally, a boy would not sing a zapateado, although it is completely appropriate for the woman playing him—but it also marks off Grabié as a Gypsy, distinct from the Granadinos in the previous number.

This contrast becomes even more pronounced in the next number, a duet between María and Don Luis. The two characters sing in completely contrasting musical styles. María's music is built around a Gypsy song with a high tessatura and significant melisma in the vocal line. Don Luis, by contrast, sings in a lower register without the use of melisma or vibrato. When the two join their voices at the end of the duet, they sing Luis's music, as Luis has temporarily brought María into his world. This is reversed almost immediately, as the next number (after a short book scene) takes place at the Gypsies' ranch. After an introduction of dance music, we are taken into another Gypsy song by María, "Tempranica me yaman" (They call me temperamental), the music of which comes from the flamenco and *cante jondo* tradition. (The same music is also used by Giménez as the orchestral prelude to the work.) The dramatic song surrounded by dance music foreshadows the famous dance sequence from Manuel de Falla's *La vida breve*—which in many ways could be considered a tragic counterpart to *La tempranica,* since Falla did not follow the soprano's dramatic arioso with comic drinking songs as Giménez does. The musical score climaxes in the next number, María's *romanza* "Sierras de Granada" (No. 5 in the vocal score), which features a vocal line with triplets, vocal melisma, and minor key singing as befits a song about a Spanish city. Then, as the scene shifts to Don Luis's house in Granada and the final scene of renunciation, the music reverts to an urban waltz. The music is a startling and abrupt change, and a reminder that Spain is changing: the elites like Don Luis who control Spanish society are urban. Only the use of the Tempranica theme to bring down the final curtain reminds us that Don Luis represents official Spain—and it is María *la tempranica* who represents the Spanish people.

Compared with the urban zarzuelas that dominated the Spanish stage in the 1890s, *La tempranica* sounds "Spanish" to foreigners, thanks to its extensive use of flamenco music and Andalucian musical forms. Unlike the waltzes and schottisches of urban zarzuela, the castanets and minor keys of these musical forms have come to signify Spain, thanks in large part to the exploitation of such folk forms in the music of Manuel de Falla and Isaac Albéniz—not to mention Georges Bizet, who used similar music as the backbone for much of the score to *Carmen*. The Spanish themselves had begun to associate flamenco music with the music of Andalucía in the 1870s thanks to the writings of Antonio Machado, who argued that flamenco combined Gypsy and Andalucian traditions.[20] Such rhetoric also tied in to the development of a genre of music generally known as *Alhambrismo,* which featured melisma in orchestral lines, alternating major and minor keys, and the use of a descending minor cadence particular to Andalucian music. Composers like Tomás Bretón and Ruperto Chapí used Alhambrismo to depict Spain's Muslim past in their orchestral works.[21] (The musical form takes its name from the Alhambra in Granada, the summer palace of the last Islamic monarchs of Spain.) The prevalence of Alhambrismo in Spanish orchestral music is what makes such Andalucian folk melodies and rhythms sound quintessentially Spanish. Musically, Spanish composers were creating a mélange of Spain's Gypsy and Moorish past that would increasingly denote Spain tunefully—which in large part has created the castanets-and-hand-clapping sound that we associate with Spanish music today.

The success of *La tempranica* led to a further outbreak of Gypsy songs on Spanish stages. It was possibly the inspiration for the next "Zarzuela de costumbres andaluzas," the 1902 hit *El puñao de rosas* (The Bunch of Roses) by Ruperto Chapí. Like Chueca and Giménez, Chapí was an urban género chico composer moving into the countryside. The plot is a standard love triangle in which Tarugo and Pepe compete for the affections of Rosario by bringing her the titular flowers. The work establishes its Adalucian roots immediately. The opening chorus uses a chromatic ascending and descending vocal line to describe the life of a group of Gypsies—one of whom will very shortly predict Rosario's romantic travails.[22] Later the score will feature a tango that gradually becomes a flamenco number, complete with hand-clapping (No. 5 in the vocal score). As in *La alegría de la huerta,* religion plays a major role for life in the patria chica. In order to demonstrate his love for Rosario, Tarugo steals a bunch of roses from a church altar to the Virgin Mary. When he finally wins her love, his penance for the theft is to collect another bouquet of roses to return to the Virgin. The plot could just as easily fit into an urban zarzuela— and librettist Carlos Arniches had written a number of urban works—but the motivating factor of stealing roses from the Virgin would not have worked in the less religious ambiance of the city.

The rise of the rural zarzuela also allowed composers and librettists to set their works in provincial cities. Madrid had dominated the imagination of género chico writers in the 1880s and 1890s, but the turn to the countryside also allowed regional capitals to become viable settings for zarzuelas. Such is the case of *La reina mora* (The Moorish Queen). This slight farce revolves around the attempts of the denizens of a Seville neighborhood to uncover the identity of the woman they have nicknamed "The Moorish Queen," who has not set foot outside of her house in two months—although her arm has emerged from a window to reward passing street musicians. Coral is actually in hiding, waiting for her fiancé Esteban to complete a prison sentence he is serving for defending her honor. This slight plot is enlivened by the accurate depiction of the customs and speech patterns of the denizens of Seville— which was the hallmark of the librettists, brothers Serafín and Joaquín Álvarez Quintero, who were possibly the most popular playwrights of pre–Civil War Spain.[23] Composer José Serrano's score leans quite heavily on Alhambrismo, especially in its use of both orchestral and vocal melisma in the numbers associated with Coral (Nos. 1 and 3 in the vocal score); this is not inappropriate, given the association of Coral with Spain's Muslim past.[24] In this way, Serrano manages to do musically what Giménez rejected in *La tempranica* and bring the provincial city into the vision of the patria chica. Giménez's use of waltz music to represent Granada walled off the city—and by extension, Don Luis—from the authentic Spain represented by Alhambrismo and Gypsies like María. Serrano demonstrates that Alhambrismo can represent urban areas, albeit exceptionally picturesque ones inhabited by picaresque types.

This initial wave of rural and regional zarzuelas was subsumed in the larger trend toward regenerationist operetta that emerged around 1910. Regional zarzuela would revive under the dictatorship of Miguel Primo de Rivera during the 1920s. This is not surprising, given the Primo de Rivera régime's complicated relationship with Spanish nationalism and Spanish regionalism. While the dictatorship did issue edicts that promoted the use of the Spanish flag and made Castilian the official language for all state occasions, these moves were prompted by a greater push for autonomy on the part of the government of Catalonia. Catalans had hoped that the dictator's relationship with the province (he had been Capitan General of Catalonia at the time of the coup, and Barcelona had provided the bedrock of his support) would encourage a loosening of ties from Madrid.[25] The dictatorship's attempts at imposing the trappings of Spanish nationalism onto the state were driven by the need to suppress the pressure for autonomy coming out of Catalonia. This had the ironic impact of strengthening regional cultures at the expense of Spanish nationalism, much as similar moves by the Franco dictatorship would in the second half of the twentieth century.

Even as the dictatorship attempted to quell regional autonomy, it was concurrently making municipal governments more important. Primo de Rivera had taken power with regenerationist claims that he would rid Spain of the caciques who had made Spanish government a sham and a farce. The way in which the dictatorship went about trying to defeat caciquismo was to strengthen local governments, believing that increased local autonomy would help to offset the influence of the caciques.[26] The process never worked in the manner that Primo de Rivera intended. The reformed municipal governments were severely underfunded, and as such the new posts were unattractive to those who might have provided impetus toward some real reform. The traditional power structure of the caciques remained in the countryside. However, this emphasis on local government arrested the centralization of the Restoration régime. The upshot of the dictatorship was that it increased the emphasis on localism and regionalism—even when such was not the intent, as with the measures against Catalan autonomy. Under the Primo de Rivera dictatorship, national identity became ever more embedded in rural Spain. Once again, the virtues of the patria chica were to override the corruption of the city.

What makes the regional zarzuelas of the 1920s distinct from their turn-of-the-century counterparts is that regions other than Andalucía get their moment upon the stage. By 1930 virtually every region had its own zarzuela. The trend seems to have gotten underway with Francisco Alonso's celebration of life in rural Salamanca in 1924's La bejarana (The Girl from Béjar); Jacinto Guerrero further immortalized the Spanish heartland of Castile and León with El huésped del Sevillano (The Guest at the Sevillano Inn) and La rosa del azafrán (The Saffron Rose). The Basque Country saw its music and several folk dances staged in Jesús Guridi's 1926 zarzuela El caserío (The Homestead); two years later, Galician bagpipes helped to form the sonic background for Pablo Luna's La chula de Pontevedra (The Dame from Pontevedra), set among Galician emigrants in Madrid. José Serrano's *Los de Aragón* from 1927 depicts the travails of a singer from . . . well, Aragón. Impoverished and unromantic Murcia gets what was arguably the best regional treatment on the lyric stage, Francisco Alonso's *La parranda* (The Street Party) from 1928. A few Catalan composers not only started writing zarzuelas, but they actually wrote them in Catalan—the most famous being Rafael Martínez Valls's 1926 work *Cançó d'amor i de guerra* (A Song of Love and War), which was deemed sufficiently noteworthy to be recorded in the 1960s with international opera star Montserrat Caballé (herself Catalan) in the lead. Under the Primo de Rivera dictatorship, the patria chica was staged not merely as romanticized Andalucía. Every corner of Spain could boast its own representation of the nation.

Yet, given the plethora of regionalism on Spanish stages in the 1920s, much of it was the same old song—literally. Following the lead of Chueca's *La alegría de la huerta,* regional music in many of these works was reduced to one folk music form: the jota. The jota is a particularly rhythmic dance form, usually in a 6/8 time signature, which allows for the interplay of duple and triple meters. The rhythm is reinforced by the fact that the jota is usually accompanied by the tambourine and the guitar. Although the jota is frequently associated with the region of Aragón, its strong and flexible rhythm allowed it to spread across Spain. It was frequently employed by zarzuela composers during the mid- and late nineteenth century—sometimes as a marker of regional identity, as in Chapí's *La bruja* and Fernández Caballero's *Gigantes y cabezudos,* and sometimes as a form of urban dance music, as in Barbieri's *El barberillo de Lavapiés* and Chueca's *La Gran Vía*—but always as a way of representing the Spanish people. It was so ubiquitous that it even made its way into one of the most significant attempts at Spanish opera. The jota from Tomás Bretón's *La Dolores* was extracted from that 1896 work and continues to be performed, usually in its orchestral setting. The jota was possibly the most frequently employed form of folk music on the Spanish musical stage.[27] It is unsurprising that eventually the jota would come to represent the idea of the patria chica as all regions of Spain came to encompass the idea in the 1920s.

Possibly the most evocative use of the jota occurs in Reveriano Soutullo and Juan Vert's 1927 evocation of rural life in Segovia, *La del soto del parral* (The Woman from the Vineyard in the Grove). "The Woman" of the title is the third corner of a love triangle, and the conflict between husband and wife Germán and Aurora—the other two corners—drives the dramatic conflict of the plot. But the composers and librettists Luis Fernández de Sevilla and Anselmo Carreño tip their audience off to the fact they are up to something more significant than a mere story of marital strife by never showing the "other woman" on stage during the course of the zarzuela. The work has several scenes in which happy peasants celebrate their happiness of living and working in the countryside, as operetta peasants are wont to do. Only Soutullo and Vert's subtle music and lush orchestrations keep things from becoming unbearably cloying. But the Introduction to the work (No. 1 in the vocal score) indicates the regional aspirations of *La del soto del parral.* The first music the audience hears as the curtain rises is set entirely in 3/4 and 3/8 time—variations on the jota's typical 6/8—with vocal lines that move back and forth between the chorus and Miguel.[28] All celebrate the pleasures of life in rural Segovia. The chorus that starts off the work is sung by peasants on their way to the hermitage for a religious service, singing about the beauty of the Segovian countryside. Then Germán celebrates his wealth and good fortune in choosing a wife with the sung declaration, "No hay en tierras de Segovia" (Not even in the countryside of Segovia), attributing his good fortune to the patria chica in music that is most obviously a jota. Even when Segovia produces stupidity, it does it better than anywhere else. The Introduction is rounded off by a male chorus tormenting Bruno, the village idiot, singing, "There is no idiot like the idiot from my home town," reinforcing the idea of the patria chica in virtually all realms of life. Here the pueblo may be specifically from Segovia, but the use of the jota moves the pueblo from the specificity of the region to the generality of the country as a whole.

Not surprisingly, the jota does its strongest work when linked with its traditional region of Aragón, as it does in another 1927 work, José Serrano's *Los de Aragón.* The work, with plot elements including a military hero returning from a colonial war in Africa; a heroine who is booed off a music-hall stage for singing a French song, and can only win the military hero by reverting to singing a jota; and a religious procession that marks a turning point in their relationship, sums up the mixture of elements of the Primo de Rivera dictatorship perfectly.[29] Although the work is subtitled "Zarzuela de costumbres aragonesas en un acto," the short playing time of the work means that the Aragonese customs are more clearly performed in the orchestra pit than onstage. The score is built around a jota, "Palomica aragonesa" (Little Aragonese Dove). It is first heard in the orchestra during the Introduction to the work, it is then sung by Gloria (the music-hall singer), and it is reprised at the Finale by Gloria and Agustín (the war hero). A second jota, "Agüita que corre al mar" (The stream that runs to the sea), introduces Agustín to the audience. This melody is then reprised in the middle of a scene set in the Basilica del Pilar, cushioned between a religious procession and the climactic confrontation between Gloria and Agustín (No. 4B in the vocal score).[30] Given that *Los de Aragón* moves directly from this confrontation to Gloria's repentant return home to her family (who were scandalized by her music-hall career), the jota reminds her of the value of the patria chica of Aragón—where she demonstrates her Spanish identity by rejecting French songs in favor of the jota. The critic for *La Época* was so stirred by Serrano's score that he gave way to patriotic fervor in his review of *Los de Aragón,* calling the jota

> the song most national, most mystical, most revolutionary, most ardent and most languid, most pure and most disturbing. When the Spanish people [pueblo español] have put to one side this paralysis that has gripped them and painted a portrait of the age of certainty and slavery; when they want to be something that will not die asphyxiated in dishonor, they will always have the invigorating lullaby of the jota.[31]

Even more telling in the long run was the fact that the same night *Los de Aragón* opened to overwhelming enthusiasm at the Teatro Centro, what should have been a far more illustrious premiere took place at the Teatro de la Zarzuela. Francisco Alonso's entire score for *La reina del Directorio* was encored, but the musical romance about the rise of Napoleon was quickly forgotten. The score to *Los de Aragón* would be recorded and remembered.[32]

Still, a jota was but one form of folk music that could serve as a signifier of Spanish nationalism during the Primo de Rivera régime. Other zarzuelas, such as Jesús Guridi's 1926 *El caserío* (The Homestead), could use more specific regional markers to denote national identity. Set in the Basque Country, the plot revolves around the attempt of Santi to force his nephew José Miguel to accept the responsibility of becoming heir to the *caserío* by testing his love for Ana Mari—who is not only Santi's niece but is also the daughter of his lost love Marichu. Santi courts Ana Mari, provoking the jealousy of José Miguel, who finally proves his worth to his uncle. Composer Guridi had become involved in Basque musical circles after his family moved to Bilbao during the early years of his musical studies.[33] By the time of the composition of *El caserío,* Guridi had been appointed the musical director of the Sociedad Coral de Bilbao, which focused on the performance of Basque music. His involvement with the choral society also prompted his composition of two Basque operas, *Mirentxu* (premiered 1910, revised 1913) and *Amaya* (premiered 1920), as well as the 1922 work for orchestra and choir *Euzko Irudiak,* which depicts three scenes from the lives of Basque fishermen. In later years he would write other Basque-themed works for orchestra, notably the *Diez melodías vascas* (Ten Basque Melodies, 1941) and the *Sinfonía pirenaica* (Pyrenees Symphony, 1945). A "cultivator of the folkloric treasure of his region" according to *El Heraldo de Madrid,* Guridi made a significant effort to establish a musical identity for the Basque Country during his career.[34]

A distinctly Basque feeling pervades *El caserío.* The Basque zortziko makes its first appearance three-quarters of the way through the first act in the form of Santi's *romanza* "Sasibill mi caserío" (Sasibill, My Homestead), his celebration of the village that is his home. On the surface, this romanza (No. 6 in the vocal score) tells the story of how Santi loved Marichu and how she abandoned him for his brother, leaving only the homestead to comfort him. Although the aria is supposedly about his love for Marichu, the zortziko rhythm gives a distinctly nationalist overtone to lyrics like these:

> Sasibill my homestead,
> warm cradle of my childhood,
> sweet relief from my pains,
> of all my loves the pride and honor . . . [35]

It is not impossible that Guridi and librettists Federico Romero and Guillermo Fernández-Shaw were making a distinct reference to the famous chorus "Va pensiero" from Verdi's *Nabucco,* which also features the theme of a homeland helping people to overcome suffering. Basque folk music then dominates Act II, which is set in the town plaza during a local fiesta. The act opens with a prelude, which is a suite of folk dances; a religious procession is followed by an *espatadanza* (a Basque sword dance); the zortziko forms the basis of the duet between José Miguel and Chomin, who are competing for the hand of Ana Mari (the "Canción de los versolaris," No. 13 in the vocal score); and "Sasibill, mi caserío" then comes back as part of the Act III finale (No. 17 in the vocal score), capping the work with the zortziko.[36]

The prevalence of folk music in Act II might suggest that Guridi is simply reverting to the traditional zarzuela practice of characterizing the Spanish people through the use of folk music. (Indeed, it could very well be a direct reference to Ruperto Chapí's 1889 zarzuela *La bruja*, which is also set in northern Spain and features the zortziko.) *El caserío* was praised for its depiction of life and customs in the Basque Country.[37] But Guridi's use of folk music to underpin a romanza is extremely rare in zarzuela. This allows the caserío of Sasibill to fulfill the function of the patria chica: the caserío forms the basis of Santi's identity against the blandishments of modern life (here, the faithless Marichu). This was the interpretation of the critic Floridor in *ABC*, who referred to the caserío as the "evocative and patriarchal name, austere home of the Basque people."[38] In fact, *El caserío* itself could be viewed as an attempt to combat the hazards of modern life with something more authentic. In a piece published in *El Sol* the day of the premiere, the newspaper argued that Guridi's score was an attempt to fight "a frenetic industrialism" and return zarzuela to its original prestige.[39] What that prestige was became clearer the following day in its review of the opening-night performance, which proclaimed that "composer and librettists have realized the heroic intent of restoring the ancient national art of the zarzuela."[40] According to *El Sol*, zarzuela itself had become the patria chica of Spain, with its authentic rural customs helping to purge the country of the problems of modern life and helping the pueblo to recover its authentic state of being.

El caserío and the other rural and regional zarzuelas written after 1898 were just that—a representation of the patria chica that supposedly housed the eternal values of the nation against the onslaught of industrial modernity. Of course, the idea that the nation is somehow the storehouse of an essential and unchanging identity is itself a construction of the modern era. But in post-1898 Spain, that idea takes on a distinctly conservative hue. This was the exact period in which the Restoration government was trying to prop up the tottering system of the turno pacífico against a rising tide of urban political mobilization. The retreat into the patria chica was a method of reinforcing the status quo of the Restoration and the system of caciquismo that maintained the elites in power at the expense of the growing urban working class. The creation of a romantic portrait of rural Spain, with its Gypsies and quaint folk music, was a desperate attempt to ignore the shifting demographic and political patterns that were increasingly taking over Spain in the early twentieth century. In the process, zarzuela composers wound up combining the rich regional heritages of Spain, where one folk dance could represent every part of rural Spain equally. But this was the genius of the patria chica. It submerged differences and asserted that any region could speak for the nation as a whole. This worked easiest for southern Spain, as Andalucía—with its Gypsies and flamenco music—had come to represent Spain in the eyes of both foreigners and Spaniards. But even the Basque Country with its history of separatist movements could represent the nation as it did in *El caserío*.

Or could it? *El caserío* might be one of the great Spanish zarzuelas, but it retains a stubbornly Basque musical identity, and it was written at a time when a rising tide of Basque and Catalan nationalism was challenging the Spanish state. Regional nationalisms played no small part in the tensions that would dominate the Second Republic in the 1930s and in the Civil War that followed. The patria chica might have been a way of using local and regional identities to promote a sense of nationalism, as the idea of Heimat did in Germany during the nineteenth century. But the use of regional identities to stand in for a larger Spanish identity was linked with a decaying and corrupt political system that still sought to lock out the actual people of the patria chica from political participation in the larger nation. Politically, regional nationalisms in Spain began to flourish in the early years of the twentieth century because they allowed another political voice for those disenfranchised by the Restoration political system. Zarzuela was one of the few ways in which these competing visions of what it meant to be Spanish were negotiated.

6

Zarzuela and the Operatic Tradition

When the influenza pandemic of 1918 reached Spain in the autumn of that year, the hit zarzuela playing in Madrid was *La canción del olvido* (The Song of Oblivion), which featured a number that had already become popular outside the show: the song "Soldado de Nápoles" (The Soldier from Naples), which rapidly became the Spanish nickname for the so-called Spanish Flu. The libretto by Federico Romero and Guillermo Fernández-Shaw manages to infuse freshness into a stock situation—the rake who is redeemed through the love of a good woman, and their sure sense of stagecraft contributed to the success of *La canción*. But in all musical theater pieces, it is the music that is responsible for the ultimate success or failure of the work, and the score to *La canción* would be the finest ever written by José Serrano. (Fernández-Shaw would later compliment the score by joking that the reason the influenza became known as the "Soldado de Nápoles" stemmed from the fact that both were equally contagious.)[1] Serrano's score is notable not only for its rapturous melodies and keen theatrical sense, but also for the way it manages to sum up the zarzuela music of the previous decade. It incorporates the sound of European operetta that composers had begun to cultivate during the 1910s, and it incorporates musical tropes from yet another genre that Spanish composers had been using during that decade—opera.

The operetta element to *La canción del olvido* is the most obvious facet of the score. Many of the numbers, notably the title song (No. 2 in the vocal score), require trained voices and are orchestrated heavily for strings and harp. Although some critics have found these numbers (especially those of leading lady Rosina, of which "La canción del olvido" is one) to be more operatic than operetta-derived, the vocal lines are more restricted in tessitura than one would expect to find in Italian opera.[2] The specifically Spanish and zarzuela-driven elements can be found in the choral numbers, which follow the zarzuela tradition of having the chorus represent a segment of the population (albeit here of Naples rather than of Spain). This is made clear by the fact that the chorus is always accompanied by a group of street musicians known as the *rondalla,* rather than by the orchestra. The guitar and lute accompaniment of the rondalla were clearly meant to evoke the street musicians who had helped to popularize zarzuela music in Spain, without necessarily losing the Neapolitan atmosphere that Serrano, Romero, and Fernández-Shaw were attempting to re-create. (The use of the rondalla is no doubt meant to recall the use of street musicians in the scores to works like *Pan y toros, El barberillo de Lavapiés,* and *La verbena de la paloma.* It also foreshadows similar treatments in *Doña Francisquita, La Calesera,* and *La parranda.*) In addition, the choral numbers tend to comment on the action, especially the central choral number and the most famous piece of music from the zarzuela, the "Soldado de Nápoles." The choral interjections serve as a mildly ironic commentary on Leonello's attempted seduction of Rosina—an irony that is doubled because Leonello has hired these serenaders to assist him.

The operatic overtones of *La canción* appear in the third scene of the work, which is the main love duet between Leonello and Rosina (No. 6 in the vocal score). The scene is a twenty-minute love duet whose scope—in terms of zarzuela music, at any rate—almost begs comparisons with the second act of Wagner's *Tristan und Isolde.* It is not simply the length of the number that evokes the shadow of Wagner: much of Serrano's orchestral underpinning uses the other numbers in the score, especially Rosina's "Canción del olvido" and Leonello's "Mujer, primorosa clavellina" (Woman, the Exquisite Carnation), as leitmotifs to reflect the emotions onstage. This love duet also manages to work in the rondalla by making the first theme of the duet a reprise of "Hermosa napolitana" (Beautiful Neapolitan Girl), which they had previously performed. In this epic love duet, Serrano managed to do something that had eluded Spanish composers for decades. He composed zarzuela music with true operatic scope. The critics noticed what Serrano had accomplished. *ABC* claimed that *La canción del olvido* had revived what it called "our classic zarzuela," while *El Imparcial* argued that "our national genre is going to recover its prestige." The opening-night audience also fêted Serrano's accomplishment with cries of "Long live Maestro Serrano! Long live Spanish composers! Long live Spain!" that rang out through the Teatro de la Zarzuela at the curtain call.[3]

In Spain as elsewhere, opera and "light" musical theater (be it operetta, light opera, or musical comedy) have had a contentious relationship with a rather ambiguous boundary between the two.[4] Recitative is usually the line in the sand. Operas are through-sung, while lighter musical theater has spoken dialogue between discrete musical numbers—unless the opera is *The Magic Flute* or the original version of *Carmen,* both of which feature dialogue, or unless the lighter work is Stephen Sondheim's *Sweeney Todd,* which is through-sung. Sometimes the boundary is in the music. Operatic music might be through-composed, while lighter musical theater relies on strophic song forms, unless one is discussing Gershwin's *Porgy and Bess,* which features quite a number of strophic song forms—not to mention most Baroque operas, which also feature repetitious strophic construction of the principal arias. Perhaps it is that opera requires trained singers with an enormous vocal range, while lighter works are constructed for actors who have only a limited vocal range. But don't tell Maria Callas or Beverly Sills that they weren't actors, and don't tell Julie Andrews or Audra MacDonald that they work in a genre that values them for their limited vocal skills. In the end, one cannot help but feel that defining opera is a little bit like defining pornography. One knows it when one sees or hears it.

While on a certain level this is a pretty pedantic question—few audience members at a performance of *Carmen* or *Porgy and Bess* have ever cared whether or not they're listening to an opera or something else—the issue of classification became a paramount question for Spanish composers.[5] Zarzuela's claim to be a uniquely Spanish form of musical theater was predicated upon the rejection of opera as a foreign intruder. It had been imported from Italy in the eighteenth century to entertain the royal court (another foreign import, the French Bourbons). Through the nineteenth century, while Spanish novelists created nationalist artworks in the vernacular, opera houses were dominated by Italian composers whose works were sung in Italian and not translated into Spanish. It was during this same period that zarzuela came to be the nationalist form of musical theater, with opera relegated to the status of an import in spite of the fact that Spanish composers made several serious attempts to create a nationalist operatic tradition. In the twentieth century, this would change. Since European ideas came to be regarded as a way to fix the problems facing Spanish society, European opera would again be brought forward as a solution. When the Spanish government finally began to support zarzuela as a national treasure in the 1920s, it did so under the aegis of a national lyric theater that was meant to promote both opera and zarzuela.

Spain is unique among the major continental European nation-states in that it never developed a nationalist school of operatic composition during the nineteenth century. (Interestingly, the other major Western nation-states that failed to do so were Great Britain and the United States—countries that also developed a strong nationalist school of lighter musical theater works.) Spain lacked the institutions to develop nationalist opera: opera houses like Madrid's Teatro Real or Barcelona's Teatre del Liceu rarely staged works by Spanish composers. Italian operas predominated. When these theaters did stage Spanish works, they were performed in Italian translation because Spanish conservatories did not train singers in their native tongue. Several Spanish composers, including Tomás Bretón and Felip Pedrell, used the new musical theories of Richard Wagner in the composition of their nationalist works, but a country whose knowledge of European music had not advanced much further than Verdi's *Il trovatore* was not fully prepared to embrace the "music of the future." Spanish composers who actually wanted to hear their music performed would have to write for the commercial stage. Composers like Francisco Asenjo Barbieri or Ruperto Chapí—who might well have written operas had they been born Italian or French—instead turned to zarzuela and the commercial theater. A Spanish school of opera never had a chance to get off the ground.[6]

Advocates of zarzuela generally avoided discussion of artistic questions when explaining why their genre of musical theater, rather than opera, was quintessentially Spanish. Instead, they embraced the commercial aspects of the genre when staking their claim. Zarzuela was nationalist because it appealed to a large number of people. And what made it appealing was the music, which was drawn from popular elements and thus had a wider appeal than opera. Zarzuela composers proved their nationalist genius by writing works that were appealing to a broad range of the population. The fullest statement of this argument is to be found in the magnum opus of music critic Antonio Peña y Goñi, *La ópera española y la música dramática en España en el siglo XIX* (Spanish Opera and Dramatic Music in Nineteenth-Century Spain), a massive if occasionally scattershot work of music history. The book opens with this salvo: "Does Spanish Opera exist? No; Spanish Opera does not exist; Spanish Opera has never existed."[7] His primary argument for this exceedingly broad claim was that Spain lacked a national tradition for opera. While geniuses could create isolated operas, it was only with the accumulation of tradition that fully nationalist art—as in France, Germany, or Italy—could develop. As Peña y Goñi elegantly put the case for zarzuela's nationalist claims, "if Nationalist Opera does not contain and synthesize the aspirations, inclinations and artistic culture of a people, can it be called nationalist?"[8] Peña y Goñi did not discount the notion that individual genius was necessary to create a lyric work, but genius proved its worth by creating music within a recognizable framework. Genius did not haul off in unforeseen artistic directions. Instead, it used the traditions and customs of the nation to create a work that would be appealing on a very broad scale.

So potent was this argument that Peña y Goñi went even further and rejected the traditional foundational myth of zarzuela. Most who discussed the subject eventually traced zarzuela's roots to performances of theatrical works at the Palacio de la Zarzuela during the reign of Philip IV. "Zarzuela" was used to distinguish Spanish lyric theater in the seventeenth century from that new import from Italy, opera. At that time the only real distinction between the two forms was that zarzuela used dialogue while opera was through-sung. The distinctions would become greater as time passed, and it was these increasing distinctions that Peña y Goñi seized upon in his argument. For him, "the zarzuela born in the Pardo Palace does not represent, nor could rationally represent the foundation of a completely new lyric-dramatic spectacle in Spain."[9] Italian opera had killed off the original zarzuela, since they had been too similar to be distinguished from each other.

What made zarzuela Spanish, in that case? It was here that Peña y Goñi introduced his musical arguments. For Peña y Goñi, "the most pure and direct product of popular song, zarzuela represents the people, it is the voice of the people as an essential element of art, an inalienable hallmark of reality."[10] One suspects that what Peña y Goñi has in mind is the traditional role of the zarzuela chorus as the embodiment of the Spanish people. This is the genre's most literal way of representing the people, and it does so musically as well as dramatically. The music is nationalist because it is music that will appeal to a wide spectrum of the Spanish population, if only because the music was popular even before it was put onstage. Again, nationalist genius is not about forging a unique artistic creation; it lies in using the traditions of a country to create a broadly appealing piece of theater. Crucial to this argument is the fact that zarzuela already had a number of composers whose commercial success had sanctified them as geniuses. According to Peña y Goñi's argument, what made these men geniuses was the fact that when they revived zarzuela in its modern form in the early 1850s, they did so through the use of popular music. They incorporated it into their scores, assuring that modern zarzuela would not be the rather pale imitation of Italian opera that eighteenth-century zarzuela had been.

Peña y Goñi focuses on three composers—Joaquín Gaztambide, Emilio Arrieta, and Francisco Asenjo Barbieri—as a sort of Holy Trinity that created the modern, popular form of zarzuela. They measured up to Peña y Goñi's definition of genius by producing music that succeeded in drawing the Spanish people into the theater. But just as with the Holy Trinity, the zarzuela trinity suffers from a paradox: all were equally honored, but one stood above the others. Gaztambide may have been the first to use popular song in zarzuela, but Peña y Goñi analyzed his work in terms of his "exquisite sensibility"—flowing melody and clear form.[11] Whatever was essential to understanding Gaztambide's work, it was not his use of folk song. Arrieta was compromised by his attempts at opera composition and his "Italian" style. Peña y Goñi had great respect for Arrieta's work—especially *Marina,* widely regarded even then as the composer's masterpiece—but Arrieta was at heart an Italian composer, trained in Milan, one in whom the foreign influence was the predominant factor.

Thus the role of savior of Spanish music, in Peña y Goñi's musical theology, devolved to Barbieri because it was Barbieri's use of popular music that made him the first nationalist composer in Spain. Peña y Goñi, always a lively writer, allowed his prose to take poetic flights of fancy when it came to discussing this particular composer. "Barbieri's muse," he argued at one point (probably in the middle of a Madrid summer), "playful and irresistible, has refreshed all of Spain with the fan of his popular songs."[12] Peña y Goñi argued this most forcefully in his analysis of *Pan y toros,* which is the most exacting of his musical analyses in *La ópera española.* Peña y Goñi compared *Pan y toros* to both *Hamlet* and *Don Quijote*—each of these works being the summit of their respective author's creative outputs. Even here, Peña y Goñi cannot deny the Italianate compositional processes of Spanish composers (indeed, the score of *Pan y Toros* has a tendency to sound very much like mid-period Verdi, only with more castanets), but stylistic quibbling is swept away in the torrent of the critic's prose:

"The cement for the edifice is, as we can see, purely Italian, but the Spanish flag waves on the apex, floating gallantly and proudly on the impulses of popular sound. . . . The dramatic impulse represented by Italian art assimilated admirably to the Spanish nature, and the humor idealized by the popular perfume on the breath of the vocalizations of Doña Pepita form a contrast of irresistible beauty." *Pan y toros* was constructed musically in the same manner as *El barberillo de Lavapiés:* the dramatic portions of the plot were carried out in an operatic Italian fashion, while the comic relief received the popular, Spanish music. But for Peña y Goñi, "its ideal was purely and exclusively Spanish."[13] No matter what role Italian music played in the formation of a work like *Pan y Toros,* it was the Spanish portion that made it an important work of nationalist standing. By splitting hairs with a vengeance, Peña y Goñi was inventing the tradition that Barbieri's zarzuelas were at the core of Spanish musical identity.

So why did erecting a Spanish flag on an Italian edifice make a piece of music distinctly Spanish instead of some sort of hybrid? For Peña y Goñi, it was because Barbieri's revival of zarzuela was built upon a Spanish form of popular music, the *tonadilla.* The tonadilla was a short theatrical piece that arose in the mid-eighteenth century as a reaction to the Italianization of zarzuela. It became rapidly popular because of its focus on daily urban life, and the music reflected this.[14] But being urban, the tonadilla was not necessarily of the folk traditions that formed the basis of other popular music. The tonadilla was more synthetic, with more influences, and was more easily malleable. And herein lay its faults. For Peña y Goñi, the tonadilla was "inept." While it often had witty and interesting lyrics, the music was eminently forgettable.[15] Barbieri recognized the popular tradition of the tonadilla but had improved upon it and thus elevated it into something quintessentially Spanish. Nationalistic genius involved improving popular forms, not turning one's back on one's national heritage.

Peña y Goñi went even further, anointing Barbieri as something of a musical saint. Not only were Barbieri's works sacred, but the composer managed to produce relics as well. One of Peña y Goñi's critical pieces was devoted solely to Barbieri's piano. This was not just a musical instrument, but a repository for the history of Spanish music: "Yes, poor, humble, and modest instrument; in you is synthesized the history of our popular music, the history of our—as poor today as you—zarzuela."[16] What is perhaps most astonishing about Peña y Goñi's mythmaking is that it took place not only while Barbieri was still alive, but while he was still actively composing. Peña y Goñi's writings that deal with the issue of zarzuela date from the mid-1870s to the mid-1880s, but Barbieri would continue writing music until his death in 1894. There was a sense in the 1880s that Barbieri was somewhat past his prime as his last popular success had been *El barberillo de Lavapiés* in 1874, but he was still very much a living figure, conducting the Sociedad de Conciertos and carrying out musicological studies culminating in the *Cancionero del Palacio* (The Palace Songbook) in 1890.

Spanish opera had no foundational figure or foundational myth because no Spanish opera was ever truly popular. Zarzuela had a figure that could accommodate nationalist mythmaking. Barbieri fulfilled Peña y Goñi's main criterion for artistic creation. He was a genius who expanded upon existing traditions.

> Barbieri has emancipated it [the tonadilla], breaking the yoke that subjugated it and maintained it a slave to the facile and ephemeral expansions of the plebeians. He gave it new body, new form, and new life, emptying into the mold his admirable vivacity and his incomparable ingenuity; he has extracted it with a strong hand from the barren terrain in which it stagnated and has encased it in zarzuela, making it pass through all gradations and subjected it to all the varieties of talent and inspiration, until he synthesized it into a powerful artistic individuality.[17]

Barbieri appears as liberator, freeing the enslaved music of the people and raising it to dizzying heights. He took what was already popular and made it even more appealing, more able to speak to the Spanish people. In the end, a nationalist genius was not necessarily a creator. A nationalist genius was a synthesizer, who could take Spanish music and make it even more broadly appealing by fusing it with a dramatic story. Nationalist lyric theater was not art for art's sake, as opera was; it was music with a theatrical purpose to draw as many people into the theater—and into a vision of the nation—as possible. The success of the género chico in the 1890s confirmed this idea that only popular music theater could speak for the Spanish nation.

Opera would become important again after 1910 when its intrinsic foreign quality would become an asset. With the need for regeneration in the wake of the War of 1898, Spain turned to European models and ideas. As we have seen, operetta was one potential method for reforming Spanish theater. But so was opera. Composers and music critics came to the conclusion that opera had the same potential to regenerate Spanish music as operetta did. Zarzuela composers began to incorporate more complex musical forms into their works, eschewing the strophic dance melodies that had predominated under the género chico. Vocal lines became more elaborate and demanded trained voices. These operatic zarzuelas made use of the new modernist tendencies in music then delighting and disturbing European audiences, particularly the unsettled and shifting harmonies of French Impressionist composers like Claude Debussy and Paul Dukas. The fuzzy line that separated music theater genres grew increasingly blurred as zarzuela composers began to incorporate elements of modernist European opera music into their works, which in turn helped to legitimize Spanish lyric theater in general as a force for regeneration.

The opera revival in Spain dates from 1907. It was in this year that the composers Vicente Lleó and Amadeo Vives, shocked by what they considered to be the decline of the quality of theatrical productions in Madrid, pooled the resources of three theaters to form what became known as the "Theatrical Trust"—a direct reference to a similar cartel of newspapers that had banded together to unseat Maura as prime minister.[18] The original idea was that each theater in the Trust would focus on developing a different aspect of the lyric repertoire. The Teatro Cómico was to specialize in cabaret performances, the Teatro Eslava in género chico, and the Teatro de la Zarzuela in both zarzuela grande and opera. Although there was discussion of presenting operas by Spanish composers, Vives initially decided to present foreign opera in Spanish translation. If the idea was worthy, the execution was not: reviewing the Trust's first operatic production, Puccini's *La bohème,* one reviewer was forced to call the translation "abominable."[19] The Trust broke up during the summer of 1908. The profits on performances from the Teatros Cómico and Eslava were funneled into lavish but underattended productions at the Zarzuela, and this eventually bankrupted the organization. Lleó would eventually recoup his losses—he remained as impresario of the Eslava—but Vives lost his entire investment.

The episode of the Theatrical Trust indicates that the zarzuela grande form was increasingly being considered an "operatic" genre. The form had never been that far distant from opera to begin within terms of its musical construction and complexity. The rise of the género chico in the 1890s had only thrown the operatic tendencies of the zarzuela grande into greater relief. The Trust had been set up as part of the wider effort to reform Spanish lyric theater, and it is indicative that Vives and Lleó felt the need to distinguish zarzuela grande from the género chico. By developing distinctions between these subgenres of zarzuela, they only accentuated the similarities between the zarzuela grande and opera. The Theatrical Trust helped to lay the groundwork for legitimizing the synthesis of opera and zarzuela. Operatic music and tropes would begin to turn up in more ambitious zarzuelas just as operetta melodies were beginning to work their way into Spanish scores. Opera's foreign identity—the very thing that had destroyed its chances of becoming the authentic form of Spanish lyric drama in the 1870s and 1880s—now became a positive virtue. Since opera was European and not Spanish, it had a greater possibility of reforming Spanish theater.

One of the key figures who first helped insert operatic tropes into zarzuela was the Catalan composer Amadeo Vives, who was the impresario of the Teatro de la Zarzuela during the period of the Theatrical Trust. His first major zarzuela was *Don Lucas del Cigarral,* staged in 1899.[20] *Don Lucas,* in many ways, is exemplary of Vives's career to come. It is a full-length zarzuela grande, staged at the height of the género chico's popularity. Vives further ensured the pedigree of his first work by having a classic seventeenth-century Spanish comedy adapted as his libretto, Francisco de Rojas Zorrilla's *Entre bobos anda el juego* (A Game Played between Fools). Vives's music for *Don Lucas* also indicates high purpose, even in what was the middle of a farcical comedy. Like the zarzuela grande of old, Vives's music indulges in sextets and concertante finales that spin out over extended periods of time, not the rapid and simple musical forms of the género chico.[21]

It is not accidental that Vives had started his theatrical career as an opera composer—his first opera, *Arthus,* received critical praise (if not public acclaim) in Barcelona—and he would at various points in his life return to the form. But more frequently he would use several tricks from his operatic composition bag and insert them into more modest stage works. One of the best examples of this occurs in his 1904 género chico piece *Bohemios* (still another adaptation of Murger's *Scènes de la vie de Bohème*). Most commentators on the work tend to treat it as a forerunner of the post-1910 operetta invasion, as indeed in many ways it is.[22] However, the work also has striking similarities to opera, from its Verdian prelude, which alternates brass and timpani with lyrical string passages, to its skillful intermingling of duets, quartets, and choruses. In fact, the entire score does not have a single solo vocal number.[23] Admittedly, these individual pieces are foreshortened in a way they would not be in opera, as Vives had only forty minutes to cover the same amount of musical ground that Puccini's *La bohème* covered in two hours, but their complexity is still far beyond what was traditional in the género chico.

Vives's attempts to meld opera into zarzuela are best represented by his 1914 work *Maruxa*. The libretto by Luis Pascual Frutos is ridiculously inane, even by musical theater standards. It revolves around amorous intrigues set among shepherds and their masters in the Galician countryside, and the quality of the plot can be best summed up by its opening sequence, which features the title shepherdess singing how much she loves her favorite sheep. Maruxa asks:

> Little sheep as white
> as my dreams.
> Isn't it true you love me
> as I love you?[24]

The disappearance of this sheep later becomes a major plot point in the first act finale, and Maruxa is arguably far more enamored of it than she is of either Pablo or Antonio, the suitors for her hand. This is not exactly the stuff of high drama. Most reviews overlooked the libretto, presumably on the assumption that if one cannot say anything nice about something, one should not say anything at all. *La Correspondencia de España* dismissed the libretto by stating, "the book . . . has not even the least minor literary importance, and there is no reason to be occupied with it. That is the most charitable thing we can do in this case." Zarzuela expert Roger Alier asserts that even Vives privately laughed at the libretto.[25]

Perhaps the very nature of the libretto drove Vives when he composed the score, as if to prove one could have a work in which score and libretto were diametric opposites. *Maruxa*'s music is sophisticated and lyrical, and contemporary critics were enraptured by Vives's melodic imagination. The critics for both *ABC* and *El Imparcial* went so far as to compare the Catalan composer with Beethoven for having captured what the *ABC* critic termed "that ingenious sentiment of Nature." But what is most striking about the reviews is the natural assumption that *Maruxa* was most emphatically an opera. The official subtitle of the work is either "lyric comedy" (*comedia lírica*) according to the score, or "lyric eclogue" (*égloga lírica*) according to the libretto. While Vives had staged previous attempts at opera in opera houses, the premiere of *Maruxa* was at the Teatro de la Zarzuela—an ambiguous choice, perhaps, given the amount of operatic activity that had gone on there, but one indicative of an attempt to place the new work as a zarzuela nonetheless. Still, most of the reviews held the assumption that the work was an opera. *ABC* opened its review with the rhetorical question, "Are all of you talking about Spanish opera?" and the other major papers followed suit.[26]

Certainly the work sounds like an opera. It is through-composed, and the vocal score lacks the traditional division into discrete numbers that most zarzuelas have.[27] If the overall length is perhaps a tad short (most full-length recordings run just shy of two hours) and the vocal lines are no more demanding in terms of tessitura than is traditional in zarzuela, the leading singers are onstage and singing for virtually that entire time span. (It may be worth noting that Maruxa was one of the few zarzuela roles recorded by Montserrat Caballé during the height of her operatic career.) Traditional zarzuela music requires only short moments of song—broken up by dialogue—from its performers. *Maruxa*'s score also contains the complex ensembles that were a hallmark of Vives's compositions. But while the work was operatic in scope, it did not lose that main prerequisite of national lyric drama, music that sounded nationalistic to its listeners. According to *El Heraldo de Madrid,* Vives "has not forgotten that popular music reveals to us only a nuance of lyric emotion . . . through personal emotions." It was this ability to blend folkloric-sounding music (which may well all have been in Vives's orchestrations: the critic Eduardo Muñoz commented heavily on the use of bagpipes in the orchestra, for example) with the more intense emotions generated by operatic music that made *Maruxa* so noteworthy.[28] The operatic element helped to save zarzuela's folk music element from the clichés of the género chico.

Maruxa was not the only operatically ambitious zarzuela premiered in 1914. José María Usandizaga's *Las Golondrinas* (The Swallows) opened in February. It is a work so operatic in scope that the composer's brother Ramón would later adapt the zarzuela into a full-fledged opera by adding recitative in Acts I and II, as well as rewriting approximately half of Act III. It is this version that is the standard performing version today (the two major recordings of the score are of the operatic performing version, as are the two published versions of the vocal score).[29] Usandizaga was no stranger to opera. His first major work and calling card was *Mendi-Mendiyan,* a work from Basque folklore with Basque musical themes that had been premiered in San Sebastián in 1910.[30] Very shortly after the wildly successful premiere of *Las Golondrinas,* he would start to work on a second Basque-themed opera, *La Llama*—although this work was cut short by the composer's tragically early death in 1915.

Usandizaga was arguably the most formidably trained of the crop of composers that came of age between 1900 and 1920 in Spain. Of this group, he had the most extensive training abroad, studying composition at the famed Schola Cantorum in Paris under the composers Vincent d'Indy and Paul Dukas from 1900 to 1906. In spite of the ingrained conservatism of both d'Indy and his academy, Usandizaga had some fairly advanced tastes in music for the first decade of the century. In Usandizaga's music one can hear the influences of Puccini, Debussy, Ravel, Mussorgsky, and Rimsky-Korsakov—which irritated the conservative d'Indy, who was otherwise pleased with his pupil's development, to no end.[31] The budding composer also made the acquaintance of Isaac Albéniz, who resided in Paris during this period. Usandizaga was thus well prepared when writer Gregorio Martínez Sierra approached him with a libretto that bore more than passing overtones to *Pagliacci*—a murderous love triangle among *commedia dell'arte* players.

What astonished the opening-night audiences and critics was *Las Golondrinas*' modernity. The critic for *El Heraldo de Madrid* found similarities between Usandizaga's work and Dukas's (especially *The Sorcerer's Apprentice* and *Ariane et Barbe-Bleue*) and to Richard Strauss's *Salome,* which was still considered fairly scandalous in 1914. *ABC* also heard similarities to Dukas in Usandizaga's orchestrations, as well as traces of Debussy. But the *ABC* critic went still further, noting that "the discovery of a composer with his astonishing methods bodes well for the definitive implementation of Spanish opera, more so than all the theorizing we will have done about it." As they would with *Maruxa* a few months later, the critics proclaimed *Las Golondrinas* to be not only opera, but eminently Spanish as well. *La Correspondencia de España* went so far as to proclaim Usandizaga the heir of Barbieri and Chapí (as well as of Vives, oddly enough), heady praise for the first Madrid production of a young composer's work.[32]

Almost all the reviews focused on Usandizaga's age (just a month away from 28 at the time of the premiere) and the modernity of his music. *El Liberal* used the perceived decline of lyric theater in Spain as the lynchpin for its review of *Las Golondrinas,* which focused on Usandizaga's ability to manage his musical material—various themes and motives run in and out throughout the work, although Usandizaga's use of leitmotifs reflects Puccini more than it does Wagner—and his orchestrations, which reflect his admiration of Debussy and Rimsky-Korsakov. *ABC* linked Usandizaga with other younger Spanish composers (including Conrado del Campo, Enrique Granados, and Joaquín Turina), all of whom it called upon to rejuvenate Spanish lyric drama and give it "the modernity that it needs."[33] There was a universal assumption behind all these reviews. Spanish lyric theater was outmoded, and only the importation of modern European music would save it. Certainly, in picking Usandizaga the critics were on the right track, since his music sounds like little else in the Spanish repertory. One of the tragedies of Spanish music is the fact that Usandizaga would die of tuberculosis the following year at the age of 29.

Critics in 1914 can be forgiven for thinking that the success of Vives and Usandizaga presaged a new era of Spanish opera. Things were so promising that Pablo Luna, the musical director of the Teatro de la Zarzuela, designed the fall season as a showcase for regenerated Spanish theater. He staged the cream of the latest successes of Spanish operetta and operatic zarzuela, including *Las Golondrinas, Maruxa,* and his own *Los cadetes de la reina,* among other works. To sing the leading roles, the two biggest zarzuela stars in Spain—Emilio Sagi-Barba and Luisa Vela, who had triumphed in the premiere of the *Las Golondrinas*—were brought in to headline the performances. The revivals, however, were only a warm-up for what was expected to be the crown jewel of Spanish lyric theater, recently consecrated by success abroad: Manuel de Falla's *La vida breve* (A Short Life), an opera whose history sums up the potential and pitfalls for Spanish lyric theater in the early twentieth century. What nobody could see at the time was the fact that *La vida breve* would be the climax of attempts to create a uniquely Spanish opera rather than a portent of things to come.

Falla, like most other Spanish composers of the period, saw the lyric stage as the surest pathway to success. He composed a number of zarzuelas (two in collaboration with Amadeo Vives) after he graduated from the Madrid Conservatory in 1899, but only one was ever staged—and that with little success. He turned to opera when he read Carlos Fernández-Shaw's poem "La chavalilla" (The Little Girl). Falla was convinced that the poem had dramatic potential and persuaded Fernández-Shaw to convert it into a libretto. Falla worked feverishly to have the opera ready in time for a 1905 Real Academia de San Fernando de Bellas Artes competition designed to promote national art. The opera prize was to be 2,500 pesetas and the promise of staged performances of the winning work.[34] *La vida breve* won the opera prize hands down, and Falla received his prize money. Performances, however, were not forthcoming. The impresario at the Teatro Real, José Arana y Elizora, was vehemently opposed to staging Spanish opera, claiming that the costs of training and rehearsing singers in Spanish were prohibitive and that the public simply would not attend.[35]

Following this debacle, Falla traveled to Paris, where the opera became his calling card and impressed modernists like Dukas and Debussy. *La vida breve* would finally receive its premiere in a French translation at the Theater of the Municipal Casino of Nice in December 1913. Shortly thereafter, Falla's opera was performed at the Opéra-Comique in Paris. Only after its triumphal reception there would the work come home to Spain and be performed in its original language.[36] The Madrid reviews were uniformly ecstatic, as was the audience. Contemporary reports note that Falla received ovations as he left the theater from crowds in the Calles de Jovellanos and los Madrazo, and that he was cheered in the Café de Castilla later that evening.[37] Like *Las Golondrinas*, *La vida breve* was praised for its musical modernism and its overtones of Dukas and Debussy (with whom, it should be remembered, Falla became acquainted only after he had completed the score). Like *Maruxa*, *La vida breve* was praised for its use of folkloric elements, especially the dances in the second act that have been the most popular parts of the opera ever since. Falla's return from Paris to Madrid, prompted by the outbreak of World War I, was seen as the crucial element in the regeneration of Spanish music and theater: "With Falla we now have reintegrated into the country another valiant champion in the service of the musical renaissance that has been initiated in Spain."[38] Falla had the European polish that would be necessary to save Spanish music.

Falla was the right man, but the vehicle by which he and the music critics hoped to save zarzuela was not. The opera revival of 1914 had been built around comparisons with European modernism, which Spanish audiences had little context to understand. Critics discussed works like *Las Golond-rinas* and *La vida breve* in terms of comparison with the European avant-garde. But while Debussy and Dukas might have been familiar to a well-read musical audience in Spain, their music had barely been performed by the Orquestra Sinfónica de Madrid or the Teatro Real in those years, despite the fervor with which they had been covered by the musical press. The first performance of Debussy's "Prélude à l'après-midi d'un faune" was met with protests on the part of the audience at its Madrid premiere in April 1906.[39] The Real gave exactly two performances of Dukas's *Ariane et Barbe-Bleue* during the 1912–1913 season, along with twelve performances of Richard Strauss's *Salome* during the entire decade. These two operas were the sum total of European modernism in Madrid's opera houses.[40] Modernism might have had the power to restore Spanish theater, but zarzuela audiences would have had no framework that would allow them to grapple with Usandizaga's or Falla's brand of Europeanism.

After 1914 Falla would continue to try to reconcile modernism with Spanish nationalism. The aural world of his music is such that he is frequently compared with such French Impressionist composers as Debussy and Maurice Ravel, but his themes and preoccupations are completely Spanish, as in his use of impressionist harmonies to evoke the country's Islamic heritage and natural beauty in the piano-and-orchestra nocturne *Noches en los jar-dines de España* (Nights in the Gardens of Spain). Falla's output would have a significant theatrical component, but few of his works are traditional in form. *El amor brujo* (Bewitched Love) uses a flamenco singer to narrate a ballet. *El retablo de maese Pedro* (Master Peter's Puppet Show) is a chamber opera staged completely with puppets and based on an episode from *Don Quijote*. Falla's only theater work to take a traditional form is the ballet *El sombrero de tres picos* (The Three-Cornered Hat), but as if to emphasize the modernism inherent in the piece, the sets and costumes for the premiere were designed by Pablo Picasso. Falla turned his back on traditional zarzuela and opera, perhaps sensing that Spanish audiences simply were not ready to experience musically challenging works.[41] Although Spain would become a more musically sophisticated country during the 1920s, that sophistication would only slowly seep from the concert halls into the theaters.

The confluence between zarzuela and opera would reach a symbolic climax as a result of a fire inspection at the Teatro Real in the spring of 1925, which revealed that Madrid's opera house was in a dangerously decrepit condition. The theater was temporarily closed pending renovations, and when it became clear those renovations would be an extremely long time in the offing, an alternate venue for opera in Madrid had to be found. (The proposed renovations were still on the drawing board when the Civil War broke out in 1936, and an incendiary bomb destroyed the interior during the siege of Madrid late in the year. The Teatro Real was reopened in 1966 as a concert hall for the Orquesta Sinfónica de Madrid. Opera was not staged at the Teatro Real again until 1997. The opera chosen for the inaugural performance was *La vida breve.*) The government settled on the Teatro de la Zarzuela and developed the idea of the Teatro Lírico Nacional, which would alternate performances of opera and zarzuela during the season to further the goal of promoting the performance of all genres of lyric theater. The composers Pablo Luna and Federico Moreno Torroba, along with librettist Luis Pascual Frutos, were selected as the impresarios for the inaugural 1926–1927 season. They served alongside Luis París, who was the artistic director. For the first time in Spanish theatrical history, state funds would be used to assist the production of zarzuelas. Government subventions had supported opera production at the Teatro Real since its opening in 1850. With this financial support, zarzuela had become part of the official apparatus of the Spanish state.

It was certainly no accident that the first production of the Teatro Lírico Nacional on 23 September 1926 was of Ruperto Chapí's 1889 zarzuela *La bruja* (The Witch). Not only was Chapí one of Spain's most revered composers, but *La bruja* was a classic zarzuela with a score of operatic complexity. It may well have been the work's position on the boundary between opera and zarzuela that led the impresarios to select it. The reaction of many critics seems to have been to look forward to the moment in which zarzuela and opera would cease to be two genres and become one. This is certainly what the critic for *El Heraldo de Madrid* prophesied: "One happy day our musicians will have brought zarzuela to the border of opera and will decide valiantly to tackle the business." Even a mundane symbolic gesture seemed to hint at the convergence of zarzuela and opera—the seats from the Teatro Real had been installed in the Teatro de la Zarzuela.[42] The season of zarzuela at the Teatro Lírico Nacional divided itself between revivals of important works like *La bruja* and *Doña Francisquita* and premieres of works that were deemed to be of special merit like Jesús Guridi's *El caserío* and Vives's *La villana.* While the season was an artistic success, it was not long before critics of the Teatro Lírico Nacional began to question its mission and its goals.

In an open letter published in *El Heraldo de Madrid* on 22 October 1926, Rafael Marquina questioned the claim made by Luna, Frutos, Moreno Torroba, and París that their goal was to establish an "autonomous body" (*Ente Autónomo*) for the production of lyric theater. As an autonomous body, the Teatro Lírico Nacional would be independent of the "industrial enterprises" that merely churned out theater for profit without higher artistic pretensions.[43] Maquina's main criticism was that the leaders of the Teatro Lírico Nacional had given no concrete plans for the ways in which the theater would promote Spanish art, relying instead upon generalities. The impresarios had turned down the services of Eugenio Casals, the artistic director of the zarzuela company at the Teatro Fuencarral, and were appearing to work against the interests of other zarzuela companies by presenting new works in addition to the classics of the zarzuela canon. All of this, Maquina argued, was inappropriate for a theater that was essentially an arm of the state.

The impresarios responded that the Teatro Lírico Nacional was not, in fact, an arm of the state. They claimed it was an independent body whose main goal was to find a way to work outside the system of industrial theater that was then prevalent. But their description of the mission of the Teatro Lírico Nacional does not sound all that different from the profit-driven industrial theater that everybody in the debate was criticizing: "Our program? . . . To better and improve our brilliant company; to premiere the works of acclaimed or new authors that gain our confidence, without neglecting the revival on the boards of the classic works of our national repertory."[44] Curiously, impresarios also rejected the idea that the Teatro Lírico Nacional was supposed to stage those zarzuelas that were closest in feel to opera, which seems disingenuous when one looks at the musical sophistication of the works staged in the autumn of 1926. All in all, it looked as if the Teatro Lírico Nacional was trying to have its cake and eat it too. The impresarios were behaving like heads of the for-profit theaters while at the same time protesting their important goal in solidifying a national culture. Maquina's argument contains a damning subtext. While never explicitly stating so, he was accusing the impresarios of profiting from both the state and the public.[45] Rather than standing for Spanish culture, the Teatro Lírico Nacional was in fact even more of a money-hungry machine than the so-called industrial theaters. Zarzuela's claim to nationalist preeminence was based on its close ties to the Spanish people through the use of folk music and mass box office appeal. But that message became muddied when it became associated with the Spanish state. Zarzuela, which had once represented vital Spain, had become a part of official Spain.

The debate over the Teatro Lírico Nacional died out over the course of the 1926–1927 season, and the impresarios of the Teatro de la Zarzuela stopped using the term to advertise their productions. The idea of a national theater would be revived in the 1930s under the Second Republic, when Amadeo Vives was appointed the head of the Junta Nacional de la Música y los Teatros Líricos.[46] But by the end of the 1920s, the confluence between opera and zarzuela had undermined the nationalist role that zarzuela had been developing since the late nineteenth century. Antonio Peña y Goñi, through his advocacy of zarzuela's popular roots, had helped to create a dichotomy between "art" and "popular culture": what would entertain the masses was nationalist, while art was ensconced at the Teatro Real and associated with a government that had separated itself from the people. But when zarzuela and opera began to merge in the 1910s, zarzuela began to move toward irrelevancy. How could popular nationalism be encased in a piece of "art"—especially a foreign art form traditionally supported by the state? The moral relevance of the theater was not that it taught lessons to the Spanish people. The morality of the theater lay in the fact that it communicated the lessons the Spanish people wished to give to their leaders.

Of course, communicating popular ideas to Spain's government had become much more difficult in the 1920s. The distinction between Spain's government and its people—the distinction between "official Spain" and "vital Spain" that José Ortega y Gasset had diagnosed—had only been reinforced by Miguel Primo de Rivera's assumption of dictatorial powers in 1923. Spanish composers had turned to opera and musical modernism to regenerate and reform Spanish society and politics at exactly the same time that the Restoration system was becoming impossibly sclerotic. The top-down reforms of Maura and the Conservative Party failed to have any lasting effect. World War I introduced new problems. Spain remained neutral during the European conflagration, but labor unrest spread as the profits flooding into the country from wartime contracts and production (for both sides) failed to make their way into the pockets of the working classes. Tensions were exacerbated by the fact that the wealthy and many political leaders tended to be pro-German while the vast majority of the Spanish population was pro-Entente.[47] Strikes became extremely common, climaxing in the Barcelona General Strike of 1919, in which over 100,000 electrical, textile, and railway workers brought the economy of Catalonia to its knees and forced the Spanish government to pass a law establishing the eight-hour workday in the country.

Such unrest helped to fuel the atmosphere in which General Miguel Primo de Rivera staged a military pronunciamiento in September of 1923. Promising to be an "iron surgeon" who would regenerate Spain by eliminating the corruption of the Restoration political system and reviving the national economy, Rivera suspended the Spanish parliament and all constitutional proceedings—temporarily, he claimed. While his investment in Spanish infrastructure did help to boost the economy, it was at the price of establishing a dictatorship that outlawed labor unions and relied on policies similar to those being established by Benito Mussolini in Italy. Despite José Ortega y Gasset's support for the régime, never had official Spain been less vital. By falling into the control of the Spanish state at the height of the Primo de Rivera dictatorship, zarzuela lost much of the legitimacy it had had as a nationalist genre of theater. But opera was not the only way in which zarzuela was distancing itself from its popular roots. Under the Primo de Rivera dictatorship, zarzuela was increasingly turning to literary classics and to Spanish history to tread a fine line between representing the Spanish people and placating a Spanish dictator. Operatic music was only the first step that would eventually divorce zarzuela from its popular origins.

7

Classicism and Historicism

B y the 1920s, European operetta was coming to seem dated and passé.
The frivolous plotlines about squabbles among Central European aristocrats seemed less amusing after they had spent four years trying to kill each
other. Musical styles were changing, thanks in large part to the jazz music that
American soldiers had brought with them to Europe during World War I. Jazz
was embraced as popular music by a continent weary of the old-fashioned
morals and culture that the war had swept away. Jazz music and short skirts
replaced the Viennese waltz and the decorous long gowns of the prewar years.
Composers like George Gershwin, Darius Milhaud, and Kurt Weill made jazz
somewhat respectable by using it in symphonic compositions. The occasional
European operetta composer tried to adapt to this changing world, such as
Emmerich Kálmán. Normally a composer who trafficked in Léhar style lyricism, in 1928 he premiered *Die Herzogin von Chicago* (The Duchess from
Chicago), which made liberal use of jazz. The plot also reflected the changes
wrought in postwar Europe. The impoverished aristocrat Prince Sandor finds
himself pursued by Miss Mary Lloyd, who believes that her father's wealth
can buy her anything she wants—including Sandor's palace, with the prince
himself as so much furniture. All ends happily, of course, but with the couple
dancing a fox-trot rather than a waltz.[1]

But *Die Herzogin von Chicago* was an exception. Most European operettas
tried desperately to ignore the sea changes of the 1920s. The output of Franz
Léhar sums up what was happening to European operetta. *The Merry Widow*
and *The Count of Luxembourg* were typical of prewar operetta, waltz music
sung by aristocratic characters and set to gossamer-thin plots. In his postwar compositions, the lush music and slight stories remained. But in order to
make his work acceptable to a world where the aristocracy were increasingly
irrelevant, Léhar set some of his postwar works in a highly fantasized histori-

cal past. *Paganini* (1925) imagines an affair between the nineteenth-century violin virtuoso and the sister of Napoleon, while *Friederike* (1928) uses the romantic travails of a young Johann Wolfgang von Goethe as the basis for the plot. (A significant chunk of Berlin audiences found a singing Goethe highly risible, and the plot was parodied in cabaret sketches that season.) Léhar's other strategy was to situate his works in exotic fantasy worlds. *The Land of Smiles* (1929) sweeps its Viennese heroine off to a China completely devoid of Chiang Kai-Shek and Mao Tse-Tung. *Guidetta* (1934), his last work, is set in a Mediterranean North Africa so stereotyped that one keeps expecting Charles Boyer to appear and ask Guidetta to come with him to the Casbah.[2]

Zarzuela was not immune to these trends. As we have seen, the increasingly close connection between opera and zarzuela in the 1920s made it seem less vital and less nationalistic than it had before. Spain may have remained neutral during the Great War, but zarzuelas with singing urban masses and happy peasants probably seemed a little out of place in a country where anarchists were organizing labor unions, and strikes made the discontent of the working classes obvious. In 1923 Spain succumbed to the blandishments of dictatorship. Miguel Primo de Rivera put a stop to labor unrest, but at the price of suspending the Cortes, banning unions, and otherwise suspending the democratic process. Spanish composers and librettists, seemingly unwilling to come to grips with the modern age, retreated into historicized fantasy just as Léhar had. Rather than shipping their casts off to exotic ports of call, zarzuelas increasingly turned to classic Spanish literature—especially the plays and novels of Spain's seventeenth-century Golden Age—as an appropriate way of distancing their plots from contemporary life.[3] Zarzuela music retreated into lush grandiosity, and while there were the occasional attempts to interject modern jazz and dance music into zarzuelas (such as the 1921 work that was Jacinto Guerrero's first significant hit, *La montería*), most 1920s scores revived the elaborate and complex musical structures of the nineteenth-century zarzuela grande, moderated occasionally by Spanish folk music or Viennese waltzes.

A suitable framework for understanding the zarzuelas of the 1920s can be found in the writings of Theodor Adorno. Adorno, one of the great pessimists of cultural analysis, tended to insist that popular culture—and specifically popular music—was a politically demobilizing force, designed to distract people from political action and to trick them into consuming the same mindless dreck over and over again while believing that they were freely choosing their entertainment.[4] This book has for the most part rejected such pessimism, arguing that popular music can politically mobilize a population. But Adorno's definition of musical kitsch from a short 1932 essay applies directly to the problem of postwar operetta and zarzuela:

> In music, at any rate, all real kitsch has the character of a *model.* It offers the outline and draft of objectively compelling, pre-established forms that have lost their content in history. . . . Hence the illusory character of kitsch . . . has its own objective origin in the downfall of forms and material into history. Kitsch is the precipitate of devalued forms and empty ornaments from a formal world that has become remote from its immediate context. . . . For kitsch precisely sustains the memory, distorted and as mere illusion, of a formal objectivity that has passed away.[5]

The retreat of operetta into historical romanticism and exotic or literary fantasy can be understood as kitsch in a technical sense. (In this chapter, "kitsch" will *not* be used as an aesthetic judgment.) Romanticism and fantasy came about as the forms and content that had traditionally underpinned operetta music and plots receded into the historical past, replaced by new types of music and social structures. But in Spain, a retreat into kitsch was also driven by political circumstance. It is certainly no coincidence that zarzuelas increasingly abandoned their political and nationalist messaging just as a conservative political dictatorship with very specific nationalist goals came to power.

As the legitimacy of the Primo de Rivera dicatatorship rested primarily on its claim to be a force for the regeneration of Spain, the development of some form of nationalist mobilization was a necessity to distinguish the new government from the failed policies of the Restoration and the turno pacífico. Taking his cue from the emerging Fascist régime of Benito Mussolini in Italy, Primo de Rivera sought to mobilize the Spanish population through military indoctrination. And to this he added Catholic religiosity as another tool to unite Spaniards into a cohesive national unit. But the dictatorship was only willing to take popular mobilization so far, as it demonstrated by banning labor unions in 1926 and by its continual attacks on Catalan nationalism. A populace nationalized in the wrong manner would certainly disturb the changes being implemented in order to "save" Spain from the inert Restoration system. Spain was now committed to an authoritarian dictatorship bent on determining what was good for Spain from above, not from below. The statist nationalism of the Primo de Rivera régime was of the authoritarian and exclusionary variety that was increasingly prevalent in interwar Europe, not the liberal and inclusive version that had predominated in the nineteenth century.[6] Zarzuela was tied to a fading idea of the nation—one in which the Spanish people rather than the state determined their own national identity and autonomy. With popular nationalism an increasingly distant idea, zarzuela had little choice but to surrender to the charms of kitsch.

Approximately one month after the Primo de Rivera pronunciamiento of 13 September 1923, the conservative daily *La Época* took the unusual step of building its leading editorial commentary around the premiere of a zarzuela, making explicit the connection between politics, culture, and the state of the country. The premiere of *Doña Francisquita* would have merited extensive coverage in *La Época* in any event, since colibrettist Guillermo Fernández-Shaw was on the staff of the newspaper. (In fact, the review of the work was one-and-one-half columns long, making it one of the lengthiest items in the newspaper that day.) *La Época* deplored the turn that Spanish composers had made toward Viennese operetta in the name of regeneration, equating it with Spanish politicians who modeled their policies after foreign politicians like René Waldeck-Rousseau, David Lloyd George, and Benito Mussolini. Instead, *La Época* argued that the true sentiment of the Spanish nation was not to be found by imitating foreigners but by looking to the strength of Spain "in light of her own history." It then proceeded to praise the composer of *Doña Francisquita*, Amadeo Vives, for doing exactly this. The praise took a decidedly political tone in its final paragraph:

> This people [pueblo] that yesterday acclaimed Vives for his gesture of resurrection of Spanish zarzuela with its classical literary model, tradition [*castiza*] in setting and situation, in songs and in dances, surely knows that we have a constitutional period in Cádiz, inaugurated by Muñoz Torrero, which is the archive of good government; they know that we have a Jovellanos, who had nothing to envy from foreign statesmen regarding his capacity of vision; they know that in our recent history we had a Cánovas, who remade Spain and its institutions. . . .[7]

While *La Época*'s historical narrative is slanted (to call the 1812 Constitution of Cádiz a specifically Spanish document misses the mark, since it was built around the same liberal principles that emanated from the French Revolution), the final ellipsis implies what *La Época*'s conservative readership could fill in for themselves. Primo de Rivera would remake Spanish government just as Vives had remade Spanish music.

That the editorial in *La Época* was not merely an isolated gesture can be seen in the fact that the more left-leaning daily *El Liberal* took the unusual step the next day of running a story about an editorial in a competing newspaper. The author of the short piece did little more than sum up *La Época*'s argument, wondering with a slightly cocked eyebrow if "*Doña Francisquita* will work a miracle that will return Spain to the jurisdiction [*fueros*] of its traditions, not only artistic, but political-constitutional as well."[8] This was then followed with a verbatim quote of the final paragraph of *La Época*'s editorial. *El Liberal* would have had to be veiled in any political criticism it offered— Primo de Rivera had instituted press censorship—but its brief summation offers little doubt that it looked askance at *La Época*'s pronouncement. But it is clear that by 1923 zarzuela had cemented its position as a key component of Spanish culture, such that it could be discussed in the same breath with major political issues of the day. It is difficult to imagine an English newspaper of the period doing this with an operetta by Ivor Novello or Noël Coward.

But the editorial in *La Época* also unwittingly lays its finger on the key problem facing zarzuelas in the 1920s. The nationalistic status of the zarzuela had risen to a point where the genre could be seriously discussed in constitutional terms. One of the crucial features that the editorial isolated in *Doña Francisquita* was its "classicism in its literary model," even though the notion that there was anything self-consciously literary about a zarzuela libretto would have surprised even the most eminent zarzuela librettists. The authors of Barbieri-style zarzuela grande spent most of their time adapting their plots from French operettas, while the authors of the género chico—for all their emphasis on a naturalist style—were busy appealing to popular taste. In spite of all the box-office receipts earned by zarzuelas in the 1920s, the status of the genre was not that of a popular art form. As part of the national heritage, it had acquired an official status and as such had to aim its ambitions higher than mere popular entertainment. This crystallization of zarzuela's pretensions would diminish the claims of the genre to represent the popular taste of the nation. It was becoming officially linked with the new dictatorship and could thus be discussed in political terms by the press, but it could not now claim to be a representation of the national identity of the Spanish people. In this way, zarzuela music and zarzuela plots came to revel in their historicity and developed into kitsch. But the historicity of zarzuela was not a direct depiction of the history of the people it was supposed to represent.

Much of the success of *Doña Francisquita* must be attributed to the plot, an intricate farce in which three pairs of mismatched lovers eventually sort themselves out. The humor is heightened by the fact that the two men competing for the title character's hand are father and son, while Francisquita and her mother are both pursuing Fernando (the son). What makes this farce more rewarding than the average zarzuela libretto is the subtle characterization of the central lovers. Fernando is one of the few characters in all of operetta who actually matures emotionally as the play progresses, a process due to Francisquita's subtle manipulations. Librettists Federico Romero and Guillermo Fernández-Shaw have to share their success with Lope de Vega, the author of the source material, *La discreta enamorada* (The Discreet Lover). The selection of *La discreta enamorada* as potential zarzuela material originated with Vives. The idea that would become *Doña Francisquita* originated in December 1922, when Vives met his future librettists at the opening-night party for Pablo Luna's *El hotel de las lunas de miel* (The Honeymoon Hotel). According to tradition, Vives took the authors back to his apartment where he gave them a copy of Vega's play, claiming that "nobody but Lope . . . had captured the ambiance of Madrid."[9]

While the notion of adapting works from Spain's Golden Age was not exactly a radical idea, zarzuela librettists had generally steered away from its canonized "classics" and its major authors: Pedro Calderón, Tirso de Molina, and Lope de Vega—although there is a certain amount of irony in this, given that Calderón is supposed to have written the libretto for the first zarzuela during the seventeenth century. The general consensus seems to have been that the major seventeenth-century dramatists and their oeuvre were unsuitable for light lyric drama, much in the way Broadway musicals (always excepting *West Side Story*) tend to avoid Shakespeare's tragedies as the basis for a fun evening at the theater. (Shakespearean comedy, on the other hand, has provided suitable inspiration for Rodgers and Hart's *The Boys from Syra-*

cuse and Cole Porter's *Kiss Me, Kate.*) Vives had turned to the works of the Spanish Golden Age for his libretti from the beginning of his career. His first popular success, *Don Lucas del Cigarral*, was adapted from a play by the minor seventeenth-century Spanish playwright Francisco de Rojas. As Vives's career progressed, he became bolder about his choices for libretto material. He was encouraged by his admirers. Upon hearing *Don Lucas*, no less an eminence than Miguel de Unamuno declared he would like to hear Vives set Calderón's *La vida es sueño* (Life is a Dream), arguably the greatest of Spain's Golden Age dramas, to music.

Theatrical critics were enchanted by the libretto to *Doña Francisquita*. They praised Romero and Fernández-Shaw for their sensitive adaptation of the exalted Lope de Vega. The opening paragraph in *La Época*'s review noted that the adaptation of a classic work had the potential to be an "unpardonable error." The critic declared that the only way in which such an adaptation could be made was that it be done with "respect," and he felt that Romero and Fernández-Shaw had shown the necessary respect to Lope de Vega. The critic for *El Sol* concurred, noting that the authors' "hard work and discretion, which governs the complications of Lope's plot, reducing them by very modest proportions," while adapting the plot, led to the work's success.[10] In each case, the upshot of the critics is clear—a play by Lope de Vega is a work of art, and one that needs to be approached with reverence.

In adapting one of Spain's literary classics, the librettists had managed to elevate what might have been merely a zarzuela, a piece of entertainment, into a work of art. *El Heraldo de Madrid* stated this most bluntly.

> *Doña Francisquita* is, besides being an excellent theatrical work, a true work of art. In these times of prose and materialism that we are disgracedly living in, the mere fact of aspiring to write something of considerable aesthetic quality, something that is on a superior plane to the vulgarity and coarseness that prevail, is worthy of praise and indubitable merit for those who carry out such work.[11]

It is difficult to imagine such praise being lavished upon even the most worthy specimens of the género chico. Most surprising is the claim that *Doña Francisquita* was a work of art that prevailed against the rampant materialism of modernity. Zarzuela had always been about materialism, since its duty had been to attract the largest number of customers into the theater in order to create a profit for the authors and the impresarios. By 1923, however, zarzuela had many more competitors for the pesetas Spaniards devoted to entertainment. Movies, cabaret, and sporting events were beginning to loom larger in the entertainment pages of the daily newspapers. *Doña Francisquita* may not have been able to fully compete with Mary Pickford, but she did not really have to. Instead, zarzuela was "art." Nor would *Doña Francisquita* be the last attempt the authors made at adapting Spanish classics for zarzuela. Four years later, Vives, Romero, and Fernández-Shaw would present *La villana* (The Peasant Girl), a musical adaptation of one of Lope de Vega's most famous works, *Peribáñez y el Comendador* (Peribáñez and the Commander). Even more than usual, Vives contributed to the construction of the libretto, making sure that the song forms and structures would not clash with the language of the adaptation.[12] The critics were enthusiastic, but the work did not last long on the stage. It seems that audiences found a light opera about droit du seigneur not to their liking. Romero and Fernández-Shaw had better luck with their adaptation of Vega's *El perro del hortelano* (The Dog in the Manger) for Jacinto Guerrero in 1930 as *La rosa del azafrán* (The Saffron Rose).

Vives's music was deemed integral to the achievement of *Doña Francisquita,* which is as it should be for any lyric piece, but critics also took note of the stylistic references he used in composing his score. Many noted the score's use of eighteenth-century popular songs as models for the musical numbers. At least one music critic also approved of Vives' subtitle for the score. Rather than calling it a "Zarzuela," at the last minute the composer changed the classification to "Comedia lírica." The music critic for *La Época* found this to his liking, noting that "when you hear the word zarzuela, you make an expression of disgust." Clearly, the notion that zarzuela was a popular art form was not appealing to the music critics, as the anonymous critic for *El Imparcial* griped: "there occur, even in works with a marked national character, the 'fox' and the 'shimmy' as an easy way of gaining applause, and the audience gives a hand to orchestral effects, to the hateful stridency of the 'jazz-band.' A work of the category of *Doña Francisquita* forcefully purifies this ambiance." By the 1920s American-style jazz was popular, and zarzuela music was in danger of becoming as quaint as high-button shoes. The critic for *ABC* claimed that Vives's music had "resuscitated Barbieri."[13] The invocation of Barbieri, who had been deified as one of Spain's greatest composers even before his death in

1894, says it all. Vives had become a kitsch composer in the best sense of the term, using the great composers of the nineteenth century as his model. The score to *Doña Francisquita* is gorgeous, but it has no grounding in the realities of 1920s Europe.

Vives's score is a self-conscious resurrection of the musical forms of the zarzuela grande that Barbieri had perfected between 1850 and 1880. Gone is the urban dance music of the género chico. Gone, too, are the Viennese-style waltzes and other trappings of Central European operetta that had flourished in the previous decade. Instead, Vives reverts to the traditional folk forms that had helped the zarzuela to establish its reputation. Street musicians play a pasa-calle as the introduction to the musical scene between Aurora, Fernando, and Cardona that establishes the love-triangle plot (No. 3 in the vocal score). Aurora herself has a bolero that leads into an orchestral fandango at the climax of the work (No. 13). The key song to establishing the play's main theme—the celebration of youthful love known as "Canción de la juventud" (Song of Youth; No. 4A in the vocal score)—is a seguidilla. This song is reprised in the finale of the play, so the audience would have left the theater with a Spanish folk-style melody ringing in their ears. But none of these forms could truly be considered "popular music" in 1923.[14]

It was not only in terms of musical style that Vives had revived the zarzuela grande. He also revived the role of the chorus in the musical action. In the nineteenth century, the chorus was critical to establishing zarzuela as a nationalist genre, since it was the chorus that represented the Spanish people. In *Doña Francsiquita* Vives uses the chorus to establish the specific setting of the work—in this case, the city of Madrid. The chorus is first allowed to go to work in full force during the "Canción de la juventud," which in addition to being the thematic crux of the work also serves as the celebration of Madrid that Vives had in mind when he first provided *La discreta enamorada* to Romero and Fernández-Shaw. The song and the chorus link the notion of youthfulness with Madrid itself, noting that "The happy song of youth / is the soul of old Madrid."[15] While not the strictly nationalist sentiment that featured in the Barbieri-style zarzuela grande, it does establish the chorus as representatives of the people of a Spanish location. The authors also use the chorus to similar effect in the Act I finale, where a wedding celebration segues directly into a chorus celebrating Madrid (No. 5). But Madrid is not Spain as a whole. Using the chorus in this way creates the distorted illusion that Adorno argued was an integral part of kitsch. Vives creates a sense of the past—but only a sense.

Vives's use of a historicizing chorus goes even deeper. Nineteenth-century zarzuela grande had generally been set in the historical past. In fact, one can see a pattern in the use of historical backdrops for zarzuela. Historical zarzuelas are almost always set approximately eighty years in the past. Hence we see the use of the late eighteenth century in the 1860s and 1870s, the use of the Napoleonic Wars in the 1890s, and the use of 1840s Madrid in the 1920s. In *Doña Francisquita* the historicism is most obvious in the opening scene of Act II, which is set at a Carnival ball. The chorus represents the local religious fraternity (*cofradía*) which helped to organize the Lenten festivities. There is an obvious contrast with the dancing habits of the 1920s—a secularized, mass-culture leisure activity—and the dancing of mid-nineteenth-century Spain, where it was reserved for special celebrations like Carnival. In essence, the chorus is used to establish that the zarzuela takes place in an era before mass culture became dominant. The chorus is used to make a similar point in the Act III opening, the famous Chorus of the Romantics. The authors revive a period in which romancing one's sweetheart in the dark meant a moonlit walk in the park, not taking her to the cinema. *Doña Francisquita*'s depiction of Madrid in the 1840s is of an innocent and quieter past, before the disruptions of modern culture that pervaded the world in which Vives was writing. It is little wonder that the critics spoke of the work in terms of a work of art, since it consciously rejected the mass culture–dominated world of the 1920s.

The backdrop of Romantic-era Madrid was used to even greater effect by Francisco Alonso in his 1925 work *La Calesera* (The Chaise-Driver's Daughter). If *Doña Francisquita* most closely resembles the zarzuela grande of the 1880s with its emphasis on romantic love, *La Calesera* reverts to the earlier style of zarzuela grande that uses history to make political points. Set in 1832, the plot of the work is built around the clash between the forces of liberalism and absolutism in the twilight of Ferdinand VII's reign. A troupe of actors finds itself rescuing the liberal aristocrat Rafael from prison, although he ends up escaping the country at the bittersweet end of the zarzuela with fellow aristocrat Elena and not his actress lover, the chaise-driver's daughter of the title. With historical hindsight, it is difficult not to read that choice as a commentary on the Primo de Rivera dictatorship. No critic at the time seems to have made the connection, although whether out of ignorance or self-preservation is open to question. Only the review in *El Imparcial* even noted the political subtext of the work, commenting that the play "offers us a picturesque episode of the persecution of the liberals in the year 1832." Whether it was the Romantic-era setting that the critic thought picturesque or the persecution of the liberals is unclear.[16]

Alonso's use of the chorus makes *La Calesera* a piece of political criticism. Unlike the traditional zarzuela grande, Alonso only uses the full chorus in its guise as the Spanish people once, during the Act I finale, in which Rafael denounces any pursuit of love while his political ideals remain in danger. This is the Hymn to Liberty, the show-stopping moment of the work (No. 4 in the vocal score).[17] With its unabashed opening line, "No hay bien más hermoso que la libertad" ("There is nothing more beautiful than liberty") and stirring music, the Hymn celebrates the freedoms that the Primo de Rivera government had a tendency to abrogate; by closing Act I with a recap of the Hymn by the full chorus, Alonso and his librettists associate the Spanish people with the protection of liberty. This sentiment would not have been out of place in Barbieri's *Pan y toros,* with its celebration of Enlightenment political ideals. The audience may well have understood this. The Hymn to Liberty had to be repeated three times at the premiere and was received with "strenuous acclamations."[18] Perhaps the 1832 backdrop would have provided camouflage had the government tried to make an issue of the work's political stance. In any event, *La Calesera* remained on the boards.

Like *Doña Francisquita, La Calesera* also used Spanish folk idioms like the seguidilla in its musical construction. Both works also harked back to the complex musical construction of the zarzuela grande that had been abandoned by the género chico in the 1880s and 1890s, since musical scenes and elaborate ensemble numbers are the rule rather than the exception in these works. Both scores also return to the use of the romanza, an operatic aria-style musical number, as the centerpiece of the romance-driven portions of the plot. But the continued use of operatic elements no longer equated to a regenerationist message. It only reinforced the idea that zarzuela had become an exemplar of kitsch. The operatic trend is most obvious in the scores of the composing team of Reveriano Soutullo and Juan Vert, whose output was crucial to the zarzuela revival of the 1920s. The duo first came to prominence with their 1924 work *La leyenda del beso* (The Legend of the Kiss), a romantic farrago revolving around a Gypsy curse. Although the music has been dismissed as "poor man's Puccini," the score's shortcomings can probably be attributed to the necessity of casting singing actors rather than trained singers in the leading roles.[19] Within its own limits, *La leyenda del beso* has a sweeping and melodic through-composed score that very rarely uses the repetitious and strophic melodies common to operetta in general and zarzuela in particular. While Soutullo and Vert's subsequent scores would not be as manifestly operatic as *La leyenda del beso,* they would demonstrate that operatic tropes had become another way that zarzuela distanced itself from its popular past.

Such distancing is evident in the team's most famous work, 1927's *La del soto del parral* (The Woman from the Vineyard in the Grove, discussed in Chapter 5). From its inception, *La del soto* seems to have been constructed to demonstrate that zarzuelas could be subtle. It may well be the only theatrical work about a love triangle in which the "other woman"—the titular character—never appears onstage. The score is not fully operatic, but when *La del soto* focuses upon the central dramatic conflict between husband Miguel and wife Aurora, Soutullo and Vert revert to the traditional romanza and duet structures that characterized similar emotional climaxes in the zarzuela grande.[20] Most notable in this regard is the duet that closes the first act (No. 5). In an operatic attempt to match the constantly shifting emotions of the characters in musical terms, the duet changes its time and key signatures with rapidity. Furthermore, rather than bringing the music to a decisive end, Soutullo and Vert choose to let it fade away into underscoring and allow a book scene to bring down the Act I curtain. While *La del soto del parral* is an unquestionably popular zarzuela, it seems to have been designed with a damn-the-groundlings attitude in mind at times. Soutullo and Vert wrote music to match the drama without fully embracing the musical imperatives that would court popularity and bring an audience to its feet. The operatic elements undermined the popular theatricality of the work, although audiences still responded enthusiastically.

The purist approach did not always work, as Amadeo Vives discovered with the other major "operatic" zarzuela of 1927, *La villana.* Once again, the through-composed score for that work ignores strophic, applause-garnering music almost completely. As with *La del soto del parral,* the romanzas and duets never quite come to a complete stop but rather fade away.[21] Vives realized that the intensely dramatic story of *La villana* would require a dramatic and operatic score, but unlike Soutullo and Vert's work (and even unlike his own

Doña Francisquita), Vives's attempt at an operatic score never managed to find a happy medium between the demands of musical drama and the marketplace. But the fact that one has to discuss zarzuela music in these terms shows just how much zarzuela had evolved since its revival in the 1850s. As with the libretti, zarzuela music could now be legitimately considered artistic. Entertainment was no longer the primary concern of those who created zarzuela. Composers and librettists now set about creating works of art.

In the attempt to create art, it is not surprising that zarzuela librettists turned to classics of Spanish theater and literature to further their cause. In particular, librettos mined the works of Spain's Golden Age, the late sixteenth and seventeenth centuries. *Doña Francisquita* and *La villana* had turned to Golden Age plays for their inspiration. The most successful attempt at reviving Spain's Golden Age, however, was Jacinto Guerrero's *El huésped del Sevillano* (The Guest at the Sevillano Inn), which premiered in 1926. The plot is set in sixteenth-century Toledo and revolves around the kidnapping of the virtuous Raquel by villainous Don Diego. She is rescued by artist Juan Luis, aided and abetted by the kitchen maid at the inn, Constancia. This plot may sound familiar to students of Golden Age Spanish literature, and it ought to: the title character, who appears midway through the second act, is none other than Miguel de Cervantes. He tells Constancia at the final curtain that the story he is writing will be about the events at the Sevillano Inn and will be named after her—"La ilustre fregona" (The Noble Scullery Maid), one of his *Novelas Ejemplares*. *El huésped del Sevillano* was designed very specifically by its authors as an exercise in kitsch. Guerrero, along with his librettists Enrique Reoyo and Juan Ignacio Luca de Tena, published a brief screed about their work in *ABC* the day before the premiere, which made their agenda quite specific. They claimed to have been inspired "by tradition and legend more than by History, perhaps; the Toledo of the swordsmen and of the Jews, of dashing gentlemen and of glorious painters."[22] Clearly, this was to be sixteenth-century Castile as viewed through rose-colored glasses, as opposed to the decidedly unromantic warts-and-all view that emerges directly out of Cervantes's works. The romanticism neatly separates Cervantes's story from its historical context, as Adorno suggested kitsch does.

Guerrero's score sharpens this nostalgic use of Spain's literary past. Guerrero and his librettists make their position most clear in a musically underscored monologue by Cervantes late in the second act. In what may be the most evocative music in the work, Cervantes declaims a series of lines in blank verse referring to the "admirable and strange mix [of] . . . / Mystics and adventurers / and poets and soldiers. / It is Castile . . . and it is Spain!"[23] The historical Cervantes would have been more likely to reflect on the drunkards, thieves, and whores that inhabited Castile, but *El huésped del Sevillano* is not aiming for documentary reality. Guerrero's score also evokes nostalgia for Spain's past through his repeated use of folk songs from the countryside around Toledo, most famously in the female chorus that opens the second act, the Chorus of the Ladies from Lagartera (No. 7 in the vocal score).[24] Guerrero's vocal score actually goes so far as to indicate exactly which musical numbers are derived from folk songs.

However, the score steps backward from classic zarzuela construction in two key ways. First, folk music is not necessarily used to characterize the chorus as the Spanish people. The crucial use of folk music in the first act is Juan Luis's famous "Song of the Sword" (No. 3 in the vocal score)—which, while undeniably thrilling, uses folk music to glorify an individual, not the people. Even when folk music is used to characterize a group of people, Guerrero uses it only for the citizens of Lagartera, a very specific section of the people. Where the zarzuela grande glorifies the Spanish people as a whole, *El huésped del Sevillano* glorifies a specific regional subset of the Spanish people, the denizens of the province around Toledo. Guerrero makes this even clearer during Cervantes's melodrama late in the second act. While speaking in nationalistic terms, the character's thoughts make it clear that this is a regional work: "Toledo, Hispanic fatherland, / crucible of the Iberian race, / blessed are those who are born / Spanish and Toledian!"[25] Once again, a musical model has been separated from its specific historical context. Barbieri would have lopped off the references to Lagartera and Toledo. While *El huésped* seems to glorify Spanish nationalism, it really glorifies particularism.

The second way in which Guerrero moves away from the traditional forms of the zarzuela grande is that he simplifies its musical construction. The romanzas and the duets are not through-composed as they would have been in the nineteenth century (or as they would have been had they been composed by Vives, for that matter). Instead, they are strophic and use a repeating musical pattern. The key number to be affected in this manner is the first act's love duet between Raquel and Juan Luis, "Insolente, presumido" (No. 4 in the vocal score). The emotion of the duet moves from incensed anger over Don Diego's behavior to a declaration of love, but Guerrero uses the same musical phrases, rather than composing new music to match the emotional situation. While Guerrero uses the broad outline of a zarzuela grande score, he readapts the formula to the necessities of 1920s popular music, with an emphasis on repeated melodies that will stick in the ear. Guerrero also doubles the melody of the vocal line in the orchestral accompaniment, a technique not prevalent in the scores of the 1870s and 1880s. While Guerrero appeals to the musical heritage of zarzuela, he does not ignore the demands of 1920s theater audiences. *El huésped* was an attempt to make the popular and the past work hand in hand, another precondition to Adorno's definition of kitsch.

Guerrero would use all of these strategies again in his last zarzuela to enter the canon, 1930's *La rosa del azafrán* (The Saffron Rose). Again, the librettists have adapted a classic Spanish work for the libretto—in this case one of Lope de Vega's best-known works, the seventeenth-century classic *El perro del hortelano*, albeit updated to the 1860s. Again, the identity emphasis within the libretto is not that of an overall Spanish identity but of a local identity (here, the action is focused on the region of La Mancha, a notion made abundantly clear from the opening song, "Aunque soy de la Mancha" ["Although I am from La Mancha"]). Again, while there are the classic romanzas and other set-piece musical forms from the zarzuela grande, much of the music has been simplified for public consumption. The score to *La rosa del azafrán* has a higher share of strophic songs and dance music than would be customary in the zarzuela grande. Both plot and music are altered in such a way as to make them more appealing to modern audiences.

By the late 1920s zarzuela had entered an odd sort of time warp. Musically, zarzuelas like *Doña Francisquita* and *La Calesera* were reviving the musical forms of the old zarzuela grande and reimagining the past through a lens of kitsch, presenting a musical version of the past divorced from its historical milieu. It is in this context that we need to understand what is possibly the most self-reflexive piece of musical theater ever written: *El último romántico* (The Last Romantic), with a libretto by José Tellaeche and a score by Soutullo and Vert. *El último romántico* is a meditation on the history of zarzuela. The action is set in Madrid in 1872 during the first act and 1887 during the second. Tellaeche dictated that the precise date of the action was to be made clear by visual references on the show curtain (*telón alegórico*) to events like the Second Carlist War or the entry of Amadeo of Savoy into Madrid. He also makes a direct reference to the Second Carlist War in the opening chorus of the piece. Throughout the stage directions, Tellaeche is at pains to make clear that the set designers need to make their sets of Madrid as historically accurate as possible. The second scene of the play is set "on the Paseo de la Fuente Castellana, just as one would have encountered today's splendid avenue between the years '70 and '75."[26] This is in part the heritage of the realism of the género chico, but it is also an attempt to re-create an era that was only fifty years past and still within living memory of some of the audience.

Soutullo and Vert's most evocative attempt to re-create that era is the opening of the second act, which takes place in front of the Teatro Felipe, the summer theater on the Paseo del Prado. Encarnación, the comic relief of the piece, confronts a group of street musicians by complaining, "Enough already of the street musicians! . . . There is too much street music / and too much of the trombone!"[27] (She's slightly wrong: as fellow trombonists will note, it is impossible to have too much of the trombone.) This complaint develops into a trio (No. 9 in the vocal score) in which Encarnación and her friends Tomás and Ceferino sum up their feelings about street musicians this way:

> They go through the streets and the plazas
> the street musicians that you hear here,
> and I'm tired already of Chueca,
> of Bretón and of Marqués.
> They only play the mazurka,
> the habanera or the schottische.
> Sometimes it's by Valverde
> and other times by Chapí.
> But it's just a joke
> that everyday
> you only hear
> them playing the *Gran Vía,*
> or *Niña Pancha,*
> or *Cható Margot,*
> *Cádiz* or other things
> that are the fashion today.[28]

Composers Soutullo and Vert, along with Tellaeche, decided that re-creating the musical ambiance was critical to understanding the time period. The opening of this number includes a musical quotation from *Niña Pancha*.[29] Later, in order to help create tension and delay a crucial recognition scene, the authors send a pair of beggars, a blind violinist accompanied by a child singer, across the stage. These beggars perform the ultrasophisticated "Vals del Caballero de Gracia" from *La Gran Vía*.

Tellaeche and the composers are extremely accurate with their theatrical history. *Cádiz* and *La Gran Vía* had premiered in 1886 (*La Gran Vía* had even had its premiere at the Teatro Felipe, which is where this scene takes place) and were still wildly popular the following year. It is not surprising that beggars would be using music from these works to make their living. We can also assume that Encarnación, Tomás, and Ceferino are avid theatergoers who are up-to-date on all the hit productions in Madrid, since *Chateau Margot* (given the Madrilenian pronunciation "*Cható Margot*") was one of the last hits of the spring 1887 season and would have premiered only a few months before the scene being enacted on stage. Soutullo and Vert's score revives the past in other ways as well. Despite the trend toward more operatic zarzuelas—a trend Soutullo and Vert played a very large role in creating—*El último romántico* abandons this mode in favor of a string of dance numbers that evoke the aural world of the género chico. Jotas, pasacalles, mazurkas, and even a can-can populate the score. For this particular piece, composing music that enhanced the drama did not necessarily mean evoking a character's state of mind. In *El último romántico*, music was meant to evoke an entire era. The reversion to the dance music of the género chico was not actually a musical step backward. It was a way of capturing the historical essence of bygone days.

El último romántico was not the only nostalgic look backward to the género chico in the 1920s. In 1920 Marciano Zurita made the first attempt at writing a history of the género chico, the *Historia del género chico*.[30] As with many subsequent attempts to document the history of zarzuela, the *Historia del género chico* was the work of an enthusiastic aficionado of the subject at hand. It is long on anecdotes and entertaining stories but short on documentary evidence. Nevertheless, Zurita isolates many of the critical elements of the género chico that are historically important but that other popular writers have missed. As one example, he attributes the success of Chueca's *La Gran Vía* to the "absolute reality" of the libretto.[31] As we have seen, it was the realism of the género chico that allowed it to articulate the new identity of an urbanizing Spain in the 1890s.

But in the 1920s Zurita was looking at a genre that was moribund. The género chico was dying, and Zurita attributed the death throes to what he termed "asphyxiation." The Madrid that had spawned the género chico was no more, and the tropes that had been the dramatic motor of the género chico would not translate into the modern world of the 1920s. Summoning up the ghosts of the past, Zurita noted that "the Spanish shawl is no longer seen in the streets other than on Maundy Thursday. The street organists have been prohibited for some time. . . . We don't know where the festivals are being held. The Gardens of the Buen Retiro have disappeared in order to build the Palace of Telecommunications. . . ." The ladies' shawl that had driven the plot lines of *La verbena de la paloma* and *Agua, azucarillos y aguardiente* had become a picturesque costume used only on special occasions, while the location of Madrid's open-air summer relaxation, with its dances and theaters, had been replaced by a glorified post office that still looks like an overwrought wedding cake. Zarzuela had sought to regenerate Spanish society, to modernize it and make it more European. And therein lay the problem: "Who doubts that all of this is going to Europeanize us? But, who doubts as well that the *género chico* cannot resist such Europeanization?"[32] The various attempts by zarzuela to fashion a new and modern Spanish identity had succeeded, but at the cost of rendering zarzuela itself obsolete.

But can we consider Zurita's history and *El último romántico* kitsch? Or were they serious attempts to understand zarzuela in its proper historical context? While both rely on nostalgia to make their points, the historical contextualization is better than average in both works. Tellaeche, Soutullo, and Vert have a very precise and accurate understanding of the historical background to their work, and their music deliberately invokes the early period of the género chico. While nobody would mistake Zurita's history for a work of rigorous scholarship, it still has a well-developed understanding of zarzuela's larger social role reflecting Spain's urban culture and the power of lyric theater in the regeneration process. But both works also recognize that zarzuela was gone with the wind, and one with Ninevah and Tyre. Their understanding of zarzuela's past also meant that those authors realized the genre's essential historical irrelevancy to the Spain of the 1920s. Where Vives and Guerrero were busy trying to re-create an era that had disappeared forever, *El último romántico* and the *Historia del género chico* recognized that zarzuela had been supplanted by a world in which Hollywood movies and football matches were popular entertainment. The only way in which zarzuela could still attempt to be a nationalist genre of theater was by engaging in historicism and literary classicism. But by separating from its popular roots—which had originally given zarzuela its claim to be a nationalist genre—zarzuela had become kitsch. This is not to say that the works in this chapter are musically inferior or somehow subpar; in fact, most of them are supreme accomplishments of musical theater. (When Plácido Domingo presented a zarzuela as part of opera seasons in Los Angeles and Washington, DC, he chose *Doña Francisquita.*) But like the contemporaneous operas of Richard Strauss and Giacomo Puccini such as *Die Frau ohne Schatten* and *Turandot,* they reflect a distinctly nineteenth-century sensibility that sits awkwardly athwart the historical realities of the post–World War I era.

Not that this was necessarily fatal in and of itself. But just as Primo de Rivera's dictatorship used the language of regeneration while undermining the popular sovereignty that could actually accomplish such change, zarzuela's classicism undermined its nationalist message. Zarzuela's populist nationalism had flourished under the Restoration because the government's weakness left space for a popular vision of national identity to thrive. By strengthening the Spanish state while quashing popular political participation, the Primo de Rivera dictatorship actually undermined Spanish nationalism at a critical juncture; never had the division between "official Spain" and "vital Spain" been more obvious. The dictatorship also accelerated the division between liberals who looked to Europe for regenerationist ideas and conservatives who wished to revive the Spain of the Catholic Monarchs Ferdinand and Isabella I. With the collapse of the dictatorship, the subsequent abdication of Alfonso XIII, and the establishment of the Second Republic in 1930, Spain was plunged into a period of oscillation between left and right that would eventually break into open civil war. Whatever headway lyric theater had made at establishing a national identity that might have prevented such a disaster was halted by the Primo de Rivera régime. At the very moment of the collapse of the Bourbon Restoration, zarzuela had ceased to be a meaningful form of Spanish nationalism. Popular theater no longer had the power to unify an increasingly urbanizing country because it no longer reflected a vision of modernization. It was retreating into the sixteenth century.

While we can best understand the zarzuelas of the 1920s as kitsch—albeit high-quality kitsch, not unlike *Downton Abbey*—this is not to deny their artistic and musical accomplishments. If anything, the turn to kitsch is one of the only ways in which zarzuela could continue to thrive as a theatrical genre. The Primo de Rivera dictatorship would hardly have countenanced music theater that celebrated the working classes of the day or pointed out the flaws in government and society, as zarzuela had during the Restoration. During a period in which the government was trying to close down any form of popular political participation, zarzuelas that celebrated the political potential of the pueblo had to disguise their politics beneath a veil of historicism. Only by a retreat into historicism and classicism could composers like Vives, Guerrero, Soutullo, and Vert hope to have their works staged. By the 1920s it was also clear that a traditional, unifying nationalist project had failed. Primo de Rivera would intensify discord between Spain's liberals and conservatives. This discord would accelerate during the Second Republic, only to culminate in the Spanish Civil War, when two competing visions of Spanish nationalism would rip the country apart. No amount of musical theater could hope to bind together such a rift. In the end, there is a limit to the nationalizing power of popular culture in the absence of state support for such a project. Music, no matter how accomplished, cannot soothe the savage breast when that breast does not want to be soothed.

Popular Music and
Popular Nationalism

The early 1930s were something of an Indian summer for the genre of zarzuela. A few works were resisting the lure of kitsch and trying to capture the nature of modern Spanish life during the 1930s. Librettists Francisco Ramos de Castro and Anselmo Carreño wrote two major pieces that attempted to move the sainete into the twentieth century. The 1934 zarzuela *La del manojo de rosas* (The Girl with the Bunch of Roses) features a romance between an automobile mechanic and a female florist. The following year's racier *Me llaman presumida* (They Call Me Vain) has not only women who drink openly in Madrid bars, but a pair of male photographers who take . . . "artistic" shots of young ladies. Adding to the modernity of the work is the fact that the climax takes place at a public defense drill for a gas attack. Francisco Alonso's music betrays his background in writing for revues. Saxophones are used prominently in the orchestration, and many of the musical numbers were clearly designed for popular airplay on the radio. These were zarzuelas that were attempting to engage with and portray modern life, as the genre had during the 1880s and 1890s.

But many more zarzuelas were attempting to ignore the gathering turmoil. (This was hardly unique to Spain. It wasn't as if Fred Astaire and Ginger Rogers were grappling with the reality of the Great Depression or Italian Fascism when traveling to Venice in *Top Hat.*) Federico Moreno Torroba, Francisco Alonso, and Pablo Sorozábal, the composers who dominated the period, created highly melodic scores indebted to the escapist heritage of operetta. Sorozábal's first major hit, 1931's *Katiuska,* was an operetta set in the Ukraine after the Bolshevik Revolution. The plot of Russian aristocrats fleeing the Red Army might have seemed topical in interwar Europe, but with a story seemingly lifted out of Alexandre Dumas—including a second-act revelation that the humble peasant Katiuska is the daughter of a disguised nobleman—any political topicality was submerged in romantic bathos. So-rozábal would similarly disguise the topicality of a plot built around cocaine smuggling with lushly escapist music in *La tabernera del puerto* (The Harbor Barmaid), which premiered on 6 April 1936 and had the distinction of being the last hit zarzuela to premiere before the outbreak of the Civil War. Other works gleefully delved into anachronism, such as Moreno Torroba's 1934 revival of the sainete in *La chulapona*. This work, with its virtually untranslatable title (a *chulapona* is Madrid's female equivalent to the London Cockney, lower-class but savvy and street-smart), is set in 1893 Madrid and has as many mazurkas, pasacalles, and Chinese shawls as *La Revoltosa* or *La verbena de la Paloma*. Heard on recordings or seen in revival today, the zarzuelas of the 1930s are glorious examples of what Spanish composers could do with musical theater forms. But placed within the larger context of the history of zarzuela, they are flies embedded in amber, remote and isolated from the wider world around them. They ignored the increasing social and political turmoil that was engulfing Spain in the years preceding the Spanish Civil War.

That political turmoil had been set in motion by the collapse of the Primo de Rivera dictatorship, and with it the last vestiges of the Restoration political system. On 26 January 1930, Miguel Primo de Rivera resigned his position as prime minister and fled Spain. In the previous two years he had lost the confidence of King Alfonso XIII and the Spanish Army, his main pillars of support. The attempt to create a "parenthesis" in order to reform the Restoration political system had failed, and Alfonso assumed control of the Spanish government by appointing General Dámaso Berenguer to take his place. Berenguer was meant to be a tool of the monarch, who had wanted to take direct control of the Spanish political system for some time. But few Spaniards were deceived by this maneuver. Berenguer's short heyday was referred to as the *dictablanda* or the "soft dictatorship," a play on the Spanish word for dictatorship, *dictadura*—"dura" in Spanish means "hard." But the failure to restore liberal parliamentary democracy undermined the legitimacy of Alfonso XIII's right to rule. He had ignored the growing political power and impatience of Spain's urban working class. In municipal elections held in April of the following year, Spaniards overwhelmingly voted for an alliance of Republican and Socialist candidates, who had formed a pact to restore liberal democracy and force the abdication of the monarch. Alfonso was then informed he could not count on the loyalty of the armed forces. He fled the country on 14 April 1931, opening the way for the formation of the Second Republic.[1]

What followed was five years of political strife in a country increasingly divided between the political Left and the political Right. The Republican-Socialist coalition that replaced the monarchy attempted to establish the most progressive democratic government in Europe at the time, but the underlying Marxist rhetoric of the Spanish Socialist Party terrified conservatives committed to a more traditional vision of Spanish society. Two years later in 1933, a conservative coalition defeated the Republican-Socialist bloc in parliamentary elections and adopted policies designed to undo the socioeconomic reforms undertaken during the first two years of the republic. Both left-wing and right-wing political groups increasingly refused to abide by the idea of constitutionalism, and both only wanted to support a régime that would further their own political agenda. The election of a Popular Front coalition of Communists, Socialists, and Republicans proved to be the final straw for conservatives, who feared an imminent Bolshevik Revolution in Spain.[2] All of this culminated in a military uprising against the government on 18 July 1936. The Spanish Civil War would demonstrate the cost of the failure to develop a coherent sense of Spanish national identity during the late nineteenth and early twentieth century: the tensions inherent in the Spanish search for national identity had never been resolved and ultimately broke out into open conflict.

One zarzuela that premiered during the years of the Second Republic tackled this tension between radical Republicanism and conservative traditionalism. *Luisa Fernanda* takes place primarily in Madrid during the late summer and early autumn of 1868. Luisa Fernanda is loved by Vidal, a wealthy farmer, and Javier, a dashing cavalry officer (who has also been carrying on an affair with the monarchist Duchess Carolina). This love triangle is an allegory of the struggle between two political systems—Republicanism as embodied by Vidal and monarchism as embodied by Javier—to gain mastery over Spain as embodied by Luisa Fernanda. The political views of the two lovers are crucial to the plot. The dramatic climax of the play is not the scene of Vidal's noble sacrifice and Javier's triumph in love, as would be expected in the operetta tradition. That moment is rushed through in a short speech seconds before the final curtain. Rather, the dramatic climax consists of the second and third scenes of Act II, in which the September Revolution breaks out and Javier has to be rescued from the Republican forces. Moreno Torroba gives this significant dramatic weight through his musical setting. The musical sequence of Javier's capture and rescue takes close to seven minutes to play out, one of the longest concentrations of music in the work.

The politics of the characters in *Luisa Fernanda* can be easy to ignore. Many critics chose to focus on the love story to the exclusion of political elements. The critic for *La Época* went so far as to claim that "the libretto of Romero and Fernández-Shaw and the score of Moreno Torroba realizes with a harmony that is charming an ideal not of Revolution—because the good taste of the authors does not permit them to mix at all in politics nor to bring to the theater passions that most often clash with the fine nature of art—but an ideal of exquisite essences."[3] It is difficult to reconcile such a statement with a zarzuela that is set at the time of a major political upheaval in Spain and actually builds its entire second act around the September 1868 Revolution, with patriotic speeches on stage. But *Luisa Fernanda* soft-pedals its political aspect by dropping it completely in the third act. Librettists Federico Romero and Guillermo Fernández-Shaw abruptly remove the action from Madrid to Javier's estate near the Portuguese border. This shift does emphasize the resolution of the love story—but in order to do so, the authors have to contort the historical backdrop of the work.

The main problem with the third act of *Luisa Fernanda* is that in order to end "happily"—i.e., so that Luisa ends up with Javier—the authors have to work around the fact that Javier was on the losing side of the September Revolution. Thus, they need to minimize the historical background which, up to this point, has been critical to the functioning of the plot. This elision of Spain's history is set up neatly at the end of Act II, since the curtain falls on the temporary victory of the royalist forces. A triumphantly royalist point of view dominates the third act. Luisa's father, Don Florito—who is characterized as "the greatest absolutist in the universe"—gets to make the announcement that the revolutionaries have succeeded and Isabel was forced to abdicate. But Don Florito's response to this shocking news is the only hint that the September Revolution swept away the old order in Spain: "I am the same as I was before the dethronement. Long live the Queen!"[4] To further negate the success of the Revolution, the authors also turn the comic-relief figure of Aníbal—hitherto an unreconstructed Republican—into an ally and emissary for Javier, who has fled across the border into Portugal. But the ultimate act that indicates the authors' unhappiness with the September Revolution is the denouement, in which the audience is supposed to assume that Luisa will be happier with the inconstant royalist rake Javier than with solid Republican citizen Vidal.[5]

This rejection of republican ideology is also built into the music of *Luisa Fernanda.* Moreno Torroba's score ostentatiously avoids the folk and dance music forms that were the traditional core of a zarzuela. In fact, only one piece of music in the score could be considered even vaguely folkish or Spanish: a habanera—which, as the name implies, comes originally from the capital of Cuba and not peninsular Spain. But the rhythms of the habanera, which Moreno Torroba weaves so heavily through the score that they serve as something of a leitmotif, are crucial to understanding the political message of the work. The music of the habanera first appears at the end of the extended musical scene that opens Act I. Having been introduced to the locale and some of the main characters of the work, the authors of *Luisa Fernanda* foreshadow the plot. An Italian street singer wanders into the midst of the action and proceeds to perform the first solo number of the zarzuela, the "Habanera del Saboyano" (The Savoyard's Habanera). Moreno Torroba gives emphasis to the Habanera through contrast. The preceding musical scene, as befitting the opening of an operetta, was built predominantly on a rather bright tempo (*allegro moderato*) with the support of the full orchestra. But for the habanera, the pulse of the music slows and the orchestration thins out to just the strings, flutes, oboe, muted trumpet, and celesta. The delicacy of the music is enough of a contrast to make the number stand out from the music surrounding it.[6]

The song itself is a cautionary tale. In the first chorus, the song describes a soldier leaving for war, promising to return to marry his sweetheart when he has earned his "General's chevrons."[7] But in the second chorus, we learn that ten years later the soldier has not returned. His sweetheart mourns him, believing he has died. What she does not know is that he has become a general and has married another woman. This warning about the constancy and fidelity of soldiers is clearly meant to prefigure the love triangle between Javier, Luisa, and Carolina. Habanera figures that recall but do not directly quote this number crop up at key points in Act I, notably when Vidal first musically declares his love for Luisa and in the finale when Luisa discovers the liaison between Javier and Carolina (Nos. 3 and 5 in the vocal score). Moreno Torroba then uses the "Habanera del Saboyano" to frame Act II. The act opens with a choral reprise of the second chorus of the "Habanera" while Javier promenades with Carolina in the background. Moreno Torroba further enhances the musical infidelity by making a dramatic segue from the melancholy "Habanera" into the bright and up-tempo "Mazurka de las Sombrillas" (The Parasol Mazurka), in which Javier flirts with Carolina (No. 6A in the vocal score). The "Habanera" comes back at the very end of Act II, when it becomes the underscoring for Luisa's request that Vidal take her away from Madrid after she has been rejected by Javier (No. 11 in the vocal score). And then something surprising happens. The habanera, which has been winding through the score for two full acts, suddenly disappears. The rhythms of the habanera are nowhere to be heard in Act III.

Assuming that Moreno Torroba was not simply trying to avoid musical overkill in plugging the "Habanera del Saboyano," why would he construct his score in this fashion? The "Habanera del Saboyano" is used to cement the correctness of libretto's dual insistence that the political mobilization of the September Revolution is a mistake and that royalist Javier is a dashing romantic hero rather than a cad. That the only "Spanish"-sounding music in the score is used to characterize Javier marks him out as the true representative of the Spanish people, just as such music was used to characterize the chorus as the Spanish people in earlier zarzuelas. The habanera is no longer needed in Act III because Javier's course of action has been proved correct, and the music is no longer required to gloss over his more unattractive features. In spite of the Revolution's success, its protagonists (Vidal and Aníbal) have been forced to retreat to the countryside and even change sides. Furthermore, even the revolutionaries realize just how misguided they were, and Vidal gives up Luisa Fernanda to Javier. When the play is read allegorically, the political radical turns Spain over to the care and comfort of the traditional royalist. If the conclusion to *Luisa Fernanda* seems dated to modern audiences used to more emancipated heroines, it makes a certain amount of sense when read within the political context of the struggle between traditionalism and progressivism in Spain.

For those who were listening, *Luisa Fernanda* was to prove prescient. Four years later, the forces of Republicanism and traditionalism would battle again over the soul of Spain. Unlike the gentlemanly resignation of the zarzuela, these two competing ideas of what Spain should look like would clash openly during the Spanish Civil War. The victory of Francisco Franco in 1939 established a conservative and authoritarian vision of the Spanish nation that attempted to seriously implement a top-down nationalist project. But the Francoist project lost legitimacy due to its exclusion and even demonization of groups not deemed to be part of Spain, among them Communists, Republicans, Liberals, Basques, and Catalans. While conservative forms of nationalism are generally built on some sort of exclusionary principle—creating a mobilizing sense of "us versus them"—the Francoist exclusions encompassed such a large number of Spaniards that they created as much dissent as nationalist feeling. The failure of Francoist nationalism would become clear during Spain's transition to democracy in the late 1970s. The 1978 Constitution created a federalist state that enshrined regionalism and granted sweeping autonomy to local governments. The ideal of the all-powerful nation-state was effectively abrogated when the Spanish government took to funding radio and television broadcasts in Catalan and Basque. For many living in Spain, Franco had made nationalism a dirty word.

The conservative turn that zarzuela had made in the 1920s and 1930s made it suitable to play a part in the Francoist nationalization project. The middle years of the dictatorship coincided with the technical advances that made the preservation of zarzuela scores possible, long-playing records and television. While there had been attempts to film zarzuela dating back to the silent era (in fact the vast majority of films based on zarzuelas were silent films—the familiarity of the plots made them excellent vehicles for early cinema), there were no new zarzuela films made after a 1949 version of *La Revoltosa*. It is unclear why Spanish studios ceased filming zarzuela. Probably there were no profits to be made, with the large budgets needed for full orchestras, singers, and dancers. (The number of musicals produced in Hollywood would drastically decline in the 1950s for the same reason.) But in the 1960s Televisión Española would have great success with broadcasts of classic zarzuelas, including *La Revoltosa*, *El huésped del Sevillano*, and *La canción del olvido*. With musical direction by zarzuela composer Federico Moreno Torroba—one of the last links with zarzuela's pre–Civil War heyday—these broadcasts were received with critical and popular success.[8] However, it is impossible to see these televised zarzuelas as anything but another tool of the Franco régime, given that they were broadcast on state television, which was the only television channel operating in the country.

The 1950s and 1960s also saw the most concerted effort at preserving zarzuela scores on disc, a project driven not by the government but by record companies. While Spanish companies had recorded excerpts of zarzuelas since the introduction of sound recording, the advent of the long-playing record in the late 1940s made it possible to capture complete scores and thus approximate the theatrical experience—especially with género chico works, since a long-playing record had enough room for both score and dialogue. Most of these recordings feature singers who performed zarzuela regularly and brought their innate theatricality into the recording studio. Occasionally, recording companies would persuade renowned Spanish opera singers to record their interpretations, leading to Montserrat Caballé's *Maruxa* or Alfredo Kraus's *La bruja*. Sometimes the recording companies would get up-and-coming singers in the early stages of international success, as when Plácido Domingo and Teresa Berganza partnered to perform *Los claveles* and *La dolorosa*. The musical direction on many of these recordings was surprisingly strong. Many were conducted either by Ataúlfo Argenta, who had a burgeoning European career before his tragic death in 1958, or by Rafael Frühbeck de Burgos before he embarked on his international career in the 1960s. Other discs featured Federico Moreno Torroba and Pablo Sorozábal, the last of the major pre–Civil War zarzuela composers, conducting classics from the repertory in addition to their own works. Most of the central repertory was put onto disc, and most of these recordings have been transferred to compact disc (although they are generally unavailable outside Spain).[9]

Yet most of these recordings were exercises in nostalgia even during the 1950s. The comic acting and singing is unbearably broad to modern ears, incorporating performance tics that can be heard on excerpts recorded in the 1920s and 1930s. Where the sets incorporate operatic singers, these problems are gone, but they also help to reinforce the idea that had developed during the 1920s that zarzuela was no longer truly popular culture. One can draw an analogy with the recording of the works of Gilbert and Sullivan, which were also being committed to long-playing records during this exact same period by Decca. Those recordings also captured broad performances and stylistic tics that dated back to the turn of the century, when a Gilbert and Sullivan performing "style" became embedded in amber. While the Decca recordings use the casts and choruses featured by the D'Oyle Carte company during the period without resorting to star casting, several sets feature the conducting of Sir Malcom Sargent—a noted orchestral conductor of the era who had trained under Sir Thomas Beecham. These records are entertaining, but they have absolutely nothing to do with the popular culture of the era and were clearly targeted at middle-class classical music enthusiasts. One cannot help but suspect something similar was going on with the long-playing zarzuela recordings. They represented the last remnants of a performing tradition, not a living and breathing repertory. (To be fair, both zarzuela and Gilbert and Sullivan performances of recent decades have abandoned the worst excesses of the 1950s and are frequently performed in a less mannered style.) In terms of Franco's agenda to create a Spanish national identity built on what might be called traditional Spanish values, zarzuela recordings fit perfectly.

The production of zarzuelas for television transmission and the phonograph recordings of zarzuelas during the 1950s and 1960s relied upon the idea that this music had a specific social meaning, and that it could be used to shape identity. The idea that music has meaning and can be related to the social structures in the society that creates and consumes it is not a universally accepted idea. Many composers and critics prefer to view music as "absolute" and insist that it must be enjoyed in terms of its musical language and forms alone. Others argue that music exists within a web of social discourse and acquires meaning—not merely whatever meaning the composer might have built into the composition, but meaning from the surroundings in which the work was composed, when it was performed, and subsequent performances. Different audiences will hear and understand music differently, and listening to music in different venues may also create different meanings. (Hearing a work in a concert hall has a very different meaning from hearing it in an elevator, for example.) Most importantly, the music that people actively choose to listen to can help to shape their identity. It informs their status within a society, it helps them to forge links with other individuals, and it helps to communicate messages about taste and values to other individuals. Music can be an extremely valuable tool for uncovering messages about identity.[10]

And if this is the case for individuals, then how much more for a society as a whole? Music is a part of virtually every civilization and society that has developed over the course of history, and many of these societies have developed music that has a claim to sound distinctly "theirs." The stately music of Edward Elgar tends to sound quintessentially English, while George Gershwin's jazzy melodies sound quintessentially American. But musical values are constructed, not essential. Elgar's musical construction was highly influenced by nineteenth-century German composers. It was none other than Richard

Strauss who was the first international figure to recognize Elgar's worth. Gershwin's jazz may be "American," but it is rooted in African and Latin American dance music and filtered through a sieve of French Creole culture. But the power of the nonverbal language of music lies in its ability to be used as a social construction. Being nonverbal, it is imprecise and emotional enough to bind disparate groups of people into a unified whole. Performers and audiences, professionals and amateurs—all can come together and enjoy music. States find music useful. Music can promote patriotism and teach messages about what it means to be a member of the nation. It can arouse historical memories and nostalgia for a past that might never have been, but is needed nonetheless to inculcate a sense of national pride. In the extreme case of Germany, the very idea of music became embedded within the idea of national identity—to be German was to be musical. But music is an essential part of the imagined communities and invented traditions of nationalism.[11]

Any study of nationalism has to deal with the two distinct channels through which national identity can be developed. National identity can be developed from the top down, as a state-sponsored project through which a government seeks to unite the diverse societal, political, and cultural strands of its citizens. But national identity can also be a bottom-up affair in which populations attempt to grapple with their history, their culture, and the society in which they live. Such popular nationalism is much messier than the state-organized version. Different groups may interpret developing competing visions of national identity, and the vision of what it means to be part of a nation can change over time. Spain is an excellent case for the study of such bottom-up nationalism, as the weakness of any state-sponsored projects meant that virtually all nationalism had to be generated by the Spanish people themselves. Given the immense amounts of distrust that the Spanish people had in the Restoration government—especially after the Disaster of 1898—a popular nationalist movement might well have been the only nationalist movement that could possibly have gained traction and created a sense of national identity.

Spain also demonstrates that such popular, bottom-up nationalism is extremely flexible and variable. National identities are not fixed; what it means to be part of a nation can change over time as social, economic, and political factors reshape the historical landscape. Popular nationalism can help people to understand and cope with these changes, integrating them into a changed idea of the nation. In the late nineteenth century, Spain had to cope with a slowly growing urban population. It would later have to deal with the defeat in the War of 1898 and the growing influence of European-style political and social reforms. And through all of this change, any national identity still had to account for the role that traditional rural society played in Spanish life. It is hard to imagine a state-sponsored, top-down nationalist project that would have had the flexibility to cope with numerous shocks in such a relatively short period of time. Popular nationalism could incorporate such changes almost instantaneously. *Gigantes y cabezudos,* the first major dramatic critique of the Spanish-American War, premiered on 29 November 1898—a mere three months after the conclusion of hostilities. For a population still dazed by the unexpected defeat, a musical representation of the suffering of the common soldiers and their loved ones back home was no doubt stirring and powerful, as was the image of women rioting against the government over food shortages. Popular forms of nationalism could even envisage a sense of national identity *without* the state. In a country where the state was weak or ineffective, not only was this powerful—it might well be the only form of national identity on offer. The weakness of the state need not imply a weakness in national identity.

But the history of Spain also demonstrates the ultimate failure of popular nationalism alone to establish a powerful and lasting national identity. Spain's confrontation with the modernizing shocks of the twentieth century eventually led to open conflict in the 1936–1939 Civil War. Every single European nation-state confronted the perils of modernity, but Spain was one of the few that collapsed into overt conflict. Some countries were halted from the slide into conflict only by the imposition of authoritarian dictatorships espousing conservative nationalist ideals, while others maintained liberal democratic values that reconfirmed the role of the individual within the nation-state. The richness of Spanish life portrayed in zarzuela was unsurpassed by that of any other popular musical theater of its era (and only rarely equaled since then); its encyclopedic embrace of different regions and social classes could seem to embrace everybody in Spain. The popularity of zarzuela music ensured that its messages would reach the widest possible audiences. But all of this could not convince conservative and traditional Spaniards that they lived in the same nation as those who embraced reform and Europeanized ideas, or vice versa. Given the lack of a guiding force from the state, popular nationalism's message was muted due to its need to cope with the rapid shocks of modernization. Zarzuela's flexibility was a double-edged sword. An all-encompassing vision meant the sacrifice of ideological purity.

Understanding popular nationalism can thus provide a potential lesson in these times of increasingly fragmented culture and polarized political discourse. Zarzuela helped the Spanish people to articulate and understand their national identity at a time of rapid social, political, and economic change. In that sense, the early twentieth century resembles the early twenty-first. Zarzuelas had to represent the identities of different groups in Spanish society who might hold different visions of the nation. Thus different productions could confidently proclaim that Spain's nationalism was centered on urban life while deeply rooted in the rural patria chica, even when these were two diametrically opposed visions. The coherent message that nationalism needs to fully take root was never going to happen in a popular culture. This should carry a warning for those of us living in the early twenty-first century. Much of our political participation is now carried out through popular culture, via social networking and through the use of the Internet. And we are already seeing that our political culture is fragmenting into narrowly defined social groupings, which then increases our political polarization. As in the late nineteenth century, more people are participating in politics than ever before. But that participation is fractured, contentious, and damaging to the polity.

This may seem a counterintuitive conclusion, as popular culture is frequently viewed as inherently democratic. Popular culture has to respond to the desires of a broad range of consumers—and certainly, democracy rests on the idea that government should rest on a framework of healthy and robust public discourse by the widest possible array of society. To suggest that too much political dialogue can damage the state and that the state has a role in creating a singular political vision smacks of authoritarianism and even totalitarianism. We view nationalism in the twenty-first century through the lens of the disasters of the twentieth, and most historians are much more ambivalent about the idea of top-down approaches to state power given the abuses that ideologies like nationalism have been put to. So much of twentieth-century nationalism has come out of exclusionary and ethnocentric ideals that it is easy to overlook the more inclusive and liberal ideals that nationalism was actually born with. The heritage of Treitschke and Otto von Bismarck is much more obvious than that of Giuseppe Mazzini and Garibaldi. In such a world, the multiplying of voices and ideas inherent in popular culture would seem like a useful and refreshing antidote to the horrors that nationalism helped to create. So how could a vision of the nation based in popular culture be bad, even if it did fail in its ostensible purpose?

It is hard to escape the idea that modern popular culture is produced by what Theodore Adorno and Max Horkheimer termed "the culture industry": corporate conglomerates that create culture that is bland, familiar, and homogenous so that even as it promises excitement and titillation, it feeds consumers pabulum that they have consumed many times before.[12] (Admittedly, Adorno and Horkheimer were discussing 1930s movies and swing music, but it sounds like a description of what passes for political commentary on the Internet these days.) Adorno and Horkheimer considered such pop culture dangerous, as it created an apolitical and ignorant audience ripe to fall into the clutches of totalitarian demagogues. (A pessimist might repeat the previous parenthetical aside here.) But late nineteenth- and early twentieth-century zarzuela, while undeniably popular culture, was created in an era before the mass culture that Adorno and Horkheimer were analyzing and that we continue to live in today. Zarzuela composers did not live in hopes of recording contracts and other mass-market techniques to popularize their work. Some composers like Chapí and Bretón shuttled back and forth between writing symphonic works for concert halls and composing lighter works for the Teatro de la Zarzuela, while many other composers who preferred to specialize in zarzuela could still turn out stunningly sophisticated and complex works that would have doomed them in later years to being pegged with the dread epithet of "highbrow." If Adorno and Horkheimer's culture industry melds neatly with totalitarian social control, the greater individualism enjoyed by nineteenth-century composers working in an era before record sales determined success allowed them greater freedom to engage in what Michael Steinberg has termed "subjectivity"—the ability to mediate between the individual and the larger structures of society and culture, even while critiquing and criticizing such structures.[13] Music is one form of subjectivity. Nationalism is another.

If nationalism and music are forms of subjectivity, this also means that they are forms of political discourse. While few would argue that nationalism is apolitical, many people still have trouble swallowing the idea that music is anything but. Such a stand can only be willing blindness after a century in which the totalitarian regimes of Hitler in Germany and Stalin in the Soviet Union regulated music to ensure that it met with their particular ideological beliefs.[14] No less an astute observer than Thomas Mann could see in music an allegory for the collapse of Germany into Fascism, which became his 1947 novel *Doktor Faustus* (one of the few works to actually communicate the sense of hearing music through text). In his 1924 parable on the fate of European civilization, *The Magic Mountain,* he places the following speech into the mouth of one of his characters:

> You have described very nicely an indubitably moral element in the nature of music: to wit, that by its peculiar and lively means of measurement, it lends an awareness, both intellectual and precious, to the flow of time. Music awakens time, awakens us to our finest enjoyment of time. Music awakens— and in that sense it is moral. Art is moral, in that it awakens. But what if it were to do the opposite? If it were to numb us, to put us asleep, counteract all activity and progress? And music can do that as well. It knows all too well the effect that opiates have. A devilish effect, gentlemen. Opiates are the Devil's tool, for they create dullness, rigidity, stagnation, slavish inertia. There is something dubious about music, gentlemen. I maintain that music is ambiguous by its very nature. I am not going too far when I declare it to be politically suspect.[15]

I would have to agree with Mann. Music is politically suspect—but it is not merely the opiate that he and Adorno suggest. True, music can distract from the cares of the day, and in the process it can create an atomized population intent on only hearing the next big hit. But music can also unite people and can bring them together into a community. There is a reason that all countries have national anthems, and there is a reason that most militaries have bands to inspire troops before they march into battle. Music cannot only suppress emotions; it can arouse them. For this reason alone, one should be aware of the political power of music, no matter how innocuous that music seems.

But at the same time, we should not forget that part of the joy of music is the sheer sensual pleasure it brings. I doubt that many Spaniards went to performances of *El barberillo de Lavapiés* or *La Gran Vía* or *Doña Francisquita* because they were thinking about the political content of the music. They went because Barbieri and Chueca and Vives were excellent composers who could write a great tune and provide an entertaining evening at the theater. Music is multivalent, and it can entertain while being political. Even when being didactic, music rarely hits its listeners over the head with its political messages the way that films and novels can. Agitprop works like Bertolt Brecht and Kurt Weill's *The Threepenny Opera* manage to be marvelously entertaining while spinning a violently anticapitalist message for the audience. (And let us not forget that the opening number became an all-American capitalist pop hit for Louis Armstrong, Bobby Darin, and Ella Fitzgerald.) There is a reason that *The Threepenny Opera* continues to be regularly performed, while even the best propaganda films of the period (like *Battleship Potemkin* or *Triumph of the Will*) are generally revived only for specialist audiences of film buffs. Zarzuela was an ideal vehicle for a nation feeling ambiguous about its national identity because of the essential ambiguity inherent in music itself.

While zarzuela is no longer popular culture today, it is still part of the Spanish heritage. The Teatro de la Zarzuela stages lavish and elaborate productions throughout the theatrical season that still entertain audiences. Other zarzuela revivals crop up around Madrid and around the country regularly. While zarzuela is no longer a truly living art form, it exists in revivals, on recordings, and increasingly on DVD. The fact that zarzuelas are still regularly revived today indicates that they have become a central part of Spanish culture. While there have been various attempts to stage zarzuela outside of Spain—in the United States, most notably at the Los Angeles and Washington Operas where Plácido Domingo has served as artistic director—the genre has never really taken root outside Spain. Unlike flamenco music, zarzuela does not seem to travel well. While it has managed to carry many different versions of nationalist discourse within the genre, it remains something of a specialty taste for those outside the Iberian Peninsula. Understanding Madrid slang or the importance of a Chinese shawl apparently requires a more refined palate than paella or gazpacho does. In today's globalized world, that perhaps demonstrates better than anything else the extent to which zarzuela represents something truly Spanish. In fact, zarzuela may have become the ne plus ultra of Spanish nationalism. In a world where many things are homogenized to be enjoyed across national borders—in a world where forms of sangria can be found in bistros in any city, usually in a pale and watered-down version—zarzuela remains defiantly and irreducibly Spanish. The national identity constructed in the late nineteenth and early twentieth century, in all its contradictory glory, remains a part of the national character today.

¡Viva la música!

Appendix

CORE ZARZUELAS

· · · · · · · · · · · · · · ·

A ny scholar studying zarzuelas is first going to have to confront the sheer number of works performed and published during the nineteenth and twentieth centuries. The teatro por horas system generated a vast number of works that were written and performed on Madrid stages. To give just one example of the quantity of works created for performance, the printed catalogue of the libretti of musical theater works in the Biblioteca Nacional de España, most of which date from the late nineteenth and early twentieth centuries, runs to three volumes.[1] Most of these works were ephemeral, at best. Some would have only run for one night, most others for only a short period of time. The teatro por horas system, to an even greater extent than theater in general, encouraged a rapid turnover in works. Since each theater performed three to four works per night rather than just one, more works failed and had to be replaced. This activity only accounts for published works, and it is impossible to gauge how many failed plays might never have been published. Still, the number of published libretti is most likely a relatively accurate reflection of the number of works staged, as the preperformance publication of libretti was common in the nineteenth century, to help theater audiences understand the words being sung.

Given the vast number of zarzuelas that were performed during the nineteenth and early twentieth centuries, how is a scholar supposed to winnow down the works being studied and discussed to a manageable number? The argument that I have made in this book relies upon the popularity of the works under discussion as a measure of their nationalist value: certain zarzuelas were popular because they embodied ideas and characteristics that resonated with Spanish theatrical audiences. But popularity is not an easy or straightforward thing to measure. Does popularity mean the amount of money grossed by a production? Does it mean the numbers of tickets sold for a work? Does it mean an outstanding critical reception in the press? Does it mean the length of the original run of a work? The number of times it has been revived? The number of productions of a work outside of Madrid after its premiere? The impact of a work on other works and other forms of cultural production? For a musical work in the twentieth century, could it mean the number of songs from a work that were recorded—or the number of times the complete work itself was recorded? Or, what is most likely, some messy combination of all of the above? Reception history is fraught with complications.

To make the situation even more complicated, some of this information is no longer available to scholars, and the missing data are usually the quantitative data. Ticket sales and financial records have vanished—even assuming that they were carefully tabulated in the first place. Records of the number of performances can be reconstructed by going through the daily theatrical listings of major newspapers, but this is an arduous and exceedingly time-consuming task. While some of this work has already been done for Madrid in the early twentieth century, coverage for other time periods and cities remains spotty and incomplete.[2] There has been no comprehensive catalogue of recordings of zarzuela music. In any event, before the advent of the long-playing record, most recordings focused on the hit tunes from each show—and popular records could still come out of flop shows. The qualitative data still survive. There are the critical notices in the newspapers. There are references to zarzuelas in other zarzuelas, in literature and in art, and in serious scholarship. (One of my more serendipitous moments of research was picking up a reproduction of a 1905 dictionary of slang at a Madrid book fair only to discover that the photograph chosen for the cover of a typical Madrid *chulo* and *chula* pair was in fact a photograph of the original production of *La verbena de la paloma*.)[3] But unless one plans on proceeding at random, how does one whittle down the immense number of theatrical works premiered between the 1880s and the 1930s?

As this study has been concerned with national identity, I wanted to fix upon those works that have achieved canonical status—zarzuelas that have become a firm part of Spanish culture—since those works would say most about Spanish national identity. To this end, the selection of the core of the zarzuelas analyzed for this book (approximately sixty-five) has been based on works that were generally available on compact disc in Madrid record stores specializing in classical music at the time this project got underway. All of these zarzuela scores were originally recorded in the 1950s and 1960s by the Spanish record companies Alhambra and Hispavox once the advent of the long-playing record made recording complete scores feasible, and were re-issued on compact disc during the 1990s and early 2000s. This method has the advantage of not only selecting works that were popular upon their premiere, but narrowing down the zarzuelas selected to those that have remained relatively popular in Spain to the present day. These are the scores that have remained in the collective national consciousness. A further twenty zarzuelas were selected because of their importance at the time of their premiere or for their thematic relevance to the topic of nationalism (and many of these scores have been reissued on compact disc during the period in which this project was in gestation, such as the classic Rafael Frühbeck de Burgos recording of *La tempranica* with Teresa Berganza). The book also includes a few further works, such as *Pan y toros* and *Luisa Fernanda*, whose premieres fall outside the period being studied but have been included to provide context about the historical development of zarzuela.

Below is a listing of the core zarzuelas studied for this book. Not all have been discussed in the text. Since the works are generally discussed by the composer in the text, works have been organized by composer. Each work is followed by the names of the librettist(s), the date of the premiere, and the theater at which the premiere took place. (For works that premiered outside of Madrid, both the provincial premiere and the Madrid premiere are listed.) This listing will aid readers in finding the full bibliographical information for each work, since libretti are listed in the bibliography by author and the scores are listed by composer.

ALBENÍZ, ISAAC

San Antonio de la Florida: Eusebio Sierra; 26 Oct. 1894, Apolo

ALONSO, FEDERICO

La bejarana (with Emilio Serrano): Luís Fernándaez Ardavín; 31 May 1924, Apolo

La Calesera: Emilio González de Castillo, Manuel Martí Alonso; 12 Dec. 1925, Zarzuela

La parranda: Luís Fernándaez Ardavín; 26 April 1928, Calderón

La picarona: Emilio González de Castillo, Luis Martin Ramon; 6 Feb. 1930, Eslava

BARBIERI, FRANCISCO ASENJO

El barberillo de Lavapiés: Luis Marriano de Lara; 18 Dec. 1874, Zarzuela

De Getafe al Paraiso: Ricardo de la Vega; 5 Jan. 1883, Variedades

Pan y Toros: José Picón; 22 Dec. 1864, Zarzuela

BRETÓN, TOMÁS

La verbena de la Paloma: Ricardo de la Vega; 17 Feb. 1894, Apolo

CHAPÍ, RUPERTO

El barquillero: José Jackson Veyán, José López Silva; 21 July 1900, Eldorado

Las bravías: Carlos Fernández-Shaw, José López Silva; 12 Dec. 1896, Apolo

La bruja: Miguel Ramos Carrión; 10 Dec. 1887, Zarzuela

El cortejo de la Irene: Carlos Fernández-Shaw; 6 Feb. 1896, Eslava

Curro Vargas: Joaquín Dicena, Antonio Paso; 10 Dec. 1898, Parish

La Czarina: José Estremera; 8 Oct. 1892, Apolo

El estreno: Serafín & Joaquín Álvarez Quintero; 19 July 1900, Apolo

Los golfos: Emilio Sánchez Pastor; 24 Sept. 1896, Apolo

Mujer y reina: Mariano Pina Domínguez; 12 Jan. 1895, Zarzuela

Música clásica: José Estremera; 20 Sept. 1880, Comedia

La patria chica: Serafín & Joaquín Álvarez Quintero; 15 Oct. 1907, Zarzuela

El puñao de rosas: Carlos Arniches, Ramón Asenso Mas; 30 Oct. 1902, Apolo

La Revoltosa: Carlos Fernández-Shaw, José López Silva; 21 Nov. 1897, Apolo

El rey que rabió: Miguel Ramos Carrión, Vital Aza; 21 April 1891, Zarzuela

El tambor de granaderos: Emilio Sánchez Pastor; 16 Nov. 1894, Eslava

La tempestad: Miguel Ramos Carrión; 11 March 1882, Zarzuela

La venta de Don Quijote: Carlos Fernández-Shaw; 19 Dec. 1902, Apolo

CHUECA, FEDERICO

Agua, azucarillos y aguardiente: Miguel Ramos Carrión; 23 June 1897, Apolo

La alegría de la huerta: Enrique García Álvarez, Antonio Paso; 20 Jan. 1900, Eslava

El año pasado por agua: Ricardo de la Vega; 1 March 1889, Apolo

El arca de Noé: Enrique Prieto, Andrés Ruesga; 26 Feb. 1890, Zarzuela

El bateo: Antonio Dominguez, Antonio Paso; 7 Nov. 1901, Eslava

El chaleco blanco: Miguel Ramos Carrión; 26 April 1890, Felipe

Las zapatillas: José Jackson Veyan; 5 Dec. 1895, Apolo

CHUECA, FEDERICO, WITH JOAQUÍN VALVERDE

Cádiz: Javier de Burgos; 20 November 1886, Apolo

La canción de la Lola: Ricardo de la Vega; 25 May 1880, Alhambra

La Gran Vía: Felipe Pérez y González; 2 July 1886, Apolo

FERNÁNDEZ CABALLERO, MANUEL

El cabo primero: Carlos Arniches, Celso Lucio; 21 May 1895, Apolo

Chateau Margaux: José Jackson Veyan; 5 Oct. 1887, Variedades

El dúo de la Africana: Miguel Echegaray; 13 May 1893, Apolo

Gigantes y cabezudos: Miguel Echegaray; 29 November 1898, Zarzuela

La Marsellesa: Miguel Ramos Carrión; 1 Feb. 1876, Zarzuela

El padrino de "El Nene" (with Mariano Hermoso Palacios): Julián Romea; 21 May 1896, Zarzuela

Los sobrinos del Capitán Grant: Miguel Ramos Carrión; 25 July 1877, Príncipe Alfonso

La viejecita: Miguel Echegaray; 30 April 1897, Zarzuela

GIMÉNEZ, GERÓNIMO

El baile de Luis Alonso: Javier de Burgos; 27 Feb. 1896, Zarzuela

La boda de Luis Alonso: Javier de Burgos; 27 Jan. 1897, Zarzuela

Los borrachos: Serafín & Joaquín Álvarez Quintero; 3 March 1899, Zarzuela

Las mujeres: Javier de Burgos; 21 May 1896, Apolo

La tempranica: Julián Romea; 19 Sept. 1900, Zarzuela

Trafalgar: Javier de Burgos; 20 Dec. 1890, Principal (Barcelona); 18 June 1891, Apolo

GUERRERO, JACINTO

La alsaciana: José Ramos Martin; 12 Sept. 1921, Tívoli (Barcelona); 14 Feb. 1922, Apolo

Los gavilanes: José Ramos Martin; 7 Dec. 1923, Zarzuela

El huésped del Sevillano: Juan Ignacio Luca de Tena, Enrique Reoyo; 3 Dec. 1926, Apolo

La montería: José Ramos Martin; 24 Nov. 1922, Circo (Zaragoza); 25 Jan. 1923, Zarzuela

La rosa del azafrán: Federico Romero, Guillermo Fernández-Shaw; 14 March 1930, Calderón

GURIDI, JESÚS

El caserío: Federico Romero, Guillermo Fernández-Shaw; 11 Nov. 1926, Zarzuela

LLEÓ, VICENTE

La corte de Faraón: Guillermo Perrín, Miguel de Palacios; 21 Jan. 1910, Eslava

LUNA, PABLO

Los cadetes de la reina: Julián Moyrón; 18 Jan. 1913, Price

La chula de Pontevedra (with Enrique Bru): Enrique Paradas, Joaquín Jiménez; 27 Jan. 1928, Apolo

Molinos de viento: Luis Pascual Frutos; 2 Oct. 1910, Cervantes (Seville); 3 Feb. 1911, Eslava

El niño judío: Antonio Paso, Enrique García Álvarez; 5 Feb. 1918, Apolo

MARQUÉS, MIGUEL

El anillo de hierro: Marcos Zapata; 7 November 1878, Zarzuela

MILLÁN, RAFAEL

La Dogaresa: Antonio López Monís; 17 Sept. 1920, Tívoli (Barcelona); 19 July 1921, Jardines del Buen Retiro

MORENO TORROBA, FEDERICO

Luisa Fernanda: Federico Romero, Guillermo Fernández-Shaw; 26 March 1932, Calderón

La Marchenera: Ricardo Gonzalez del Toro, Fernando Luque; 7 April 1928, Zarzuela

NIETO, MANUEL

El barbero de Sevilla (with Gerónimo Giménez): Guillermo Perrín, Miguel de Palacios; 5 Feb. 1901, Zarzuela

Cuadros disolventes: Guillermo Perrín, Miguel de Palacios; 3 June 1896, Príncipe Alfonso

SERRANO, JOSÉ

La alegría de batallón: Carlos Arniches, Felix Quintana; 11 March 1909, Apolo

Alma de Dios: Carlos Arniches, Enrique García Álvarez; 17 Dec. 1907, Cómico

El amigo Melquiades (with Quinito Valverde): Carlos Arniches; 14 May 1914, Apolo

Los de Aragón: Juan José Lorente; 26 Oct. 1927, Centro

La canción del olvido: Federico Romero, Guillermo Fernández-Shaw; 17 Nov. 1916, Lírico (Valencia); 1 March 1918, Zarzuela

Los claveles: Luis Fernández de Sevilla, Anselmo Carreño; 6 April 1929, Fontalba

La Dolorosa: Juan José Lorente; 23 May 1930, Apolo (Valencia); 24 Oct. 1930, Reina Victoria

Moros y cristianos: Maximiliano Thous, Elías Cerdá; 28 April 1905, Zarzuela

La reina mora: Serafín & Joaquín Álvarez Quintero; 11 Dec. 1903, Apolo

SOUTULLO, REVERIANO, AND JUAN VERT

La leyenda del beso: Antonio Paso Díaz, Enrique Reoyo; 18 Jan. 1924, Apolo

La del soto del parral: Luis Fernández Ardavín, Anselmo Carreño; 26 Oct. 1927, La Latina

El último rómantico: José Tellaeche; 9 March 1928, Apolo

TORREGROSA, TOMÁS LÓPEZ

La fiesta de San Antón: Carlos Arniches; 24 Nov. 1898, Apolo
El santo de la Isidra: Carlos Arniches; 19 Feb. 1898, Zarzuela

USANDIZAGA, JOSÉ MARÍA

Las golondrinas: Gregorio Martínez Sierra; 5 Feb. 1914, Price

VALVERDE, QUINITO, AND RAMÓN ESTELLÉS

La marcha de Cádiz: Celso Lucio, Enrique García Álvarez; 11 Oct. 1896, Eslava

VIVES, AMADEO

Bohemios: Guillermo Perrín, Miguel de Palacios; 24 March 1904, Zarzuela
Doña Francisquita: Federico Romero, Guillermo Fernández-Shaw; 17 Oct. 1923, Apolo
Don Lucas del Cigarral: Tomas Lucena, Carlos Fernández-Shaw, 18 Feb. 1899, Parish
La Generala: Guillermo Perrín, Miguel de Palacios; 14 June 1912, Gran Teatro
Maruxa: Luis Pascual Frutos; 28 May 1914, Zarzuela
La villana: Federico Romero, Guillermo Fernández-Shaw; 1 Oct. 1927, Zarzuela

A NOTE ON THE CITATION
OF ZARZUELA LIBRETTI

· · · · · · · · · · · · · ·

Libretti for zarzuela come in a multiplicity of editions and formats. For the most part, I have used the libretti published at the time of the premiere. But not always: many of the most prominent *género chico* works were published in a famous 1962 anthology (Antonio Valencia, ed., *El género chico [Antología de textos completos]*). In other places I have used reprints. For many works, I have used the libretti reissued by the Teatro de la Zarzuela as part of the souvenir programs for their productions, which also feature useful and enlightening scholarly essays. For those zarzuelas whose scores have been republished in a critical edition by the Instituto Complutense de Ciencias Musicales, I have used the libretti published with the musical score because they frequently have variant texts (such as scenes or dialogue added to a production after the premiere). To make citation as useful as possible given the number of possible libretti, I have avoided citing text by page number. Instead, text is cited by the act and scene divisions within a work, which tend to remain static across the various editions. Most published libretti tend to follow a standard method of numbering and dividing scenes. Capital Roman numerals are used for act divisions. Arabic numerals are used for scene divisions (thus, most género chico works will not have a capital Roman numeral in the citation). Lowercase Roman numerals are used to demark the entry or exit of a new character within a scene, what is sometimes referred to as a "French scene." Since these occur fairly frequently in zarzuelas, they are generally as convenient as a page number for locating text—and are far more convenient when the reader has access to a different edition of a libretto. For readers interested in exactly which edition of a libretto I used for this book, it will be indicated at the first citation of a work in the notes and again in the bibliography. Where no libretto is cited in the bibliography, I have used the critical edition published in the corresponding ICCM score.

NOTES

....

OVERTURE

1. The best biography of Arrieta is María Encina Cortizo, *Emilio Arrieta: De la ópera a la zarzuela* (Madrid: ICCMU, 1998).

2. Antonio Peña y Goñi, "El entierro de Barbieri," *Blanco y Negro* 3 March 1894: 1–3. The most comprehensive Barbieri biography is Emilio Casares Rodicio, *Francisco Asenjo Barbieri*, 2 vols. (Madrid: ICCMU, 1994).

3. Antonio Peña y Goñi, "La música de Arrieta," *La Época* 12 Feb. 1894, and "Sobre motivos de Arrieta," *La Época* 13 Feb. 1894.

4. Antonio Peña y Goñi, *Impresiones musicales: Colección de artículos de crítica y literatura músical* (Madrid: Manuel Minuesa de Rios, 1878) 284. The italics are Peña y Goñi's.

5. Antonio Peña y Goñi, "El maestro seguidilla," *La Época* 19 Feb. 1894.

6. Antonio Peña y Goñi, "La música de Barbieri," *La Época* 20 Feb. 1894.

7. On the development of European musical life in the nineteenth century, see William Weber, *Music and the Middle Class: The Social Structure of Concert Life in London, Paris, and Vienna between 1830 and 1848,* 2nd ed. (Aldershot: Ashgate, 2004); F. M. Scherer, *Quarter Notes and Banknotes: The Economics of Music Composition in the Eighteenth and Nineteenth Centuries* (Princeton: Princeton UP, 2004); Celia Applegate, *Bach in Berlin: Nation and Culture in Mendelssohn's Revival of the* St. Matthew Passion (Ithaca: Cornell UP, 2005); James H. Johnson, *Listening in Paris: A Cultural History* (Berkeley: U of California P, 1995); Carl Dahlhaus, *Nineteenth-Century Music,* trans. J. Bradford Robinson (Berkeley: U of California P, 1989).

8. On the history of the Teatro Real, see Joaquín Turina Gómez, *Historia del Teatro Real* (Madrid: Alianza, 1997) esp. 75–81.

9. For brief English-language overviews of the history of zarzuela, see the first two chapters of Christopher Webber's *The Zarzuela Companion,* ed. Louise K. Stein and Roger Alier (Lanham, MD: Scarecrow Press, 2002), or Louise K. Stein and Roger Alier's entry, "Zarzuela," in *The New Grove Dictionary of Music and Musicians,* 2001 ed. See also Christopher Webber and Ignaco Jassa Haro, eds., *Zarzuela.net,*. 19 Oct. 2014. www.zarzuela.net.

10. The best overview of this period is Roland J. Vasquez's "The Quest for National Opera in Spain and the Re-invention of the Zarzuela (1809–1849)," diss., Cornell U, 1992.

11. The best discussion of the work and its significance is María Encina Cortizo, "Jugar con fuego," *Diccionario de la Zarzuela España e Hispanoamérica,* 2006 ed.

12. For a cogent analysis of these early zarzuelas, see Emilio Casares Rodicio, "La Música

del siglo XIX español. Conceptos fundamentales," *La música española en el siglo XIX,* ed. Emilio Casares Rodicio and Celsa Alonso González (Oviedo: U de Oviedo, 1995) 79.

13. Emilio Cotarelo y Mori, *Historia de la zarzuela o sea el drama lírico en España, desde su origen a fines del siglo XIX* (Madrid: Tipografía de Archivos, 1934; Madrid: Ediciones del ICCMU, 2001) 571. See also Emilio García Carretero, *Historia del Teatro de la Zarzuela de Madrid,* vol. 1 (Fundación de la Zarzuela Española, 2003–2005) 4–5.

14. Mori 572.

15. Casares Rodicio, *Francisco Asenjo Barbieri,* vol. 1, 193–194; and Salvador Valverde, *El mundo de la zarzuela* (n.p.: Palabras, 1976) 109.

16. Benedict Anderson, *Imagined Communities,* rev. ed. (London: Verso, 2006); Eric Hobsbawm and Terence Ranger, eds., *The Invention of Tradition* (Cambridge: Cambridge UP, 1983); and Eugene Weber, *Peasants into Frenchmen: The Modernization of Rural France* (Stanford: Stanford UP, 1976). Among other classics of the state as nationalizing force, see Ernest Gellner, *Nations and Nationalism* (Ithaca: Cornell UP, 1983); Eric Hobsbwam, *Nations and Nationalism Since 1780: Programme, Myth, Reality,* 2nd ed. (Cambridge: Cambridge UP, 1992); and George L. Mosse, *The Nationalization of the Masses: Political Symbolism and Mass Movements in Germany from the Napoleonic Wars through the Third Reich* (Ithaca: Cornell UP, 1971).

17. Good examples of the localized view of nationalism include Alon Confino, *The Nation as a Local Metaphor: Württemberg, Imperial Germany, and National Memory, 1871–1918* (Chapel Hill: U of North Carolina P, 1997); Caroline Ford, *Creating the Nation in Provincial France: Religion and Political Identity in Brittany* (Princeton: Princeton UP, 1993); Herman Lebovics, *True France: The Wars over Cultural Identity, 1900–1945* (Ithaca: Cornell UP, 1992); Anthony Smith, *National Identity* (Reno: U of Nevada P, 1991). On the wider implications of the interaction between state and popular nationalism, see Liah Greenfeld, *Nationalism: Five Roads to Modernity* (Cambridge: Harvard UP, 1992); and Aviel Roshwald, *The Endurance of Nationalism: Ancient Roots and Modern Dilemmas* (Cambridge: Cambridge UP, 2006).

18. See the collected essays in Joost Augusteijn and Eric Storm, eds., *Region and State in Nineteenth-Century Europe: Nation-Building, Regional Identities, and Separatism* (New York: Palgrave Macmillan, 2012).

19. José Álvarez Junco, "El nacionalismo español como mito movilizador: Cuatro guerras," *Cultura y movilización en la España contemporánea,* ed. Rafael Cruz and Manuel Pérez Ledesma (Madrid: Alianza, 1997) 35–68.

20. The two essential works for understanding Spanish nationalism before the Civil War are José Álvarez Junco, *Mater dolorosa: La idea de España en el siglo XIX* (Madrid: Taurus, 2001), and E. Inman Fox, *La invención de España: Nacionalismo liberal e identidad nacional* (Madrid: Cátedra, 1998). See also Enrique A. Sanabria, *Republican and Anticlerical Nationalism in Spain* (New York: Palgrave Macmillan, 2009); Alejandro Quiroga, *Making Spaniards: Primo de Rivera and the Nationalization of the Masses* (New York: Palgrave Macmillan, 2007); Juan Carlos Sánchez Illán, *La nación inacabada: Los intelectuales y el proceso de construcción nacional (1900–1914)* (Madrid: Biblioteca Nueva, 2002); Juan Pablo Fusi, *España: La evolución de la identidad nacional* (Madrid: Temas de Hoy, 2000); Carlos Serrano, *El nacimiento de Carmen: Símbolos, mitos y nación* (Madrid: Taurus, 1999); and Carolyn Boyd, *Historia Patria: Politics, History, and National Identity in Spain, 1875–1975* (Princeton: Princeton UP, 1997).

21. On conservative nationalism elsewhere in Europe, see Herman Lebovics, *True France: The*

Wars over Cultural Identity, 1900–1945 (Ithaca: Cornell UP, 1992), and Geoff Eley, *Reshaping the German Right: Radical Nationalism and Political Change after Bismarck,* rev. ed. (Ann Arbor: U of Michigan P, 1991).

22. Ernest Renan, "What is a Nation?" in (among many other places) *The Nationalism Reader,* ed. Omar Bahbour and Micheline R. Ishay (Amherst: Humanity Books, 1999) 143–155. On the conservative-liberal divide in Spain, see Boyd, *Historia Patria* and Henry Kamen, *The Disinherited: Exile and the Making of Spanish Culture, 1492–1975* (New York: HarperCollins, 2007).

23. The description and all quotations that follow are from Ricardo de la Vega, *La verbena de la paloma,* Scene i, *El género chico (Antología de textos completos),* ed. Antonio Valencia (Madrid: Taurus, 1962) 251–277. For an explanation of how zarzuela libretti will be cited in this book, see the Note on Citation.

24. "El aciete de ricino / ya no es malo de tomar. / Se administra en piloritas / y el efecto es siempre igual."

25. No. 1 in the vocal score, Tomás Bretón, *La verbena de la paloma, o El boticario y las chulapas y celos mal reprimidos: Sainete lírico en un acto,* ed. Ramón Barce (Madrid: Instituto Complutense de Ciencias Musicales, 1994). "Parlante" is the Spanish translation of the Italian "parlando," which means "speech over music."

26. "También la gente del pueblo / tiene su corazoncito, / y lágrimas en los ojos / y celos mal reprimidos. / . . . / ¡Y por una morena chulapa / me veo *perdío,* / y a la cara me sale el coraje / que tengo *escondío!"*

27. "Por ser la Virgen / de la Paloma, / un mantón de China-na, / China-na, / te voy a regalar."

28. J. A., "Teatro de Apolo," *El Liberal* 18 Feb. 1894; Pedro Bofil, "Veladas teatrales," *La Época* 18 Feb. 1894.

CHAPTER ONE

1. The best account of the teatro por horas is María Pilar Espín Templado, *El teatro por horas en Madrid (1870–1910)* (Madrid: Instituto de Estudio Madrileños, 1995), a shorter version of her more comprehensive dissertation, "El teatro por horas en Madrid (1870–1910) (Subgéneros que comprende, autores príncipales y análisis de algunas obras representativas)," tésis doctoral, Universidad Complutense de Madrid, 1986. For an exhaustive study in English, see Nancy Jane Hartley Membrez, "The *teatro por horas:* History, Dynamics and Comprehensive Bibliography of a Madrid Industry, 1867–1922" diss., U of California, Santa Barbara, 1987.

2. Among other works on the uses of early popular culture, see Deborah Heckert, "Working the Crowd: Elgar, Class, and Reformulations of Popular Culture at the Turn of the Twentieth Century," *Edward Elgar and His World,* ed. Byron Adams (Princeton: Princeton UP, 2007) 287–316; Jorge Uría, "La cultura popular en la Restauración: El declive de un mundo tradicional y desarrollo de una sociedad de mases," *La cultura española en la Restauración,* ed. Manuel Suárez Cortina (Santander: Sociedad Menéndez Pelayo, 1999) 103–144; Peter Bailey, *Popular Culture and Performance in the Victorian City* (Cambridge: Cambridge UP, 1998); Vanessa L. Schwartz, *Spectacular Realities: Early Mass Culture in Fin-de-siècle Paris* (Berkeley: U of California P, 1998); Rosalind H. Williams, *Dream Worlds: Mass Consumption in Late Nineteenth-Century France* (Berkeley: U of California P, 1982).

3. Carlos Gómez Amat, *Historia de la música Española*, vol. 5, *Siglo XIX* (Madrid: Alianza, 1988) 100–101, 121–122, 287–293; and Robert Hughes, *Barcelona* (New York: Alfred A. Knopf, 1992) 289–298.

4. Virgilio Pinto Crespo, ed., *Madrid: Atlas histórico de la ciudad, 1850–1939* (Madrid: Fundación Caja Madrid, 2001) 342–349.

5. James H. Johnson, *Listening in Paris: A Cultural History* (Berkeley: U of California P, 1995).

6. For the development of theaters in Madrid, see Deborah L. Parsons, *A Cultural History of Madrid: Modernism and the Urban Spectacle* (Oxford and New York: Berg, 2003) 68–75; Fernanda Andura Varela, "Del Madrid teatral del XIX: La llegada de la luz, el teatro por horas, los incendios, los teatros de verano," *Cuatro siglos de teatro en Madrid* (Madrid: Consorcio Madrid Capital Europea de la Cultura, 1992) 85–115; and Angel Luis Fernández Muñoz, *Arquitectura teatral en Madrid: Del corral de comedias al cinematógrafo* (Madrid: El Avapiés, 1988).

7. For overviews of Spanish theater in the nineteenth century, see David Thatcher Gies, *The Theatre in Nineteenth-Century Spain* (Cambridge: Cambridge UP, 1994), and Nancy J. Membrez, "The Mass Production of Theatre in Nineteenth-Century Madrid," *The Crisis of Institutionalized Literature in Spain*, ed. Wlad Godzich and Nicholas Spadaccini (Minneapolis: Prisma Institute, 1988) 309–356.

8. Membrez, "El *teatro por horas*" 15–16.

9. On Spanish theater before the nineteenth century, see Melvina McKendrick, *Theatre in Spain, 1490–1700* (Cambridge: Cambridge UP, 1989); and Walter Cohen, *Drama of a Nation: Public Theater in Renaissance England and Spain* (Ithaca: Cornell UP, 1985).

10. For discussions of the sainete, see Clinton Young, "Sainete," *The Columbia Encyclopedia of Modern Drama*, 2007 ed., and Ramón Barce, "El sainete lírico (1880–1915)," *La música española en el siglo XIX*, ed. Emilio Casares Rodicio and Celsa Alonso González (Oviedo: U of Oviedo, 1995) 195–201.

11. Membrez, "El *teatro por horas*" 68–74. For a wider discussion of the press in late nineteenth-century Spain, see David Ortiz, *Paper Liberals: Press and Politics in Restoration Spain* (Westport, CT: Greenwood, 2000).

12. For a general overview of the 1868 Revolution, see Jorge Vilches, *Progreso y libertad: El partido progresista en la revolución liberal española* (Madrid: Alianza, 2001); Gregorio de la Fuente Monge, *Los revolucionarios de 1868: Elites y poder en la España liberal* (Madrid: Marcial Pons, 2000); and Julio Montero Díaz, "La Crisis del moderantismo y la experiencia del Sexenio democrático," *Historia contemporánea de España (siglo XIX)*, ed. Javier Paredes (Barcelona: Ariel Historia, 1998) 242–258. For an English-language overview, see C. A. M. Hennessy, *The Federal Republic in Spain: Pi y Margall and the Federal Republican Movement, 1868–1874* (Oxford: Oxford UP, 1962).

13. The classic studies of the Restoration political system, focusing on caciquismo, are Robert W. Kern, *Liberals, Reformers and Caciques in Restoration Spain, 1875–1900* (Albuquerque: U of New Mexico P, 1974); and José Varela Ortega, *Los amigos políticos: Partidos, elecciones y caciquismo en la Restauración (1875–1900)* (Madrid: Alianza, 1977; Madrid: Marcial Pons, 2001).

14. The best description of the zarzuela grande model is in Emilio Casares Rodicio, "La Música del siglo XIX español. Conceptos fundamentales," *La música española en el siglo XIX*, ed. Emilio Casares Rodicio and Celsa Alonso González (Oviedo: U de Oviedo, 1995) 79.

15. José Picón, *Pan y toros: Zarzuela en tres actos y en verso* (Madrid: José Rodriguez, 1889), I.ii.

16. For a historical summary of this period, see John Lynch, *Bourbon Spain, 1700–1808* (Oxford: Basil Blackwell, 1989) 251–254, 261–268.

17. Although why Queen Isabella banned *Pan y toros* is fairly obvious from the tone of the libretto, why it took her three years to do so remains something of a mystery. See Casares Rodicio, *Francisco Asenjo Barbieri,* vol. 1, 296; and John Edward Henken, "Francisco Asenjo Barbieri and the Nineteenth-Century Revival in Spanish National Music," diss., UCLA, 1987. 204–205.

18. Fidel Gómez Ochoa, "El conservadurismo canovista y los orígenes de la Restauración: La formación de un conservadurismo moderno," *La Restauración, entre el liberalismo y la democracia,* ed. Manuel Suárez Cortina (Madrid: Alianza, 1997) 109–155.

19. Francisco Asenjo Barbieri, *Pan y toros,* ed. Emilio Casares and Xavier de Paz (Madrid: Instituto Complutense de Ciencias Musicales, 2001).

20. Francisco Asenjo Barbieri, *El barberillo de Lavapiés: Zarzuela en tres actos,* ed. Maria Encina Cortizo and Ramón Sobrino (Madrid: Instituto Complutense de Ciencias Musicales, 1994).

21. "¡La verdadera hidalguía / la escribe Dios en el alma!" Marcos Zapato, *El anillo de hierro. Drama lírico en tres actos y en verso,* I.ix. The full text of the libretto can be found in Marcos Zapato, *Colección de obras dramáticas de Marcos Zapato* 1: 140–291 (Madrid: R. Velasco, 1887).

22. *La Correspondencia de España* 8 Nov. 1878.

23. For a fuller sketch of Marqués's life, see Carlos Gómez Amat, *Historia de la música española, vol. 5, Siglo XIX* (Madrid: Alianza, 1988) 183–187.

24. "El Anillo de Hierro," *Crónica de la Música* 14 Nov. 1878: 3; *La Correspondencia de España* 8 Nov. 1878.

25. See Nos. 1A, 3, and 8A in the vocal score: Miguel Marqués, *El anillo de hierro. Drama lírico en tres actos;* piano reduction, Isidoro Hernandez (Madrid: Romero y Marzo, n.d.).

26. A. Leon, "La tempestad," *Crónica de la Música* 15 March 1882: 4–5.

27. See, for example, *El Heraldo de Madrid* 28 Nov. 1890.

28. See Plaza Sixto, "Sociología del teatro musical español," diss., Georgetown U, 1986. 112–113.

29. Miguel Ramos Carrión, *La bruja: Zarzuela en tres actos* (Madrid: Teatro de la Zarzuela, 2002), 3.xx.

30. Ramos Carrión, "Mágicos conjuros, / hechizo y brujería," *La bruja,* 2.xxi.

31. Ruperto Chapí, *La Bruja: Ópera cómica en tres actos,* piano reduction Valentín Arín (Madrid: Pablo Martin, n.d.).

32. José María Esperanza y Sola, *Treinta años de crítica musical: Colección póstuma de los trabajos,* vol. 2 (Madrid: La viuda é hijos de Tello, 1906) 339.

33. Siegried Kracauer, *Jacques Offenbach and the Paris of His Time* (1937; New York: Zone Books, 2002).

CHAPTER TWO

1. "Sección de espectáculos," *El Imparcial* 26 May 1880. The story is recounted in José Deleito y Peñuela, *Origen y apogeo del "género chico"* (Madrid: Revista de Occidente, 1949) 13–15.

2. Ricardo de la Vega, *La canción de la Lola*, 1.i. The full text of the libretto is in *El género chico (Antología de textos completos)*, ed. Antonio Valencia (Madrid: Taurus, 1962) 23–48.

3. The description is from "Sección de espectáculos," *El Imparcial* 26 May 1880. For the music itself, see the vocal score: Federico Chueca and Joaquín Valverde, *La canción de la Lola: Zarzuela en un acto* (Madrid: Zozaya, n.d.).

4. Anselm Gerhard, *The Urbanization of Opera: Music Theater in Paris in the Nineteenth Century*, trans. Mary Whittall (Chicago: U of Chicago P, 1998).

5. Emilio Casares Rodicio, "La música del siglo XIX español: Conceptos fundamentales," *La música española en el siglo XIX*, ed. Emilio Casares Rodicio and Celsa Alonso González (Oviedo: U de Oviedo, 1995) 79–80.

6. Brigitte Magnien, "Cultura urbana," *1900 en España*, ed. Serge Salaün and Carlos Serrano (Madrid: Espasa-Calpe, 1991) 108.

7. Santos Juliá, David Ringrose, and Cristina Segura, *Madrid: Historia de una capital* (Madrid: Alianza, 1994) 415. On Spanish urbanization in general, see Francisco Quirós Linares, *Las ciudades españolas en el siglo XIX* (Gijón: Ediciones Trea, 2009).

8. Juliá, Ringrose, and Segura 428–432.

9. "Somos las calles, somos las plazas / y los callejones de Madrid / que por un recurso mágico / nos podemos hoy congregar aquí." Felipe Pérez y González's libretto is in the vocal score: Federico Chueca and Joaquín Valverde, *La Gran Vía: Revista madrileña cómico-lírica, fantástico-callejera en un acto*, ed. María Encina Cortizo and Ramón Sobrino (Madrid: Instituto Complutense de Ciencias Musicales, 1996), 1.i.

10. Steven L. Driever, "The Historical Geography of the Proposals for Madrid's Gran Vía, 1860–1904," 34th Annual Congress of the Society for Spanish and Portuguese Historical Studies, Universidad Complutense de Madrid, 3 July 2003. For a more general background to the urban reforms of the period, see Juliá, Ringrose, and Segura 405–432.

11. "¡Pobre chica / la que tiene servir! / Más valiera / que se llegase a morir." Pérez y González, *La Gran Vía*, 2.ii.

12. "Pobres amas / las que tiene que sufrir / a esas truchas / de criadas de servir"; "Me faltaron dos pendientes / de azabache superior, / y, por fin, de tantas faltas, / faltóme mi esposo, que fue lo peor." Pérez y González, *La Gran Vía*, 2.iii.

13. Pérez y González, *La Gran Vía*, 3.iii.

14. See Angel Luis Fernández Muñoz, *Arquitectura teatral en Madrid: Del corral de comedias al cinematógrafo* (Madrid: El Avapiés, 1988).

15. Direct statistics about theater prices and audiences are difficult to come by. For the best summaries on the subject, see Nancy J. Membrez, "The *teatro por horas*: History, Dynamics and Comprehensive Bibliography of a Madrid Industry, 1867–1922," diss., U of California, Santa Barbara, 1987) 113–121; and María Pilar Espín Templado, *El teatro por horas en Madrid (1870–1910)* (Madrid: Insitituo de Estudios Madrileños, 1995) 72–75.

16. Ricardo de la Vega's libretto is in the vocal score: Federico Chueca, *El año pasado por agua: Revista general de 1888 en un acto*, ed. José Luis Navarro (Madrid: Instituto Complutense de Ciencias Musicales, 1997), 3.xi.

17. See Espín Templado, *El teatro por horas en Madrid* 75–76.

18. Jesus Cruz, *The Rise of Middle-Class Culture in Nineteenth Century Spain* (Baton Rouge: Louisiana State UP, 2011) 169–198; Virgilio Pinto Crespo, ed., *Madrid: Atlas histórico de la ciu-*

dad, 1850–1939 (Madrid: Fundación Caja Madrid, 2001) 368; and Antonio Barrera Maraver, *Crónicas del género chico y de un Madrid divertido* (Madrid: El Avapiés, 1983) 22–32.

19. Ramón Barce, "El sainete lírico," *La música española en el siglo XIX,* ed. Emilio Casares Rodicio and Celsa Alonso González (Oviedo: U de Oviedo, 1995) 223–229; see also his "El folklore urbano y la música de los sainetes líricos del último cuarto del siglo XIX: La explicación escénica de los bailes," *Revista de Musicología* 16.6 (1993): 3217–3225.

20. The only full-length biography of Federico Chueca is Florentino Hernández Girbal, *Federico Chueca: El alma de Madrid* (Madrid: Ediciones Lira, 1992); see also Carlos Gómez Amat, *Historia de la música española,* vol. 5, *Siglo XIX, 211–219* (Madrid: Alianza, 1988), and Christopher Webber, *The Zarzuela Companion* (Lanham: Scarecrow, 2002) 73–74.

21. See Federico Chueca, *Agua, azucarillos y aguardiente: Pasillo veraniego en un acto,* ed. Benito Lauret (Madrid: Instituto Complutense de Ciencias Musicales, 1996).

22. See Barce, "El sainete lírico" 226–227.

23. Miguel Ramos Carrión, *Agua, azucarillos y aguardiente,* 2.v. The libretto is published in Chueca's vocal score cited above.

24. "¿Cuándo me iré / a mi lugar, / que el farruco me manda a llamar?" Ramos Carrión, *Agua, azucarillos y aguardiente,* 2.v.

25. Ramos Carrión, *Agua, azucarillos y aguardiente,* 2.xvii.

26. Barce, "El sainete lírico" 223–224, 228.

27. See the vocal score: Tomás Bretón, *La verbena de la paloma, o El boticario y las chulapas y celos mal reprimidos: Sainete lírico en un acto,* ed. Ramón Barce (Madrid: Instituto Complutense de Ciencias Musicales, 1994).

28. Ricardo de la Vega, *La verbena de la paloma,* 2.vi.

29. See the vocal score: Ruperto Chapí, *La Revoltosa: Sainete lírico en un acto,* piano reduction, V. Arin (Madrid: Casa Dotesio, n.d.).

30. "La mujer / debe tener . . . / Pupila pa distinguir, / y corazón pa querer, / y buen gusto pa elegir." José López Silva and Carlos Fernández-Shaw, *La Revoltosa,* 1.vi, *El género chico (Antología de textos completos),* ed. Antonio Valencia (Madrid: Taurus, 1962) 321–372.

31. J. A., "Teatro de Apolo," *El Imparcial* 18 Feb. 1894.

32. L., "Teatro de Apolo: «El santo de la Isidra»," 20 Feb. 1898.

33. Carlos Arniches, *El santo de la Isidra,* 1.i., *El género chico (Antología de textos completos),* ed. Antonio Valencia (Madrid: Taurus, 1962) 587–619.

34. "Estreno en Apolo," *El Heraldo de Madrid* 20 Feb. 1898.

35. L., "Teatro de Apolo: «El santo de la Isidra»," *El Liberal* 20 Feb. 1898. For further discussion of Arniches's realism, see Juan A. Ríos Carratalá, "Del castizo al fresco: tipología y ambientes del teatro cómico (1890–1910) y su adaptación al cine," *La escena española en la encrucijada (1890–1910),* ed. Serge Salaün, Evelyne Ricci, and Marie Salgues (Madrid: Fundamentos, 2005) 28–37.

36. Some of my discussion for what follows is drawn from José María Gomez Labad, *El Madrid de la zarzuela (Visión regocijada de un pasado en cantables)* (Madrid: Editoral Tres, 1983), Part II, "Tipos Populares" 51–194—although Gomez Labad makes no mention of the heavy female presence in his listings.

37. "Estos son los calzones / de un señorito, / de un señorito. / ¡Ay, qué frío habrá pasado / este invierno el pobrecito! / Tiene ventiladores / por delante y por detrás. / ¡Marecita de mi alma,

/ cómo está la sociedá!" Miguel Rámos Carrión, *El chaleco blanco,* 2.xix in Federico Chueca's vocal score *El chaleco blanco: Episodio cómico-lírico en un acto,* ed. Claudio Prieto (Madrid: Instituto Complutense de Ciencias Musicales, 1996).

38. Arturo Barea, *The Forging of a Rebel,* trans. Ilsa Barea (London: Granta, 2001) 10.

39. See Benedict Anderson, *Imagined Communities: Reflections on the Origin and Spread of Nationalism,* 2nd ed. (London: Verso, 1991), esp. 9–46.

CHAPTER THREE

1. Caroline P. Boyd, *Historia Patria: Politics, History, and National Identity in Spain, 1875–1975* (Princeton: Princeton UP, 1997).

2. See Scott Eastman, *Preaching Spanish Nationalism across the Hispanic Atlantic, 1759–1823* (Baton Rouge: Louisiana State UP, 2012); and José Álvarez Junco, *Mater dolorosa: La idea de España en el Siglo XIX* (Madrid: Taurus, 2001).

3. For further background on Burgos, see Alberto Romero Ferrer's introduction to *Cádiz, El baile de Luis Alonso* (Cádiz: Publicaciones de la Univerdad de Cádiz, 1997) 35–37.

4. See Miguel Roa's "Introducción" to the vocal score of Federico Chueca, *Cádiz: Episodio nacional cómico-lírico-dramático en dos actos* (Madrid: Instituto Complutense de Ciencias Musicales, 1997) xviii–xix.

5. Javier de Burgos, *Cádiz,* I.1.i. See the libretto in the vocal score cited above.

6. "Necesita enviar más franchutes / que granos de arena contiene el mar; / Porque ancianos, mujeres, chiquillos / y todas las clases de la sociedad / a pedradas, a palos, a tiros, / con uñas, con dientes, sabrán pelear." Burgos, *Cádiz,* I.1.i.

7. "Teatro de Apolo: Cádiz en Viena," *Madrid Cómico* 25 Nov. 1886: 2–3; "Los estrenos," *La Época* 21 Nov. 1886.

8. Burgos, *Cádiz,* II.6.xiii.

9. Miguel de Unamuno, *En torno al casticismo* (1902; Madrid: Alianza, 2000). See also Carlos Barriuso, *Los discursos de la modernidad: Nación, imperio y estética en el fin de siglo español (1895–1924)* (Madrid: Biblioteca Nueva, 2009) 21–64; Stephen G. H. Roberts, "Unamuno and the Restoration Political Project: A Re-evaluation," *Spain's 1898 Crisis: Regenerationism, Modernism, Post-Colonialism,* ed. Joseph Harrison and Alan Hoyle (Manchester: Manchester UP, 2000) 68–80; and H. Ramsden, *The 1898 Movement in Spain: Towards a Reinterpretation with Special Reference to* En torno al casticismo *and* Idearium español (Manchester: Manchester UP, 1974).

10. Unamuno, *En torno al casticismo* 53–54.

11. See Ramsden 118–127.

12. Unamuno, *En torno al casticismo* 22.

13. Burgos, *Cádiz,* II.6.xiii.

14. See Fernández Muñoz 119–122, and Juan Arnau, *Historia de la Zarzuela* (Madrid: Zacosa, 1979), vol. 1, 172–173. The Teatro Apolo was torn down in 1929; it stood near the modern-day confluence of the Calle de Alcalá and the Gran Vía.

15. See José Álvarez Junco, "El nacionalismo español como mito movilizador: Cuatro guerras," *Cultura y movilización en la España contemporánea,* ed. Rafael Cruz and Manuel Pérez Ledesma (Madrid: Alianza, 1997) 36–42.

16. *El Heraldo de Madrid* 19 June 1891.

17. Carlos Serrano, *El nacimiento de Carmen: Símbolos, mitos y nación* (Madrid: Taurus, 1999) 137. It should be noted that Serrano has a quite different opinion of *Cádiz,* which he describes on page 138 as having "un papel de suma relevancia en la historia cultural de los españoles del siglo pasado."

18. "En mi tierra ser valientes/todos, como en esta tierra. / Valor el mismo; variar / solamente las maneras. / Inglaterra, valor frío. / España, valor calienta." Miguel Echegaray, *La viejecita,* 1.iii, *El género chico (Antología de textos completos),* ed. Antonio Valencia (Madrid: Taurus, 1962) 375–412.

19. "Fuego es el vino / del suelo español; / fuego es el aire / y fuego es el sol; / fuego en mis venas / ya siento correr / para amar y beber / y luchar y vencer." Echegaray, *La viejecita,* 1.i.

20. Echegaray, *La viejecita,* 2.xvii.

21. Luis Bermejo, "Los éxitos: *La viejecita,*" *Blanco y negro* 22 May 1897: 7.

22. Emilio Sánchez Pastor, *El tambor de granaderos,* 1.i., *El género chico (Antología de textos completos),* ed. Antonio Valencia (Madrid: Taurus, 1962) 455–487.

23. Sánchez Pastor, *El tambor de granaderos,* 1.iii.

24. "Cuánto quieren nuestros reyes / al emperador se ve; / luego cumple bien las leyes / el que ataca al rey José." Sánchez Pastor, *El tambor de granaderos,* 1.v.

25. Sánchez Pastor, *El tambor de granaderos,* 2.xiii.

26. "¡Pobres soldados / que juran sin fe!"; "Por mi amor tan solo / sufre esa tortura." Sánchez Pastor, *El tambor de granaderos,* 1.x.

27. "Yo, ni beso ni juro esa infamia, / de la patria ignominia y baldón. / . . . / ¡Qué me importa la vida sin honra! / ¡Es mejor por la patria morir! / . . . / Me la dan para herir a la patria / en el nombre del vil invasor."; "¡Muy bien hecho! . . . ¡Que viva el muchacho / que a la patria prefiere ser fiel!" Sánchez Pastor, *El tambor de granaderos,* 1.x.

28. *El Heraldo de Madrid* 17 Nov. 1894; El Abate Pirracas, "El tambor de granaderos," *La Correspondencia de España* 17 Nov. 1894; Zeda, "Veladas teatrales," *La Época* 17 Nov. 1894; J. A., "Teatro Eslava," *El Liberal* 17 Nov. 1894.

29. On the relationship of 1898 to Spanish nationalism, see Christopher Schmidt-Nowara, *The Conquest of History: Spanish Colonialism and National Histories in the Nineteenth Century* (Pittsburgh: U of Pittsburgh P, 2006); and Joseph Harrison and Alan Hoyle, eds., *Spain's 1898 Crisis: Regenerationism, Modernism, Post-Colonialism* (Manchester: Manchester UP, 2000).

30. "Tocamos más que Wagner / Rossini y Mozart." Celso Lucio and Enrique García-Álvarez, *La marcha de Cádiz,* 1.ix, in *El género chico (Antología de textos completos),* ed. Antonio Valencia (Madrid: Taurus, 1962) 491–512.

31. "La marcha aquí terminó; / si no te parece mal, / aplaude, lo pido yo, / por el himno nacional." Lucio and García-Álvarez, 3.ix.

32. On the history of Spanish national anthems, see Carlos Serrano, *El nacimiento de Carmen* 107–130, and María Nagore Ferrer, "Historia de un fracaso: El 'himno nacional' en la España del siglo XIX," *Arbor* 187.751 (Sept.–Oct. 2011): 827–845.

33. "La Marcha de 'Cádiz,'" *El Liberal* 27 Dec. 1896.

34. "Los cochinos de Chicago / dicen que han tomado á mal / el que muchos los comparen / con Sherman, Morgan y Call. / Porque tiene los cochinos / muy buen lomo y buen jamón, / y aquellos sujetos sólo / tienen lengua . . . de escorpión." "Villancicos de la guerra," *El Liberal* 20 Dec. 1896.

35. See *El Heraldo de Madrid* 21 Feb. 1896.

36. Matamoros, "Crónicas madrileñas: El himno nacional," *La Época* 17 Feb. 1896.

37. Antonio Peña y Goñi, "Crónicas madrileñas: ¡Vi-va es-paña!" *La Época* 29 Feb. 1896.

38. Florentino Hernández Girbal, *Federico Chueca: El alma de Madrid* (Madrid: Ediciones Lira, 1992) 328–332.

39. See *El Heraldo de Madrid* 25 Nov. 1896.

40. See Sebastian Balfour, *The End of the Spanish Empire, 1898–1923* (Oxford: Clarendon, 1997).

CHAPTER FOUR

1. "La plazuela ha votado, / y que ha votado que no." Miguel Echegaray, *Gigantes y cabezudos,* 1.i, *El género chico (Antología de textos completos),* ed. Antonio Valencia (Madrid: Taurus, 1962) 413–454.

2. Pamela Beth Radcliff, "Women's Politics: Consumer Riots in Twentieth-century Spain," *Constructing Spanish Womanhood: Female Identity in Modern Spain,* ed. Victoria Loree Enders and Pamela Beth Radcliff (Albany: State U of New York P, 1999) 301–323.

3. "Con nosotras, que débiles somos, los hombres no pueden, / y al mirarnos furiosas se asustan y el campo nos ceden. / . . . / Aunque traiga el alcalde un cañón, / no nos echa de aquí si hay unión." Echegaray, *Gigantes y cabezudos,* 1.x.

4. Zeda and M. Barber, "Veladas teatrales," *La Época* 30 Nov. 1898.

5. Zeda and M. Barber, "Veladas teatrales," *La Época* 30 Nov. 1898. See the vocal score: Manuel Fernández Caballero, *Gigantes y cabezudos: Zarzuela en un acto* (Madrid: Unión Musical Española, 1927).

6. Joan Connelly Ullman, *The Tragic Week: A Study of Anticlericalism in Spain, 1875–1912* (Cambridge: Harvard UP, 1968); Temma Kaplan, *Red City, Blue Period: Social Movements in Picasso's Barcelona* (Berkeley: U of California P, 1992); Francisco J. Romero Salvadó, *Spain 1914–1918: Between War and Revolution* (London and New York: Routledge), 1999).

7. On regenerationism, see Guadalupe Gómez-Ferrer and Raquel Sánchez, eds., *Modernizar España: Proyectos de reforma y apertura internacional (1898–1914)* (Madrid: Biblioteca Nueva, 2007); Joseph Harrison and Alan Hoyle, eds., *Spain's 1898 Crisis: Regenerationism, Modernism, Post-Colonialism* (Manchester: Manchester UP, 2000); Enric Ucelay da Cal, "The Restoration: Regeneration and the Clash of Nationalisms, 1875–1914," *Spanish History Since 1808,* ed. José Álvarez Junco and Adrian Shubert (London: Arnold, 2000) 121–136; and Sebastian Balfour, *The End of the Spanish Empire, 1898–1923* (Oxford: Clarendon, 1997).

8. For an in-depth discussion of these efforts at theatrical reform, see Clinton D. Young, "Theatrical Reform and the Emergence of Mass Culture in Spain," *Sport in Society* 11.6 (Nov. 2008): 630–642.

9. Richard Traubner, *Operetta: A Theatrical History,* rev. ed. (New York & London: Routledge, 2003) 244.

10. Caramanchel, "Cosas de Teatros: El género chico en el siglo XX," *La Correspondencia de España* 1 Jan. 1901.

11. Lara, "El género chico: Palenque abierto," *El Heraldo de Madrid* 29 Oct. 1904.

12. See "Revista de Teatros: Teatro de la Zarzuela," *La Correspondencia Musical* 15 Oct. 1885: 3.

13. The main reviews of the Madrid production cited in this paragraph are S. A., "La viuda alegre," *El Heraldo de Madrid* 9, Feb. 1909; Floridor, "Los estrenos: Price, «La viuda alegre»," *ABC,* 9 Feb. 1909: 10. The operetta had actually been adapted from an 1861 French comedy by Henri Meilhac, *L'attaché d'ambassade.*

14. Amadeo Vives, *Sofía* (Madrid: Espasa-Calpe, 1973) 135–141. At one point, Vives mentions in passing that he is about to premiere an opera, which allows us to date the article to 1910, the year *Colomba* premiered at the Teatro Real.

15. S.-A., "Eslava: El Conde de Luxemburgo," *El Heraldo de Madrid* 20 Oct. 1910; José Juan Cádenas, "*ABC* en Madrid: El conde de Luxemburgo," *ABC* 19 Oct. 1910: 3.

16. Cádenas, "*ABC* en Madrid": 3.

17. Cádenas, "*ABC* en Madrid": 4. The term *chulo* in the original is a more-or-less untranslatable term referring to a specific stereotype of the lower-class citizen of Madrid as a cocky and self-assured, street-smart character—not unlike the Cockney stereotype in England.

18. "Teniendo tan grave herida . . . / después de la operación . . . / se casa con esa niña?" See 1.ii in the libretto, published in Vicente Lleó, *La corte de Faraón,* ed. Josep Soler (Madrid: ICCM, 1997).

19. "Los teatros," *La Época,* 24 Jan. 1910.

20. Vicente Lleó, *La corte de Faraón,* ed. Josep Soler (Madrid: ICCM, 1997).

21. "Es muy duro / y molesto, yo te lo aseguro, / . . . / el derecho que tiene el marido / sobre la mujer." See 2.i.

22. See Angel Sagardía, *Pablo Luna* (Madrid: Espasa-Calpe, 1978) 15–25.

23. See Pablo Luna, *Molinos de viento: Opereta en un acto* (1935; Madrid: Unión Musical Española, 1973).

24. "Eslava: Molinos de viento," *ABC,* 4 Feb. 1911: 12.

25. M. de Z., "Los teatros," *La Correspondencia de España,* 4 Feb. 1911: 6.

26. *Comedias y comediantes,* July 1912.

27. A., "Veladas teatrales," *La Época* 6 Feb. 1918. The Cook Agency was one of the first modern travel agents in Europe.

28. Floridor, "Notas teatrales," *ABC* 6 Feb. 1918.

29. Leopoldo Bejarano, "Los estrenos," *El Liberal* 6 Feb. 1918.

30. J. A., "Los estrentos de ayer," *El Sol* 6 Feb. 1918.

31. "De España vengo, soy española. / En mis ojos me traigo la luz de su cielo / y en mi cuerpo la gracia de la manola. / De España vengo, de España soy / y mi cara serran va pregonando / que he nacido en España por donde voy." II.1. Enrique García Álvarez and Antonio Paso, *El niño judío* (Madrid: Teatro de la Zarzuela, 2003).

32. See Emilio Casares Rodicio, *Francisco Asenjo Barbieri,* vol. 1 (Madrid: ICCMU, 1994) 68–71; Luis G. Iberni, *Ruperto Chapí* (Madrid: ICCMU, 1995) 41–45; Florentino Hernandez Girbal, *Federico Chueca: El alma de Madrid* (Madrid: Ediciones Lira, 1992) 72–87.

33. Florentino Hernández Girbal, *Amadeo Vives: El músico y el hombre* (Madrid: Ediciones Lira, 1971) 34–40; Sol Burgete, *Amadeo Vives* (Madrid: Espasa-Calpe, 1978) 26.

34. Angel Sagardía, *El compositor José Serrano: Vida y obra* (Madrid: Organización Sala Editorial, 1972) 14–18; Vicente Vidal Corella, *El maestro Serrano y los felices tiempos de la zarzuela* (Valencia: Prometo, 1973) 24–27 and 42–44.

35. Vidal Corella 45–48.

36. Vidal Corella 42–44.

37. Gabriel Hernández Gonzalez (Javier de Montillana), *Bretón* (Salamanca: Talleres Gráficos Nuñez, 1952) 21–25.

38. Carlos Gómez Amat and Joaquín Turina Gómez, *La Orquesta Sinfónica de Madrid: Noventa años de historia* (Madrid: Alianza, 1994), and Tomás Marco, *Spanish Music in the Twentieth Century,* trans. Cola Franzen (Cambridge: Harvard UP, 1993) 14–17.

39. Vidal Corella 65–67, and Sagardía 23.

40. "Muerte de Chapí," *El Heraldo de Madrid* 25 March 1909, and "La muerte de Chapí," *ABC* 26 March 1909: 7–9.

41. The series included: "La Marsellesa" 14 Dec. 1907; "Pan y toros" 25 Jan. 1908; "Cádiz" 4 April 1908; "Jugar con fuego" 16 May 1908; "Fiesta nacional" 20 July 1908; "La canción de la Lola" 2 Oct. 1908; "Los diamantes de la corona" 6 Nov. 1908; and "La gran vía" 4 Dec. 1908.

42. *El Heraldo de Madrid* 28 May 1906. The paper noted, perhaps defensively, that the public was "apasionado de lucha."

43. "El incendio de ayer: El Teatro de la Zarzuela, destruido," *El Liberal* 9 Nov. 1909. See also "Incendio del Teatro de la Zarzuela," *ABC* 9 Nov. 1909: 11–13, and "El incendio de la Zarzuela," *El Imparcial* 9 Nov. 1909.

44. José Ortega y Gasset, "Vieja y nueva política," vol. 1, *Obras Completas* 265–308 (Madrid: Revista del Occidente, 1961).

45. See Enrique A. Sanabria, *Republicanism and Anticlerical Nationalism in Spain* (New York: Palgrave Macmillan, 2009), and José Álvarez Junco, *The Emergence of Mass Politics in Spain: Populist Demagoguery and Republican Culture, 1890–1910* (Brighton and Portland, OR: Sussex Academic, 2002), a translation of *El emperador del Paralelo: Lerroux y la demagogia populista* (Madrid: Alianza, 1990).

46. See María Jesús González, *El universo conservador de Antonio Maura: Biografía y proyecto de Estado* (Madrid: Biblioteca Nueva, 1997) esp. 129–175.

47. Young, "Theatrical Reform" 633–634.

CHAPTER FIVE

1. Christopher Webber, *The Zarzuela Companion* (Lanham, MD: Scarecrow, 2002).118–121.

2. For a discussion of regional nationalisms, see Juan Pablo Fusi, *España: La evolución de la identidad nacional* (Madrid: Temas de Hoy, 2000) 197–247; Josep Maria Fradera, *Cultura nacional en una sociedad dividida: Cataluña, 1838–1868,* trans. Carles Mercadal Vidal (1992; Madrid: Macial Pons Historia, 2003); José Luis de Granja Sainz, "Nacionalismo, ideología y cultura en el País Vasco," and Justo Beramendi, "Nacionalismo y cultura en Galicia," *La cultura española de la Restauración,* ed. Manuel Suárez Cortina (Santander: Sociedad Menéndez Pelayo, 1999) 525–564 and 585–605; E. Inman Fox, *La invención de España: Nacionalismo liberal e identidad nacional* (Madrid: Cátedra, 1998) 65–96.

3. For an overview of the historiography on the subject, see Fernando Molina and Miguel Cabo Villaverde, "An Inconvenient Nation: Nation-Building and National Identity in Modern

Spain. The Historiographical Debate," *Nationhood from Below: Europe in the Long Nineteenth Century,* ed. Maarten Van Ginderachter and Marnix Beyen (New York: Palgrave Macmillan, 2012) 59–62. See also Francesc Mezquita Patuel, *¿Una nación débil? Aproximación a los discuros nacionales en España* (n.p.: 05ediciones, 2009).

4. Walter Aaron Clark, *Isaac Albéniz: Portrait of a Romantic* (Oxford: Oxford UP, 1999) 63–69, and 223–253.

5. Ferran Archilés and Marta García Carrión, "En la sombra del estado: Esfera pública nacional y homogeneización cultural en la España de la Restauración," *Historia Contemporánea* 45 (2012): 511–512.

6. Clark 281–282; see also 223–248 for a musical analysis of *Iberia.*

7. Ernest Gellner, *Nations and Nationalism* (Ithaca: Cornell UP, 1983), and Eugene Weber, *Peasants into Frenchmen: The Modernization of Rural France, 1870–1914* (Stanford: Stanford UP, 1976).

8. The best overview of mass mobilization is Pamela Beth Radcliff, "The Emerging Challenge of Mass Politics," *Spanish History Since 1808,* ed. José Álvarez Junco and Adrian Shubert (London: Arnold, 2000) 137–154. For more in-depth studies of Republican politics, see Pamela Beth Radcliff, *From Mobilization to Civil War: The Politics of Polarization in the Spanish City of Gijón, 1900–1937* (Cambridge: Cambridge UP, 1996), and José Álvarez Junco, *The Emergence of Mass Politics in Spain.*

9. Federico Chueca, *La alegría de la huerta: Zarzuela en un acto y tres cuadros,* piano reduction M. Brull (Madrid: Almagro y Compañía, n.d.).

10. Enrique García Álvarez and Antonio Paso, *La alegría de la huerta,* 1.iv, *El género chico (Antología de textos completes),* ed. Antonio Valencia (Madrid: Taurus, 1962) 525–551.

11. "Y cuando regreso / de la Fuensantica / limpia de pecados, / a eso de las diez, / tengo los garbanzos / tan mantecosicos / que hay que macharcarlos / en el almirez." García Álvarez and Paso, *La alegría de la huerta* 544, 3.i.

12. Benito Pérez Galdós, *Doña Perfecta* (Madrid: Cátedra, 2001) 120–132.

13. Henry Kamen, *Imagining Spain: Historical Myth and National Identity* (New Haven & London: Yale UP, 2008) 74–95.

14. Julían Romea, *La tempranica,* 1.ii and 1.v, *El género chico (Antología de textos completes),* ed. Antonio Valencia (Madrid: Taurus, 1962) 555–583.

15. On regional literature, see Alison Sinclair, "The Regional Novel: Evolution and Consolidation," *The Cambridge Companion to the Spanish Novel: From 1600 to the Present,* 2009 ed., 49–64. On the idea of *heimat,* see Alon Confino, *The Nation as a Local Metaphor: Württemberg, Imperial Germany, and National Memory, 1871–1918* (Chapel Hill: U of North Carolina P, 1997), and Celia Applegate, *A Nation of Provincials: The German Idea of Heimat* (Berkeley: U of California P, 1990).

16. Lou Charnon-Deutsch, *The Spanish Gypsy: The History of a European Obsession* (University Park: Pennsylvania State UP, 2004) 179–183.

17. Charnon-Deutsch 183–196.

18. Throughout this chapter, I have used the term *Gypsy* rather than the currently accepted *Roma* to emphasize the fact that I am discussing dramatic constructs rather than real, historical Roma subjects. I have borrowed this convention from Charnon-Deutsch 14.

19. Gerónimo Giménez, *La tempranica: Zarzuela en un acto,* ed. Claudio Prieto (Madrid: Instituto Complutense de Ciencias Musicales, 1999).

20. Charnon-Deutsch 202–210.

21. See Ramón Sobrino's "Alhambrismo," liner notes to *En la Alhambra: Obras de Chapí, Bretón, Monasterio and Carreras,* CD, Almaviva, 1999.

22. Ruperto Chapí, *El puñao de rosas: Zarzuela en tres cuadros y en prosa* (Madrid: Sociedad Anónima Casa Dotésio, n.d.).

23. See Mariano Sánchez de Palacios, *Serafín y Joaquín Álvarez Quintero* (Madrid: Gráficas Valera, 1971). For a brief English-language overview, see "Álvarez Quintero, Joaquín and Serafín," *The Columbia Encyclopedia of Modern Drama,* 2007 ed.

24. José Serrano, *La Reina mora: Sainete lírico en un acto* (Madrid: Unión Musical Española, 1930).

25. Shlomo Ben-Ami, *Fascism from Above: The Dictatorship of Primo de Rivera in Spain, 1923–1930* (Oxford: Clarendon, 1983) 194–202.

26. James H. Rial, *Revolution from Above: The Primo de Rivera Dictatorship in Spain, 1923–1930* (Fairfax, VA: George Mason UP, 1986) 79–98.

27. See Emilio Casares Rodicio's article, "Jota," *Diccionario de la Zarzuela España e Hispanoamérica,* 2006 ed.

28. Reveriano Soutullo and Juan Vert, *La del soto del parral: Zarzuela en dos actos* (Madrid: Sociedad de Autores Españoles, 1927).

29. Juan José Lorente, *Los de Aragón: Zarzuela de costumbres aragonesas* (Madrid: Unión Musical Española, 1967). For an analysis of the libretto, see "Los de Aragón," *Diccionario de la Zarzuela Español e Hispanoamérica,* 2006 ed.

30. José Serrano, *Los de Aragón: Zarzuela en un acto,* ed. J. F. Pacheco (Madrid: Unión Musical Española, 1927).

31. "Acontecimientos teatrales: Estrenos e inauguraciones de Pascua," *La Época* 18 April 1927.

32. "'La reina del Directorio' en la Zarzuela," *ABC* 17 April 1927: 30.

33. The best biography of Guridi is Victor Sánchez Sánchez's entry, "Jesús Guridi," *Diccionario de la Zarzuela España e Hispanoamérica,* 2006 ed. English readers can find a brief introduction to Guridi and his works in Santiago Gorostiza, liner notes, Jesús Guridi, *Sinfonía pirenaica,* CD, Naxos, 2005.

34. "Movimiento teatral: Zarzuela, 'El caserío,'" *El Heraldo de Madrid* 12 Nov. 1926: 6.

35. "Sasibill mi caserío, / tibia cuna de mi niñez, / alivio suave de mis dolores, / de mis amores orgullo y prez. . . ." Federico Romero and Guillermo Fernández-Shaw, *El caserío: Comedia lírica en tres actos* (Madrid: Unión Musical Española, 1967), I.

36. Jesús Guridi, *El caserío: Cómedia lírica en tres actos* (1927; Madrid: Union Musical Española, n.d.).

37. See Melchor Fernández Almagro, "Veladas teatrales," *La Época* 12 Nov. 1926, and El Bachiller Relamido, "Movimiento teatral," *El Heraldo de Madrid* 12 Nov. 1926: 6.

38. Floridor, "Informaciones de espectaculos de teatros, toros y deportes," *ABC* 12 Nov. 1926.

39. "Una nueva obra de Jesús Guridi: *El caserío,*" *El Sol* 11 Nov. 1926: 4.

40. S., "En la Zarzuela: Estreno de 'El caserío,' de Guridi, Fernández Shaw y Romero," *El Sol* 12 Nov. 1926: 2.

CHAPTER SIX

1. See Ramón Barce, "El sainete lírico (1880–1915)," *La música española en el siglo XIX,* ed. Emilio Casares Rodicio and Celsa Alonso González (Oviedo: U de Oviedo, 1995) 207–208, and Christopher Webber, *The Zarzuela Companion* (Lanham & Oxford: Scarecrow, 2002) 197.

2. The best musical analysis of *La canción del olvido* can be found in Miguel Roa and Ramón Sobrino, "Introducción," José Serrano, *La canción del olvido: Zarzuela en un acto,* ed. Miguel Roa and Ramón Sobrino (Madrid: Instituto Complutense de Ciencias Musicales, 1993), ii–xi.

3. "De espectaculos: Notas teatrales," *ABC* 2 March 1918: 13; J. de L., "Los teatros," *El Imparcial* 2 March 1918; L. P., "Noticias e informaciones teatrales," *La Correspondencia de España* 2 March 1918: 5.

4. For context on this relationship outside Spain, see John Dizikes, *Opera in America: A Cultural History* (New Haven: Yale UP, 1993), and Lawrence W. Levine, *Highbrow/Lowbrow: The Emergence of Cultural Hierarchy in America* (Cambridge: Harvard UP, 1988).

5. For the significance of such distinctions, see Pierre Bordieu, *Distinction: A Social Critique of the Judgment of Taste* (Cambridge: Harvard UP, 1984).

6. For a more thorough discussion of the subject, see Clinton D. Young, "Why Did Spain Fail to Develop Nationalist Opera?" *Bulletin of the Association for Spanish and Portuguese Historical Studies* 38.1 (2013): 117–137.

7. Antonio Peña y Goñi, *La ópera española y la música dramática en España en el siglo XIX. Apuntes históricos* (Madrid: Imprenta y estereotipia de *El Liberal,* 1881) 14.

8. Peña y Goñi, *Ópera española* 21.

9. Peña y Goñi, *Ópera española* 313.

10. Antonio Peña y Goñi, *Discursos leídos ante la Real Academia de Bellas Artes de San Fernando en la recepción pública de Don Antonio Peña y Goñi el día 10 de abril de 1892* (Madrid: Manuel Ginés Hernández, 1892) 37.

11. Peña y Goñi, *Ópera española* 398.

12. Peña y Goñi, *Ópera española* 451.

13. Peña y Goñi, *Ópera española* 424–425 and 428.

14. See Roger Alier, *La Zarzuela* (Barcelona: Ma Non Troppo, 2002) 48–49.

15. Peña y Goñi, *Ópera española* 428.

16. Antonio Peña y Goñi, *Impresiones musicales: Colección de artículos de crítica y literatura musical* (Madrid: Manuel Minuesa de los Rios, 1878) 262.

17. Peña y Goñi, *Ópera española.* 428.

18. Some of this is summarized from Nancy J. Membrez, "The *teatro por horas:* History, Dynamics and Comprehensive Bibliography of a Madrid Industry, 1867–1922," diss., U of California, Santa Barbara, 1987) 486–487. Ascertaining exact dates and data regarding the Trust is difficult. Membrez, for example, asserts that the Trust began operation in the fall of 1906 (based primarily on Hérnadez Girbal's biography of Vives, one of those works whose data must be treated with a certain amount of suspicion); I can find no references in the press to the Trust earlier than the autumn of 1907.

19. Antonio Garrido, "Teatro de la Zarzuela," *La Ilustración Española y Americana* 30 September 1907.

20. Tomás Luceño and Carlos Fernández-Shaw, *Don Lucas del Cigarral: Zarzuela en tres actos* (Madrid: R. Velasco, 1899).

21. See Vives's vocal score, *Don Lucas del Cigarral: Zarzuela en tres actos* (Madrid: Pablo Martin, n.d.). The music's complexity can be seen especially in No. 1 (the opening sextet) and No. 13 (a septet that evolves into a concertante number).

22. See, for example, Carlos Gómez Amat's "*Bohemios,* zarzuela peculiar," liner notes, Amadeo Vives, *Bohemios,* CD, Auvidis Valois, 1994.

23. Amadeo Vives, *Bohemios: Zarzuela en un acto* (1935; Madrid: Unión Musical Española, 1971).

24. "Ovejita tan blanca / como mis sueños. / ¿No es verdad que me quieres / como te quiero?" Luis Pascual Frutos, *Maruxa,* I.i.

25. X., "Los teatros: Maruxa," *La Correspondencia de España* 29 May 1914; Roger Alier, *La zarzuela* (Barcelona: Ma Non Troppo, 2002) 469. Part of the problem with the libretto might arise from the fact that originally *Maruxa* was supposed to be a one-act work and was expanded to a full-length evening only after Vives received it. See S. A., "La vida escénica," *El Heraldo de Madrid* 29 May 1914.

26. "Los estrenos," *ABC* 29 May 1914: 15. See also Eduardo Muñoz, "Teatro de la Zarzuela," *El Imparcial* 30 May 1914.

27. See Amadeo Vives, *Maruxa: Comedia lírica en dos actos* (Madrid: Unión Musical Española, 1915).

28. S. A., "La vida escénica," *El Heraldo de Madrid* 29 May 1914; for Muñoz's comments, see his review in *El Imparcial* 30 May 1914.

29. José Maria Usandizaga, *Las Golondrinas: Drama lírico en tres actos* (San Sebastián: Casa Erviti, n.d.), is a piano score; for the full score, see José Maria Usandizaga and Ramón Usandizaga, *Las Golondrinas: Opera en tres actos,* ed. Ramón Lazkano (Madrid: Instituto Complutense de Ciencias Musicales, 1999).

30. For the background to *Medi-Mendiyan,* see José Montero Alonso, *Usandizaga* (Madrid: Espasa-Calpe, 1985) 38–43.

31. Montero Alonso, *Usandizaga.* 34–37. On the conservatism of the Schola Cantorum, see Jann Pasler, *Composing the Citizen: Music as Public Utility in Third Republic France* (Berkeley: U of California P, 2009). 617–620.

32. S. A., "Vida teatral," *El Heraldo de Madrid* 6 Feb. 1914; "Los estrenos," *ABC* 6 Feb. 1914: 8; Caramanchel, "Los teatros," *La Correspondencia de España* 6 Feb. 1914: 5.

33. Tristán, "Teatro de Price: Las Golondrinas," *El Liberal* 6 Feb. 1914; "Los estrenos," *ABC* 6 Feb. 1914: 8.

34. On the early career of Falla, see Federico Sopeña, *Vida y obra de Falla* (Madrid: Turner Música, 1988) 25–37, and Tomás Marco, *Spanish Music in the Twentieth Century,* trans. Cola Franzen (Cambridge: Harvard UP, 1993) 18–20.

35. See the memoirs of Arana y Elizora's assistant José Bilbao: *Teatro Real: Recuerdos de las cinco temporadas del empresario Arana* (Madrid: Editorial Norma, 1936; Madrid: Comunidad de Madrid, 1996) 148–151. Ironically, Bilbao suggests that contests should have been held to promote the writing of Spanish opera, forgetting about *La vida breve.*

36. The best short history of the travails of *La vida breve* was published in *ABC* the morning of the premiere: "Una ópera española: La vida breve" 14 Nov. 1914: 18. A more thorough history,

with selections of correspondence between Fernández-Shaw and Falla, can be found in Guillermo Fernández-Shaw's *Larga historia de* La vida breve (Madrid: Revista de Occidente, 1972).

37. See "De teatros," *El Liberal* 15 Nov. 1914.

38. "Vida teatral," *El Heraldo de Madrid* 15 Nov. 1914.

39. Gómez Amat and Turina Gómez, *La Orquesta Sinfónica de Madrid* 49.

40. See the statistical appendix to Joaquín Turina Gómez, *Historia del Teatro Real* (Madrid: Alianza, 1997).

41. For a further discussion, see Carol A. Hess, *Manuel de Falla and Modernism in Spain, 1898–1936* (Chicago: U of Chicago P, 2001).

42. "El Teatro Lírico Nacional," *El Heraldo de Madrid* 24 Sept. 1926.

43. See Rafael Maquina, "Movimiento teatral: Teatro Lírico Nacional," *El Heraldo de Madrid* 22 Oct. 1926.

44. Pablo Luna, Luis Pascual Frutos, Federico Moreno Torroba, and Luis París, "Teatro lírico nacional: Respuesta al Sr. D. Rafael Maquina," *El Heraldo de Madrid* 28 Oct. 1926.

45. "El teatro lírico nacional: Apostillas a una replica," *El Heraldo de Madrid* 10 Nov. 1926.

46. Sol Burgete, *Amadeo Vives* (Madrid: Espasa-Calpe, 1978) 99–100. On cultural organization during the Second Republic, see Sandie Holguín, *Creating Spaniards: Culture and National Identity in Republican Spain* (Madison: U of Wisconsin P, 2002).

47. Francisco J. Romero Salvadó, *Spain 1914–1918: Between War and Revolution* (London and New York: Routledge, 1999).

CHAPTER SEVEN

1. Richard Traubner, *Operetta: A Theatrical History,* rev. ed. (New York & London: Routledge, 2003) 272; see also Richard Traubner, liner notes, Emmerich Kálman, *Die Herzogin von Chicago,* CD, Decca, 1999.

2. Traubner, *Operetta* 257–263.

3. See Chapter XI ("El centenario de *El Quijote:* La subjetivación de la política") of Eric Storm's *La perspectiva del progreso: Pensamiento político en la España del cambio de siglo (1890–1914)* (Madrid: Biblioteca Nueva, 2001) for a discussion of how Golden Age literature became a central part of Spanish nationalism.

4. Max Horkheimer and Theodor Adorno, "The Culture Industry: Enlightenment as Mass Deception," *Dialectic of Enlightenment: Philosophical Fragments* (1947; Stanford: Stanford UP, 2002) 94–136.

5. Theodor Adorno, "Kitsch," *Essays on Music,* ed. Richard Leppart, trans. Susan H. Gillespie (Berkeley: U of California P, 2002) 501.

6. The classic study of the dictatorship is Shlomo Ben-Ami, *Fascism from Above: The Dictatorship of Primo de Rivera in Spain, 1923–1930* (Oxford: Clarendon, 1983); see also Javier Tusell and Genoveva Quiepo de Llano, "The Dictatorship of Primo de Rivera, 1923–1931," *Spanish History Since 1808, ed.* José Álvarez Junco and Adrian Shubert (London: Arnold, 2000) 207–220. Nationalism under the dictatorship is covered in Alejandro Quiroga, *Making Spaniards: Primo de Rivera and the Nationalization of the Masses, 1923–1930* (New York: Palgrave Macmillan, 2007).

7. "La Tradición Española," *La Época* 18 Oct. 1923. The original text ends with the ellipsis as quoted.

8. "El tríunfo de *Doña Francisquita* y el régimen constitucional," *El Liberal* 19 Oct. 1923.

9. See Florentino Hernández Girbal, *Amadeo Vives: El músico y el hombre* (Madrid: Ediciones Lira, 1971) 130–133 and 269.

10. Melchor Fernandez Almargro, "Veladas teatrales: Estreno de 'Doña Francisquita'—El libreto," *La Época* 18 Oct. 1923; E. Diez-Canedo, "El teatro," *El Sol* 18 Oct. 1923.

11. José Forns, "Estreno en Apolo de 'Doña Francisquita: El maestro Vives obtiene un exito clamoroso," *El Heraldo de Madrid* 18 Oct. 1923.

12. See the correspondence in the Archivo Epistolar Fernández-Shaw in the Biblioteca de la Fundación Juan March: AE 17 Músicos, #492, 496, 498.

13. Víctor Espinós, "Veladas teatrales: Estreno de 'Doña Francisquita'—La música," *La Época* 18 Oct. 1923; "Un triunfo grande del maestro Vives," *El Imparcial* 18 Oct. 1923; Floridor, "Espectaculos y deportes," *ABC* 18 Oct. 1923.

14. Amadeo Vives, *Doña Francisquita: Comedia Lírica en tres actos* (Madrid: Unión Musical Española, 1968).

15. "Canto alegre de la juventud / que eres alma del viejo Madrid." Federico Romero and Guillermo Fernández-Shaw, *Doña Francisquita,* ed. Xosé Aviñoa (Madrid: Ediciones Daimon, 1986), I.x.

16. A. F. L., "Los últimos estrenos: Zarzuela—"La calesera," *El Imparcial* 13 Dec. 1925.

17. Federico Alonso, *La Calesera: Zarzuela en tres actos* (Madrid: Editorial Música Española, 1926).

18. A. F. L., "Los últimos estrenos: Zarzuela—"La calesera," *El Imparcial* 13 Dec. 1925.

19. This somewhat harsh evaluation is by Christopher Webber in *The Zarzuela Companion* (Lanham, MD, & Oxford: Scarecrow, 2002) 231.

20. Reveriano Soutullo and Juan Vert, *La del soto del parral: Zarzuela en dos actos* (Madrid: Sociedad de Autores Españoles, 1927).

21. Amadeo Vives, *La villana: Zarzuela en tres actos* (Madrid: Sociedad de Autores Españoles, 1927).

22. Enrique Reoyo, Juan Luca de Tena, and Jacinto Guerrero, "Antes de un estreno," *ABC* 3 Dec. 1926.

23. "Mezcla admirable y extraña . . . / Místicos y aventuereros / y poetas y guerreros. / ¡Es Castilla . . . y es España!" Juan Ignacio Luca de Tena and Enrique Reoyo, *El huésped del sevillano,* II.2.

24. Jacinto Guerrero, *El huésped del sevillano: Zarzuela en dos actos,* ed. Jesús Villa Rojo (Madrid: Instituo Complutense de Ciencias Musicales, 1995).

25. "Toledo, solar hispano, / crisol de la raza iberia, / ¡dichoso aquel que naciera / español y toledano!" Luca de Tena and Reoyo, II.2.

26. José Tellaeche, *El último romántico: Zarzuela de costumbres, en dos actos, divididos en cuatro cuadros* (Madrid: La Farsa, 1928), I.1 and I.2.

27. "¡Basta ya de murga! . . . ¡Ya esto es mucha murga / y es mucho trombón!" Tellaeche, *El último romántico,* II.1.

28. "Van por calles y por plazas / los murguistas que aquí veis, / y estoy harta ya de Chueca, / de Bretón y de Marqués. / Tocan sólo la mazurca, / la habanera o el schotís. / Unas veces de Val-

verde / y otras veces de Chapí. / Pero es mucha broma / que todos los días / se oiga solamente / tocar la *Gran Vía,* / o la *Niña Pancha,* / o *Cható Margot,* / *Cádiz* u otras cosas / que se estilan hoy." Tellaeche, *El último romántico,* II.1.

29. Reveriano Soutullo and Juan Vert, *El último romántico: Zarzuela en dos actos* (Madrid: Unión Musical Española, 1968).

30. Marciano Zurita, *Historia del género chico* (Madrid: Prensa Popular, 1920).

31. Zurita 46.

32. Zurita 124, 125, and 126.

FINALE

1. On Alfonso XIII and the end of the Restoration system, see Raymond Carr, *Spain, 1808–1975,* 2nd ed. (Oxford: Clarendon, 1982) 581–602; Miguel Martorell Linares, "El rey en su desconcierto: Alfonso XIII, los viejos políticos y el ocaso de la monarquía," *Alfonso XIII: Un político en el trono,* ed. Javier Moreno Luzón (Madrid: Marcial Pons Historia, 2003) 373–402; and Javier Tusell and Genoveva G. Queipo de Llano, *Alfonso XIII: El rey polémico* (Madrid: Taurus, 2001) 565–652.

2. The literature on the Second Republic is vast and growing, but the best overviews in English remain Gabriel Jackson, *The Spanish Republic and the Civil War, 1931–1939* (Princeton: Princeton UP, 1965), and Stanley G. Payne, *Spain's First Democracy: The Second Republic, 1931–1936* (Madison: U of Wisconsin P, 1993).

3. "La nueva temporada teatral: Estrenos e inauguraciones," *La Época* 28 March 1932: 1.

4. Federico Romero y Guillermo Fernández-Shaw, *Luisa Fernanda: Comedia lírica en tres actos,* in *Luisa Fernanda, La Chulapona, Monte Carmelo* (Barcelona: Editorial Cisne, n.d.), III.1.

5. For a discussion of Moreno Torroba's essential conservatism, see Walter Aaron Clark and William Craig Krause, *Federico Moreno Torroba: A Musical Life in Three Acts* (Oxford: Oxford UP, 2013)—although the authors insist that *Luisa Fernanda* is an apolitical work: see 93–107.

6. Federico Moreno Torroba, *Luisa Fernanda: Comedia lírica en tres actos,* ed. Federico Moreno Torroba-Larregla (Madrid: ICCMU, 2003).

7. "Entorchados / de brigadier." Romero and Fernández-Shaw, *Luisa Fernanda,* I.1.

8. "Filmografía," *Diccionario de la zarzuela España e Hispanoamérica,* 2006 ed.

9. For a brief history of zarzuela recordings, see "Fonografía," *Diccionario de la zarzuela España e Hispanoamérica,* 2006 ed. I: 788–794. The best current discography of recordings and advice for purchasing zarzuela recordings can be found in the "Zarzuela.net CD Magazine." www .zarzuela.net/cd/cdmagfp.htm (last accessed 19 October 2014).

10. Some examples of scholarship that examines how music acquires meaning include Martin Clayton, Trevor Herbert, and Richard Middleton, eds., *The Cultural Study of Music: A Critical Introduction* (New York and London: Routledge, 2003); Lawrence Kramer, *Musical Meaning: Towards a Critical History* (Berkeley: U of California P, 2002); and Tia DeNora, *Music in Everyday Life* (Cambridge: Cambridge UP, 2000).

11. On music as a vernacular language, see Benedict Anderson, *Imagined Communities: Reflections on the Origin and Spread of Nationalism,* rev. ed. (London: Verso, 2006) 77. On the use of music in constructing social and national identities, see Jann Pasler, *Composing the Citizen: Music*

as Public Utility in Third Republic France (Berkeley: U of California P, 2009); Jeffrey H. Jackson, *Making Jazz French: Music and Modern Life in Interwar Paris* (Durham: Duke UP, 2003); the essays in Celia Applegate and Pamela Potter, eds., *Music and German National Identity* (Chicago: U of Chicago P, 2002); and Uta G. Poiger, *Jazz, Rock, and Rebels: Cold War Politics and American Culture in a Divided Germany* (Berkeley: U of California P, 2000).

12. Max Horkheimer and Theodor W. Adorno, "The Culture Industry: Enlightenment as Mass Deception," in *Dialectic of Enlightenment: Philosophical Fragments* 94–136 (1947; Stanford: Stanford UP, 2002).

13. Michael P. Steinberg, *Listening to Reason: Culture, Subjectivity, and Nineteenth-Century Music* (Princeton: Princeton UP, 2004) 1–23.

14. Michael H. Kater, *The Twisted Muse: Musicians and Their Music in the Third Reich* (Oxford: Oxford UP, 1997); David Caute, *The Dancer Defects: The Struggle for Cultural Supremacy During the Cold War* (Oxford: Oxford UP, 2003); and Elizabeth Wilson, *Shostakovich: A Life Remembered* (Princeton: Princeton UP, 1994).

15. Thomas Mann, *The Magic Mountain,* trans. John E. Woods (New York: Vintage, 1996) 112.

APPENDIX

1. Nieves Iglesias Martinez, ed., *Catalogo del teatro lírico español en la Biblioteca Nacional,* 3 vols. (Madrid: Ministero de Cultura, 1986–1991).

2. Dru Dougherty and María Francisca Vilches de Frutos, *La escena madrileña entre 1918 y 1926: Análsis y documentación* (Madrid: Editorial Fundamentos, 1990), and María Francisca Vilches and Dru Dougherty, *La escena madrileña entre 1926 y 1931: Un lustro de transición* (Madrid: Fundamentos, 1997).

3. Luis Besses, *Diccionario de argot español o lenguaje jergal gitano, delincuente profesional y popular* (Barcelona: Sucesores de Manuel Soler, 1905; Cádiz: Servicio de Publicaciones de la Universidad de Cádiz, 1989).

BIBLIOGRAPHY

• • • • • • • • • • • • • •

ARCHIVAL SOURCES

Biblioteca de la Fundación Juan March (Madrid): Archivo Epistolar Fernández-Shaw

Ruperto Chapí—Carlos Fernández-Shaw: AE 5 Músicos #190–230, 303, 304; CFS 152 Músicos (Chapí) #313, 314

Manuel Fernández Caballero—Carlos Fernández-Shaw: AE 5 Músicos #1–4

Jacinto Guerrero—Guillermo Fernández-Shaw: AE 15 Músicos #147–160; AE 16 Músicos #395–398, 400; GFS #390

Jesús Guridi—Guillermo Fernández-Shaw: AE 15 Músicos (Guridi) #120, 122–137, 140–146; AE 16 Músicos (Guridi) #328, 329, 331, 333–338, 340, 342–351; GFS 442 Músicos (Guridi) #635, 637, 638, 649–651, 653–655, 657–659, 663, 667–669, 677–681

José Serrano—Guillermo Fernández-Shaw: AE 15 Músicos #15–22

Amadeo Vives—Carlos Fernánez-Shaw: AE 5 Músicos #128–159, 308; CFS 152 Músicos (Vives) #312

Amadeo Vives—Guillermo Fernández-Shaw: AE 17 Músicos, #472, 474, 479, 483, 484, 486–490, 492, 493, 495–498, 501–508, 513–517, 600–614; GFS 441 Músicos (Vives) #616, 617, 619–626, 629–633, 675, 676, 682, 683, 685–692, 696, 698–702

PERIODICALS
[all published in Madrid except as noted]

ABC, January 1903–October 1930

Blanco y Negro, May 1891–November 1907

Boletín de Espectáculos, February 1885–September 1885

Comedias y Comediantes, November 1909–July 1912

La Correspondencia de España, December 1874–January 1924

La Correspondencia Musical, January 1881–December 1886

Crónica de la Música, September 1878–December 1882

La Época, January 1875–October 1930

El Heraldo de Madrid, October 1890–October 1930

La Ilustración Española y Americana, December 1874–December 1921

La Ilustración Musical Hispano Americana (Barcelona), January 1888–December 1896

El Imparcial, January 1875–October 1930

El Liberal, March 1880–October 1930

Madrid Cómico, December 1880–April 1881 and February 1883–December 1891

La Música Ilustrada Hispano Americana (Barcelona), December 1898–May 1902

La Opera Española, September 1875–January 1877

El Sol, March 1918–October 1930

El Teatro, November 1900–December 1905

MUSICAL SCORES

Alonso, Federico. *La Calesera: Zarzuela en tres actos.* Madrid: Editorial Música Española, 1926.

———. *La Parranda: Zarzuela en tres actos.* Madrid: Sociedad de Autores Españoles, 1928.

———. *La Parranda: Zarzuela en tres actos.* Ed. Manuel Moreno Buendía. Madrid: Instituto Complutense de Ciencias Musicales, 1996.

Barbieri, Francisco Asenjo. *El barberillo de Lavapiés: Zarzuela en tres actos.* Ed. Maria Encina Cortizo and Ramón Sobrino. Madrid: Instituto Complutense de Ciencias Musicales, 1994.

———. *Pan y toros.* Ed. Emilio Casares and Xavier de Paz. Madrid: Instituto Complutense de Ciencias Musicales, 2001.

Bretón, Tomás. *Los amantes de Teruel: Drama lírico en cuatro actos y un prologo.* Ed. Francesc Bonastre. Madrid: Instituto Complutense de Ciencias Musicales, 1998.

———. *La Dolores: Drama lírico en tres actos.* Ed. Angel Oliver. Madrid: Instituto Complutense de Ciencias Musicales, 1999.

———. *La verbena de la paloma, o El boticario y las chulapas y celos mal reprimidos: Sainete lírico en un acto.* Ed. Ramón Barce. Madrid: Instituto Complutense de Ciencias Musicales, 1994.

Chapí, Ruperto. *El barquillero: Zarzuela en un acto.* Madrid: Unión Musical Española, 1935.

———. *La bruja: Ópera cómica en tres actos.* Piano reduction, Valentín Arín. Madrid: Pablo Martin, n.d.

———. *Los golfos: Sainete en un acto.* Piano reduction, V. Arin. Madrid: Pablo Martin, n.d.

———. *El puñao de rosas: Zarzuela en tres cuadros y en prosa.* Madrid: Sociedad Anónima Casa Dotésio , n.d.

———. *La Revoltosa: Sainete lírico en un acto.* Piano reduction, V. Arin. Madrid: Casa Dotesio, n.d.

———. *El rey que rabió: Zarzuela en tres actos.* Ed. Tomás Marco. Madrid: Instituto Compultense de Ciencias Musicales, 1996.

———. *La tempestad: Melodrama fantástico en tres actos.* Madrid: Sociedad Anónima Casa Dotesio, n.d.

Chueca, Federico. *Agua, azucarillos y aguardiente: Pasillo veraniego en un acto.* Ed. Benito Lauret. Madrid: Instituto Complutense de Ciencias Musicales, 1996.

———. *La alegría de la huerta: Zarzuela en un acto y tres cuadros.* Piano reduction, M. Brull. Madrid: Almagro y Compañía, n.d.

———. *El año pasado por agua: Revista general de 1888 en un acto.* Ed. José Luis Navarro. Madrid: Instituto Complutense de Ciencias Musicales, 1997.

———. *El bateo: Sainete en un acto.* Ed. María Encina Cortizo and Ramón Sobrino. Madrid: Instituto Complutense de Ciencias Musicales, 1993.

———. *El chaleco blanco: Episodio cómico-lírico en un acto.* Ed. Claudio Prieto. Madrid: Instituto Complutense de Ciencias Musicales, 1996.

Chueca, Federico, and Joaquín Valverde. *Cádiz: Episodio nacional cómico-lírico-dramático en dos actos.* Ed. Miguel Roa. Madrid: Instituto Complutense de Ciencias Musicales, 1997.

———. *La canción de la Lola: Zarzuela en un acto.* Madrid: Zozaya, n.d.

———. *La Gran Vía: Revista madrileña cómico-lírica, fantástico-callejera en un acto.* Ed. María Encina Cortizo and Ramón Sobrino. Madrid: Instituto Complutense de Ciencias Musicales, 1996.

Fernández Caballero, Manuel. *El cabo primero: Zarzuela cómica en un acto.* Madrid: Zozaya, n.d.

———. *Château-Margaux: Zarzuela en un acto.* Piano reduction, V. Arin. Madrid: Sociedad Anónima Casa Dotesio, n.d.

———. *El dúo de la Africana: Zarzuela en un acto.* Madrid: Zozaya, [1893?].

———. *Gigantes y cabezudos: Zarzuela en un acto.* Madrid: Unión Musical Española, 1927.

———. *Los sobrinos del Capitán Grant: Novela cómico-lírica-drámatica en cuatro actos.* Ed. Xavier de Paz. Madrid: Instituto Complutense de Ciencias Musicales, 2002.

Giménez, Gerónimo. *La Tempranica: Zarzuela en un acto.* Ed. Claudio Prieto. Madrid: Instituto Complutense de Ciencias Musicales, 1999.

Guerrero, Jacinto. *El huésped del sevillano: Zarzuela en dos actos.* Ed. Jesús Villa Rojo. Madrid: Instiuo Complutense de Ciencias Musicales, 1995.

———. *La montería: Zarzuela en dos actos.* Ed. Benito Lauret. Madrid: Instituto Complutense de Ciencias Musicales, 1995.

Guridi, Jesús. *El caserío: Comedía lírica en tres actos.* 1927. Madrid: Union Musical Española, n.d.

Lleó, Vicente. *La corte de Faraón.* Ed. Josep Soler. Madrid: Instituto Complutense de Ciencias Musicales, 1997.

Luna, Pablo. *Molinos de viento: Opereta en un acto.* 1935. Madrid: Unión Musical Española, 1973.

——— and Enrique Brú. *La chula de Pontevedra: Sainete in dos actos.* Madrid: Sociedad de Autores Españoles, 1928.

Marqués, Miguel. *El anillo de hierro: Drama lírico en tres actos.* Piano reduction, Isidoro Hernandez. Madrid: Romero y Marzo, n.d.

Moreno Torroba, Federico. *Luisa Fernanda: Comedia lírica en tres actos.* Ed. Federico Moreno Torroba-Larregla. Madrid: ICCMU, 2003.

———. *La Marchenera: Zarzuela en tres actos.* Madrid: Sociedad de Autores Españoles, 1928.

Serrano, José. *La canción del olvido: Zarzuela en un acto.* Ed. Miguel Roa and Ramón Sobrino. Madrid: Instituto Complutense de Ciencias Musicales, 1993.

———. *Los claveles: Sainete en un acto, dividio en tres cuadros.* Piano reduction, J. F. Pacheco. Madrid: Unión Musical Española, 1929.

———. *Los de Aragón: Zarzuela en un acto.* Piano reduction, J. F. Pacheco. Madrid: Unión Musical Española, 1927.

———. *La Reina mora: Sainete lírico en un acto.* Madrid: Unión Musical Española, 1930.

Soutullo, Reveriano, and Juan Vert. *La del soto del parral: Zarzuela en dos actos.* Madrid: Sociedad de Autores Españoles, 1927.

———. *El último romántico: Zarzuela en dos actos.* Madrid: Unión Musical Española, 1968.

Usandizaga, José Maria. *Las Golondrinas: Drama lírico en tres actos.* San Sebastián: Casa Erviti, n.d.

——— and Ramón Usandizaga. *Las Golondrinas: Opera en tres actos.* Ed. Ramón Lazkano. Madrid: Instituto Complutense de Ciencias Musicales, 1999.

Vives, Amadeo. *Bohemios: Zarzuela en un acto.* 1935. Madrid: Unión Musical Española, 1971.

———. *Doña Francisquita: Comedia Lírica en tres actos.* Madrid: Unión Musical Española, 1968.

———. *Don Lucas del Cigarral: Zarzuela en tres actos.* Madrid: Pablo Martin, n.d.

———. *Maruxa: Comedia lírica en dos actos.* Madrid: Unión Musical Española, 1915.

———. *La villana: Zarzuela en tres actos.* Madrid: Sociedad de Autores Españoles, 1927.

PUBLISHED LIBRETTI

Álvarez Quintero, Serafín, and Joaquín Álvarez Quintero. *Los borrachos: Sainete en cuatro cuadros y en prosa.* Madrid: R. Velasco, 1899.

———. *El estreno: Zarzuela cómico en tres cuadros sin exposición, nudo, ni desenlace.* Madrid: Regino Velasco, 1912.

———. *La mala sombra.* Madrid: R. Velasco, 1908.

———. *La patria chica: Zarzuela en un acto.* Madrid: R. Velasco, 1910.

———. *La reina mora: Sainete en tres cuadros.* Madrid: Unión Musical Española, 1967.

Arniches, Carlos. *La fiesta de San Antón: Sainete lírico de costumbres madrileñas.* Madrid: R. Velasco, 1898.

———. *El santo de la Isidra.* Valencia,587–619.

——— and Ramón Asensio Mas. *El puñao de rosas: Zarzuela de costumbres andaluzas en un acto, dividido en tres cuadros.* Madrid: R. Velasco, 1914.

——— and Enrique García Álvarez. *Alma de Dios: Comedia lírica de costumbres populares.* Madrid: R. Velasco, 1908.

——— and Celso Lucio. *El cabo primero: Zarzuela cómica en un acto.* Madrid: R. Velasco, 1895.

——— and Félix Quintana. *La alegría del batallón: Cuento militar.* Madrid: R. Velasco, 1909.

Burgos, Javier. *El baile de Luis Alonso: Sainete lírico en un acto, dividido en tres cuadros, en verso.* In *Cádiz/El baile de Luis Alonso,* ed. Alberto Romero Ferrer. Cádiz: Servicio de Publicaciones, Universidad de Cádiz, 1997. 64–118.

———. *La boda de Luis Alonso o la noche del encierro: Sainete lírico en un acto, dividido en tres cuadros.* Madrid: R. Velasco, 1897.

———. *Las mujeres: Sainete lírico en un acto, dividido en cuatro cuadros, en verso.* Madrid: R. Velasco, 1896.

———. *Trafalgar: Episodio nacional, lírico dramático en dos actos, dividido en once cuadros, en verso.* Madrid: R. Velasco, 1891.

Dicenta, Joaquín, and Manuel Paso. *Curro Vargas: Drama lírico en tres actos y en verso.* Madrid: R. Velasco, 1899.

Echegaray, Miguel. *El dúo de la Africana.* Valencia 215–247.

———. *Gigantes y cabezudos.* Valencia 413–454.

———. *La viejecita.* Valencia 375–412.

Estremera, José. *La czarina: Zarzuela en un acto y en prosa.* Madrid: R. Velasco, 1894.

———. *Música clásica: Disparate cómico-lírico.* Madrid: Cosme Rodriguez, 1888.

Fernández Ardavín, Luis. *La bejarana: Zarzuela en dos actos.* Madrid: Sucesor de R. Velasco, 1924.

Fernández de Sevilla, Luis, and Anselmo C. Carreño. *Los claveles: Sainete lírico en un acto y tres cuadros.* In *Los claveles/Agua, azucarrillos y aguardiente.* Madrid: Teatro de la Zarzuela, 2002. 57–90.

———. *La del soto del parral: Zarzuela en dos actos y tres cuadros.* Madrid: Teatro de la Zarzuela, 2000.

Fernández-Shaw, Carlos. *El cortejo de la Irene: Zarzuela en un acto.* Madrid: R. Velasco, 1896.

———. *La venta de Don Quijote: Comedia lírica en un acto, en prosa y en verso.* Madrid: R. Velasco, 1903.

———and José López Silva. *La Revoltosa.* Valencia 321–372.

García Álvarez, Enrique and Antonio Paso. *La alegría de la huerta.* Valencia 525–551.

———. *El niño judío.* Madrid: Teatro de la Zarzuela, 2003.

———. *El niño judío: Zarzuela en dos actos.* Madrid: R. Velasco, 1918.

González del Castillo, Emilio, and Luis Martínez Román. *La Calesera: Zarzuela en tres actos.* Madrid: Grafica Renacimiento, 1925.

———. *La picarona: Zarzuela en tres actos.* Madrid: Grafica Victoria, 1930.

González del Toro, Ricardo, and Fernando Luque. *La marchenera: Zarzuela en tres actos y en prosa.* Madrid: La Farsa, 1928.

Jackson Veyan, José. *Chateau Margaux: Juguete cómico-lírico en un acto y en verso.* Madrid: R. Velasco, 1912.

———. *Las zapatillas: Cuento cómico-lírico en un acto y cuatro cuadros y en verso.* Madrid: R. Velasco, 1896.

López Monís, Antonio. *La dogaresa: Zarzuela en dos actos, en prosa.* Barcelona: Publicaciones Rafols, 1920.

López Silva, José, and Carlos Fernández-Shaw. *Las bravías.* In *Sainetes Madrileños* 7–70. Madrid: Biblioteca Renacimiento, 1911.

López Silva, José, and José Jackson Veyán. *El barquillero: Zarzuela en un acto y tres cuadros, en prosa y verso.* Madrid: Los hijos de M. G. Hernández, 1900.

Lorente, Juan José. *La Dolorosa.* Ed. Xosé Aviñoa. Ediciones Daimon, 1985.

———. *La Dolorosa: Zarzuela de costumbres aragonesas.* Madrid: Unión Musical Española, 1967.

———. *Los de Aragón: Zarzuela de costumbres aragonesas.* Madrid: Unión Musical Española, 1967.

Luceño, Tomás, and Carlos Fernández-Shaw. *Don Lucas del Cigarral: Zarzuela en tres actos.* Madrid: R. Velasco, 1899.

Lucio, Celso, and Enrique García-Álvarez. *La marcha de Cádiz.* Valencia 491–521.

Martínez Sierra, Gregorio. *Las golondrinas: Drama lírico en tres actos.* Madrid: Renacimiento, 1914.

Moyrón, Julian. *Los cadetes de la reina: Zarzuela en un acto.* Madrid: R. Velasco, 1913.

Paradas, Enrique, and Joaquín Jimenez. *La chula de Pontevedra: Sainete en dos actos.* Madrid: Talleres Graficos Piñera, 1928.

Pascual Frutos, Luís. *Maruxa: Egloga lírica en dos actos.* Madrid: R. Velasco, 1914.

———. *Molinos de viento: Opereta en un acto.* Madrid: R. Velasco, 1910.

Perrín, Guillermo, and Miguel de Palacios. *El barbero de Sevilla: Zarzuela cómica en un acto.* Madrid: R. Velasco, 1901.

———. *Bohemios: Zarzuela en un acto, dividido en tres cuadros.* Madrid: R. Velasco, 1912.

———. *Cuadros disolventes: Apropósito cómico-lírico-fantástico inverosimil en un acto y cinco cuadros.* Madrid: R. Velasco, 1896.

————. *La Generala: Opereta cómica en dos actos y en prosa.* Madrid: R. Velasco, 1912.

Picón, José. *Pan y toros: Zarzuela en tres actos y en verso.* Madrid: José Rodriguez, 1889.

Piña Domínguez, Mariano. *Mujer y reina: Zarzuela melodramática en tres actos.* Madrid: José Rodríguez, 1895.

Prieto, Enrique, and Andrés Ruesga. *El arca de Noé: Problema cómico-lírico social en un acto y dos cuadros, en verso.* Madrid: José Rodríguez, 1890.

Ramos Carrión, Miguel. *Agua, azucarillos y aguardiente: Pasillo veraniego en un acto y dos cuadros.* In *Los claveles/Agua, azucarrillos y aguardiente.* Madrid: Teatro de la Zarzuela, 2002. 103–138.

————. *La bruja: Zarzuela en tres actos.* Madrid: Teatro de la Zarzuela, 2002.

————. *La bruja: Zarzuela en tres actos, en prosa y verso.* Madrid: R. Velasco, 1895.

————. *La marsellesa: Zarzuela histórica original, en tres actos y en verso.* Madrid: J. Rodríguez, 1879.

————. *Los sobrinos del Capitán Grant: Novela cómico-lírico-dramático en cuatro actos y diecisiete cuadros.* Madrid: Teatro de la Zarzuela, 2001.

————. *La tempestad: Melodrama en tres actos, en prosa y verso.* Madrid: Cedaceros, 1893.

Ramos Martín, José. *La Alsaciana: Zarzuela en un acto, dividido en dos cuadros.* Madrid: Sociedad de Autores Españoles, 1923.

————. *Los gavilanes: Zarzuela en tres actos y cinco cuadros.* Madrid: Teatro de la Zarzuela, 2002.

Reoyo, Enrique, Antonio Paso, and Silva Aramburu. *La leyenda del beso: Zarzuela en dos actos.* Madrid: Tipografia Fenix, 1924.

Romea, Julián. *El padrino de «El Nene» o ¡Todo por el arte! Sainete lírico en tres cuadros, en prosa.* Madrid: R. Velasco, 1896.

————. *La Tempranica.* Valencia 555–583.

Romero, Federico, and Guillermo Fernández-Shaw. *El caserío: Comedia lírica en tres actos.* Madrid: Unión Musical Española, 1967.

————. *Doña Francisquita.* Ed. Xosé Aviñoa. Madrid: Ediciones Daimon, 1986.

————. *Luisa Fernanda: Comedia lírica en tres actos.* In *Luisa Fernanda, La Chulapona, Monte Carmelo.* Barcelona: Editorial Cisne, n.d.

————. *La rosa del azafrán.* Madrid: Imprenta Ciudad Lineal, 1930.

————. *La villana: Zarzuela en tres actos.* Madrid: La Farsa, 1927.

Sánchez Pastor, Emilio. *Los golfos: Sainete madrileño lírico y en verso.* Madrid: R. Velasco, 1896.

————. *El tambor de granaderos.* Valencia 455–487.

Sierra, Eusebio. *San Antonio de la Florida: Zarzuela cómica en un acto y dos cuadros, en prosa.* Madrid: R. Velasco, 1894.

Tellaeche, José. *El último romántico: Zarzuela de costumbres, en dos actos, divididos en cuatro cuadros.* Madrid: La Farsa, 1928.

Thous, Maximiliano, and Elías Cerdá. *Moros y cristianos: Zarzuela de costumbres valencianas e n un acto, dividido en tres cuadros.* Madrid: R. Velasco, 1905.

Vega, Ricardo de la. *La canción de la Lola.* Valencia 23–48.

———. *De Getafe al paraiso o la familia del Tío Maroma.* Valencia 51–98.

———. *La verbena de la paloma.* Valencia 251–277.

Valencia, Antonio, ed. *El género chico (Antología de textos completos).* Madrid: Taurus, 1962.

Zapata, Marcos. *El anillo de hierro: Drama lírico en tres actos y en verso.* In *Colección de obras dramaticas de Marcos Zapata.* Vol. 1. Madrid: R. Velasco, 1887. 140–291.

OTHER SOURCES CITED

Adorno, Theodor. "Kitsch." Trans. Susan H. Gillespie. *Essays on Music.* Ed. Richard Leppart, Berkeley: U of California P, 2002. 501–505.

Alier, Roger. *La Zarzuela.* Barcelona: Ma Non Troppo, 2002.

Álvarez Junco, José. *The Emergence of Mass Politics in Spain: Populist Demagoguery and Republican Culture, 1890–1910.* Trans. of *El emperador del Paralelo: Lerroux y la demagogia populista* (Madrid: Alianza, 1990). Brighton and Portland, OR: Sussex Academic Press, 2002.

———. *Mater Dolorosa: La idea de España en el siglo XIX.* Madrid: Taurus, 2001.

———. "El nacionalismo español como mito movilizador: Cuatro guerras." *Cultura y movilización en la España contemporánea.* Ed. Rafael Cruz and Manuel Pérez Ledesma. Madrid: Alianza, 1997. 35–68.

Anderson, Benedict. *Imagined Communities: Reflections on the Origin and Spread of Nationalism.* Rev. ed. London: Verso, 2006.

Andura Varela, Fernanda. "Del Madrid teatral del XIX: La llegada de la luz, el teatro por horas, los incendios, los teatros de verano." *Cuatro siglos de teatro en Madrid.* Madrid: Consorcio Madrid Capital Europea de la Cultura, 1992.

Applegate, Celia. *Bach in Berlin: Nation and Culture in Mendelssohn's Revival of the* St. Matthew Passion. Ithaca: Cornell UP, 2005.

———. *A Nation of Provincials: The German Idea of Heimat.* Berkeley: U of California P, 1990.

——— and Pamela Potter, eds. *Music and German National Identity.* Chicago: U of Chicago P, 2002.

Archilés, Ferran, and Marta García Carrión. "En la sombra del estado: Esfera pública nacional y homogeneización cultural en la España de la Restauración." *Historia Contemporánea* 45 (2012): 483–518.

Arnau, Juan. *Historia de la zarzuela.* 4 vols. Madrid: Zacosa, 1979.

Augusteijn, Joost, and Eric Storm, eds. *Region and State in Nineteenth-Century Europe: Nation-Building, Regional Identities, and Separatism.* New York: Palgrave Macmillan, 2012.

Bailey, Peter. *Popular Culture and Performance in the Victorian City.* Cambridge: Cambridge UP, 1998.

Balfour, Sebastian. *The End of the Spanish Empire, 1898–1923.* Oxford: Clarendon, 1997.

Barce, Ramón. "El folklore urbano y la música de los sainetes líricos del último cuarto del siglo XIX: La explicación escénica de los bailes." *Revista de Musicología* 16.6 (1993): 3217–3225.

———. "El sainete lírico (1880–1915)." *La música española en el siglo XIX,* ed. Emilio Casares Rodicio and Celsa Alonso González. Oviedo: U of Oviedo, 1995.

Barea, Arturo. *The Forging of a Rebel.* Trans. Ilsa Barea. London: Granta, 2001.

Barrera Maraver, Antonio. *Crónicas del género chico y de un Madrid divertido.* Madrid: El Avapiés, 1983.

Barriuso, Carlos. *Los discursos de la modernidad: Nación, imperio y estética en el fin de siglo español (1895–1924).* Madrid: Biblioteca Nueva, 2009.

Ben-Ami, Shlomo. *Fascism from Above: The Dictatorship of Primo de Rivera in Spain, 1923–1930.* Oxford: Clarendon, 1983.

Beramendi, Justo. "Nacionalismo y cultura en Galicia." *La cultura española de la Restauración.* Ed. Manuel Suárez Cortina. Santander: Sociedad Menéndez Pelayo, 1999. 585–605.

Besses, Luis. *Diccionario de argot español o lenguaje jergal gitano, delincuente profesional y popular.* Barcelona: Sucesores de Manuel Soler, 1905. Cádiz: Servicio de Publicaciones de la Universidad de Cádiz, 1989.

Bilbao, José. *Teatro Real: Recuerdos de las cinco temporadas del empresario Arana.* Madrid: Editorial Norma, 1936. Madrid: Comunidad de Madrid, 1996.

Bordieu, Pierre. *Distinction: A Social Critique of the Judgment of Taste.* Cambridge: Harvard UP, 1984.

Boyd, Caroline P. *Historia Patria: Politics, History, and National Identity in Spain, 1875–1975.* Princeton: Princeton UP, 1997.

Burgete, Sol. *Amadeo Vives.* Madrid: Espasa-Calpe, 1978.

Carr, Raymond. *Spain, 1808–1975.* 2nd ed. Oxford: Clarendon, 1982.

Carratalá, Juan A. Ríos. "Del castizo al fresco: tipología y ambientes del teatro cómico (1890–1910) y su adaptación al cine." *La escena española en la encrucijada (1890–1910).* Ed. Serge Salaün, Evelyne Ricci, and Marie Salgues. Madrid: Fundamentos, 2005.

Carretero, Emilio García. *Historia del Teatro de la Zarzuela de Madrid.* 2 vols. Madrid: Fundación de la Zarzuela Española, 2003–2005.

Casares Rodicio, Emilio. *Francisco Asenjo Barbieri.* 2 vols. Madrid: Instituto Complutense de Ciencias Musicales, 1994.

———. "La Música del siglo XIX español. Conceptos fundamentales." *La música española en el siglo XIX.* Ed. Emilio Casares Rodicio and Celsa Alonso González. Oviedo: U de Oviedo, 1995. 13–122.

————, ed. *Diccionario de la Zarzuela España e Hispanoamérica*. 2nd ed. Madrid: ICCM, 2006.

———— and Celsa Alonso González, eds. *La música española en el siglo XIX*. Oviedo: U de Oviedo, 1995.

Caute, David. *The Dancer Defects: The Struggle for Cultural Supremacy During the Cold War*. Oxford: Oxford UP, 2003.

Charnon-Duetsch, Lou. *The Spanish Gypsy: The History of a European Obsession*. University Park: Pennsylvania State UP, 2004.

Clark, Walter Aaron. *Isaac Albéniz: Portrait of a Romantic*. Oxford: Oxford UP, 1999.

———— and William Craig Krause. *Federico Moreno Torroba: A Musical Life in Three Acts*. Oxford: Oxford UP, 2013.

Clayton, Martin, Trevor Herbert, and Richard Middleton, eds. *The Cultural Study of Music: A Critical Introduction*. New York and London: Routledge, 2003.

Cody, Gabriele H., and Evert Sprinchorn, eds. *The Columbia Encyclopedia of Modern Drama*. New York: Columbia UP, 2007.

Cohen, Walter. *Drama of a Nation: Public Theater in Renaissance England and Spain*. Ithaca: Cornell UP, 1985.

Confino, Alon. *The Nation as a Local Metaphor: Württemberg, Imperial Germany, and National Memory, 1871–1918*. Chapel Hill: U of North Carolina P, 1997.

Cotarelo y Mori, Emilio. *Historia de la zarzuela o sea el drama lírico en España, desde su origen a fines del siglo XIX*. Madrid: Tipografía de Archivos, 1934; Madrid: Ediciones del ICCMU, 2001.

Cruz, Jesus. *The Rise of Middle-Class Culture in Nineteenth Century Spain*. Baton Rouge: Louisiana State UP, 2011.

Dahlhaus, Carl. *Nineteenth-Century Music*. Trans. J. Bradford Robinson. Berkeley: U of California P, 1989.

Deleito y Peñuela, José. *Origen y apogeo del "género chico."* Madrid: Revista de Occidente, 1949.

DeNora, Tia. *Music in Everyday Life*. Cambridge: Cambridge UP, 2000.

Díaz, Julio Montero. "La Crisis del moderantismo y la experiencia del Sexenio democrático." *Historia contemporánea de España (siglo XIX)*, ed. Javier Paredes. Barcelona: Ariel Historia, 1998. 242–258.

Dizikes, John. *Opera in America: A Cultural History*. New Haven: Yale UP, 1993.

Dougherty, Dru, and María Francisca Vilches de Frutos. *La escena madrileña entre 1918 y 1926: Análsis y documentación*. Madrid: Editorial Fundamentos, 1990.

Driever, Steven L. "The Historical Geography of the Proposals for Madrid's Gran Vía, 1860–1904." Paper presented at the 34th Annual Congress of the Society for Spanish and Portuguese Historical Studies, Universidad Complutense de Madrid, 3 July 2003.

Eastman, Scott. *Preaching Spanish Nationalism across the Hispanic Atlantic, 1759–1823*. Baton Rouge: Louisiana State UP, 2011.

Eley, Geoff. *Reshaping the German Right: Radical Nationalism and Political Change after Bismarck.* Rev. ed. Ann Arbor: U of Michigan P, 1991.

Encina Cortizo, María. *Emilio Arrieta: De la ópera a la zarzuela.* Madrid: Instituto Complutense de Ciencias Musicales, 1998.

Esperanza y Sola, José María. *Treinta años de crítica musical: Colección póstuma de los trabajos.* 3 vols. Madrid: La viuda é hijos de Tello, 1906.

Espín Templado, María Pilar. *El teatro por horas en Madrid (1870–1910).* Madrid: Instituto de Estudio Madrileños, 1995.

———. "El teatro por horas en Madrid (1870–1910) (Subgéneros que comprende, autores príncipales y análisis de algunas obras representativas)." Tésis doctoral, Universidad Complutense de Madrid, 1986.

Fernández Muñoz, Angel Luis. *Arquitectura teatral en Madrid: Del corral de comedias al cinematógrafo.* Madrid: El Avapiés, 1988.

Fernández-Shaw, Guillermo. *Larga historia de* La vida breve. Madrid: Revista de Occidente, 1972.

Ford, Caroline. *Creating the Nation in Provincial France: Religion and Political Identity in Brittany.* Princeton: Princeton UP, 1993.

Fox, Inman. *La invención de España: Nacionalismo liberal e identidad nacional.* Madrid: Cátedra, 1998.

Fradera, Josep Maria. *Cultura nacional en una sociedad dividida: Cataluña, 1838–1868.* Trans. Carles Mercadal Vidal. 1992. Madrid: Macial Pons Historia, 2003.

Fusi, Juan Pablo. *España: La evolución de la identidad nacional.* Madrid: Temas de Hoy, 2000.

Galdós, Benito Pérez. *Doña Perfecta.* Madrid: Cátedra, 2001.

Gellner, Ernest. *Nations and Nationalism.* Ithaca: Cornell UP, 1983.

Gerhard, Anselm. *The Urbanization of Opera: Music Theater in Paris in the Nineteenth Century.* Trans. Mary Whittall. Chicago: U of Chicago P, 1998.

Gies, David Thatcher. *The Theatre in Nineteenth-Century Spain.* Cambridge: Cambridge UP, 1994.

Gómez Amat, Carlos. "*Bohemios,* zarzuela peculiar." Liner notes, Amadeo Vives, *Bohemios.* CD. Auvidis Valois, 1994.

———. *Historia de la música española.* Vol. 5. *Siglo XIX.* Madrid: Alianza, 1988.

——— and Joaquín Turina Gómez. *La Orquesta Sinfónica de Madrid: Noventa años de historia.* Madrid: Alianza, 1994.

Gómez-Ferrer, Guadalupe, and Raquel Sánchez, eds. *Modernizar España: Proyectos de reforma y apertura internacional (1898–1914).* Madrid: Biblioteca Nueva, 2007.

Gomez Labad, José María. *El Madrid de la zarzuela (Visión regocijada de un pasado en cantables).* Madrid: Editoral Tres, 1983.

Gómez Ochoa, Fidel. "El conservadurismo canovista y los orígenes de la Restauración: La formación de un conservadurismo moderno." *La Restauración, entre el liberalismo y la democracia.* Ed. Manuel Suárez Cortina. Madrid: Alianza, 1997. 109–155.

González, María Jesús. *El universo conservador de Antonio Maura: Biografía y proyecto de Estado.* Madrid: Biblioteca Nueva, 1997.

Gorostiza, Santiago. Liner notes. Jesús Guridi, *Sinfonía pirenaica.* CD. Naxos, 2005.

Greenfeld, Liah. *Nationalism: Five Roads to Modernity.* Cambridge: Harvard UP, 1992.

Harrison, Joseph, and Alan Hoyle, eds. *Spain's 1898 Crisis: Regenerationism, Modernism, Post-Colonialism.* Manchester: Manchester UP, 2000.

Heckert, Deborah. "Working the Crowd: Elgar, Class, and Reformulations of Popular Culture at the Turn of the Twentieth Century." *Edward Elgar and His World,* ed. Byron Adams. Princeton: Princeton UP, 2007. 287–316.

Henken, John Edward. "Francisco Asenjo Barbieri and the Nineteenth-Century Revival in Spanish National Music." Diss. UCLA, 1987.

Hennessy, C. A. M. *The Federal Republic in Spain: Pi y Margall and the Federal Republican Movement, 1868–1874.* Oxford: Oxford UP, 1962.

Hernández Girbal, Florentino. *Amadeo Vives: El músico y el hombre.* Madrid: Ediciones Lira, 1971.

———. *Federico Chueca: El alma de Madrid.* Madrid: Ediciones Lira, 1992.

Hernández Gonzalez, Gabriel (Javier de Montillana). *Bretón.* Salamanca: Talleres Gráficos Nuñez, 1952.

Hess, Carol A. *Manuel de Falla and Modernism in Spain, 1898–1936.* Chicago: U of Chicago P, 2001.

Hobsbawm, E. J. "Mass-Producing Traditions: Europe, 1870–1914." *The Invention of Tradition,* ed. Eric Hobsbawm and Terence Ranger. Cambridge: Cambridge UP, 1983. 263–307.

———. *Nations and Nationalism Since 1780: Programme, Myth, Reality.* 2nd ed. Cambridge: Cambridge UP, 1992.

——— and Terence Ranger, eds. *The Invention of Tradition.* Cambridge: Cambridge UP, 1983.

Holguín, Sandie. *Creating Spaniards: Culture and National Identity in Republican Spain.* Madison: U of Wisconsin P, 2002.

Horkheimer, Max, and Theodor Adorno. "The Culture Industry: Enlightenment as Mass Deception." *Dialectic of Enlightenment: Philosophical Fragments.* 1947. Stanford: Stanford UP, 2002. 94–136.

Iberni, Luis G. *Ruperto Chapí.* Madrid: Instituto Complutense de Ciencias Musicales, 1995.

Iglesias Martinez, Nieves, ed. *Catálogo del teatro lírico español en la Biblioteca Nacional.* 3 vols. Madrid: Ministero de Cultura, 1986–1991.

Jackson, Gabriel. *The Spanish Republic and the Civil War, 1931–1939.* Princeton: Princeton UP, 1965.

Jackson, Jeffrey H. *Making Jazz French: Music and Modern Life in Interwar Paris.* Durham: Duke UP, 2003.

Johnson, James H. *Listening in Paris: A Cultural History.* Berkeley: U of California P, 1995.

Juliá, Santos, David Ringrose, and Cristina Segura. *Madrid: Historia de una capital.* Madrid: Alianza, 1994.

Kamen, Henry. *The Disinherited: Exile and the Making of Spanish Culture, 1492–1975.* New York: HarperCollins, 2007.

———. *Imagining Spain: Historical Myth and National Identity.* New Haven & London: Yale UP, 2008.

Kaplan, Temma. *Red City, Blue Period: Social Movements in Picasso's Barcelona.* Berkeley: U of California P, 1992.

Kater, Michael H. *The Twisted Muse: Musicians and Their Music in the Third Reich.* Oxford: Oxford UP, 1997.

Kern, Robert W. *Liberals, Reformers and Caciques in Restoration Spain, 1875–1900.* Albuquerque: U of New Mexico P, 1974.

Kracauer, Siegfried. *Jacques Offenbach and the Paris of His Time.* 1937. New York: Zone Books, 2002.

Kramer, Lawrence. *Musical Meaning: Towards a Critical History.* Berkeley: U of California P, 2002.

Lebovics, Herman. *True France: The Wars over Cultural Identity, 1900–1945.* Ithaca: Cornell UP, 1992.

Levine, Lawrence W. *Highbrow/Lowbrow: The Emergence of Cultural Hierarchy in America.* Cambridge: Harvard UP, 1988.

Linares, Francisco Quirós. *Las ciudades españolas en el siglo XIX.* Gijón: Ediciones Trea, 2009.

Linares, Miguel Martorell. "El rey en su desconcierto: Alfonso XIII, los viejos políticos y el ocaso de la monarquía." *Alfonso XIII: Un político en el trono.* Ed. Javier Moreno Luzón. Madrid: Marcial Pons Historia, 2003.

Lynch, John. *Bourbon Spain, 1700–1808.* Oxford: Basil Blackwell, 1989.

Magnien, Brigitte. "Cultural urbana." *1900 en España.* Ed. Serge Salaün and Carlos Serrano. Madrid: Espasa-Calpe, 1991. 107–129.

Mann, Thomas. *The Magic Mountain.* Trans. John E. Woods. New York: Vintage, 1996.

Marco, Tomás. *Spanish Music in the Twentieth Century.* Trans. Cola Franzen. Cambridge: Harvard UP, 1993.

McKendrick, Melvina. *Theatre in Spain, 1490–1700.* Cambridge: Cambridge UP, 1989.

Membrez, Nancy J. "The Mass Production of Theatre in Nineteenth-Century Madrid." *The Crisis of Institutionalized Literature in Spain.* Ed. Wlad Godzich and Nicholas Spadaccini. Minneapolis: Prisma Institute, 1988. 309–356.

———. "The *teatro por horas*: History, Dynamics and Comprehensive Bibliography of a Madrid Industry, 1867–1922." Diss. U of California, Santa Barbara, 1987.

Molina, Fernando, and Miguel Cabo Villaverde. "An Inconvenient Nation: Nation-Building and National Identity in Modern Spain. The Historiographical Debate." *Nationhood from Below: Europe in the Long Nineteenth Century.* Ed. Maarten Van Ginderachter and Marnix Beyen. New York: Palgrave Macmillan, 2012. 47–72.

Monge, Gregorio de la Fuente. *Los revolucionarios de 1868: Elites y poder en la España liberal.* Madrid: Marcial Pons, 2000.

Montero Alonso, José. *Usandizaga.* Madrid: Espasa-Calpe, 1985.

Mosse, George L. *The Nationalization of the Masses: Political Symbolism and Mass Movements in Germany from the Napoleonic Wars through the Third Reich.* Ithaca: Cornell UP, 1971.

Nagore Ferrer, María. "Historia de un fracaso: El 'himno nacional' en la España del siglo XIX." *Arbor* 187.751 (Sept.–Oct. 2011): 827–845.

Narotzky, Susana, and Gavin Smith. *Immediate Struggles: People, Power, and Place in Rural Spain.* Berkeley: U of California P, 2006.

Ortega y Gasset, José. "Vieja y nueva política." In *Obras completas.* Vol. 1. [1914.] Madrid: Revista del Occidente, 1961. 265–308.

Ortiz, David. *Paper Liberals: Press and Politics in Restoration Spain.* Westport, CT: Greenwood, 2000.

Parsons, Deborah L. *A Cultural History of Madrid: Modernism and the Urban Spectacle.* Oxford and New York: Berg, 2003.

Pasler, Jann. *Composing the Citizen: Music as Public Utility in Third Republic France.* Berkeley: U of California P, 2009.

Patuel, Francesc Mezquita *¿Una nación débil? Aproximación a los discuros nacionales en España.* N.p.: 05ediciones, 2009.

Payne, Stanley G. *Spain's First Democracy: The Second Republic, 1931–1936.* Madison: U of Wisconsin P, 1993.

Peña y Goñi, Antonio. *Discursos leídos ante la Real Academia de Bellas Artes de San Fernando en la recepción pública de Don Antonio Peña y Goñi el día 10 de abril de 1892.* Madrid: Manuel Ginés Hernández, 1892.

———. *Impresiones musicales: Colección de artículos de crítica y literatura musical.* Madrid: Manuel Minuesa de los Rios, 1878.

———. *La ópera española y la música dramática en España en el siglo XIX. Apuntes históricos.* Madrid: Imprenta y estereotipia de *El Liberal,* 1881.

Pinto Crespo, Virgilio, ed. *Madrid: Atlas histórico de la ciudad, 1850–1939.* Madrid: Fundación Caja Madrid, 2001.

Poiger, Uta G. *Jazz, Rock, and Rebels: Cold War Politics and American Culture in a Divided Germany.* Berkeley: U of California P, 2000.

Quiroga, Alejandro. *Making Spaniards: Primo de Rivera and the Nationalization of the Masses, 1923–1930.* New York: Palgrave Macmillan, 2007.

Radcliff, Pamela Beth. "The Emerging Challenge of Mass Politics." *Spanish History Since 1808.* Ed. José Álvarez Junco and Adrian Shubert. London: Arnold, 2000. 137–154.

———. *From Mobilization to Civil War: The Politics of Polarization in the Spanish City of Gijón, 1900–1937.* Cambridge: Cambridge UP, 1996.

———. "Women's Politics: Consumer Riots in Twentieth-century Spain." *Constructing Spanish Womanhood: Female Identity in Modern Spain.* Ed. Victoria Loree Enders and Pamela Beth Radcliff. Albany: State U of New York P, 1999. 301–323.

Ramsden, H. *The 1898 Movement in Spain: Towards a Reinterpretation with Special Reference to* En torno al casticismo *and* Idearium español. Manchester: Manchester UP, 1974.

Renan, Ernest. "What is a Nation?" *The Nationalism Reader.* Ed. Omar Bahbour and Micheline R. Ishay. Amherst: Humanity Books, 1999.

Rial, James H. *Revolution from Above: The Primo de Rivera Dictatorship in Spain, 1923–1930.* Fairfax, VA: George Mason UP, 1986.

Roberts, Stephen G. H. "Unamuno and the Restoration Political Project: A Re-evaluation." *Spain's 1898 Crisis: Regenerationism, Modernism, Post-Colonialism.* Ed. Joseph Harrison and Alan Hoyle. Manchester: Manchester UP, 2000. 68–80.

Romero Ferrer, Alberto. "Introducción." *Cádiz, El baile de Luis Alonso,* by Javier de Burgos. Cádiz: Publicaciones de la Univerdad de Cádiz, 1997. 7–52.

Romero Salvadó, Francisco J. *Spain 1914–1918: Between War and Revolution.* London and New York: Routledge, 1992.

Roshwald, Aviel. *The Endurance of Nationalism: Ancient Roots and Modern Dilemmas.* Cambridge: Cambridge UP, 2006.

Sagardía, Angel. *El compositor José Serrano: Vida y obra.* Madrid: Organización Sala Editorial, 1972.

———. *Pablo Luna.* Madrid: Espasa-Calpe, 1978.

Sainz, José Luis de Granja. "Nacionalismo, ideología y cultura en el País Vasco." *La cultura española de la Restauración.* Ed. Manuel Suárez Cortina. Santander: Sociedad Menéndez Pelayo, 1999. 525–564.

Salaün, Serge, and Carlos Serrano, eds. *1900 en España.* Madrid: Espasa-Calpe, 1991.

Sanabria, Enrique A. *Republican and Anticlerical Nationalism in Spain.* New York: Palgrave Macmillan, 2009.

Sánchez de Palacios, Mariano. *Serafín y Joaquín Álvarez Quintero.* Madrid: Gráficas Valera, 1971.

Sánchez Illán, Juan Carlos. *La nación inacabada: Los intelectuales y el proceso de construcción nacional (1900–1914).* Madrid: Biblioteca Nueva, 2002.

Scherer, F. M. *Quarter Notes and Banknotes: The Economics of Music Composition in the Eighteenth and Nineteenth Centuries.* Princeton: Princeton UP, 2004.

Schmidt-Nowara, Christopher. *The Conquest of History: Spanish Colonialism and National Histories in the Nineteenth Century.* Pittsburgh: U of Pittsburgh P, 2006.

Schwartz, Vanessa L. *Spectacular Realities: Early Mass Culture in Fin-de-siècle Paris.* Berkeley: U of California P, 1998.

Serrano, Carlos. *El nacimiento de Carmen: Símbolos, mitos y nación.* Madrid: Taurus, 1999.

Sinclair, Alison. "The Regional Novel: Evolution and Consolidation." *The Cambridge Companion to the Spanish Novel: From 1600 to the Present.* Ed. Harriet Turner and Adelaida López de Martínez. Cambridge: Cambridge UP, 2009. 49–64.

Sixto, Plaza. "Sociología del teatro musical español." Diss. Georgetown University, 1986.

Smith, Anthony. *National Identity.* Reno: U of Nevada P, 1991.

Sobrino, Ramón. "Alhambrismo." Liner notes to *En la Alhambra: Obras de Chapí, Bretón, Monasterio and Carreras.* CD. Almaviva, 1999.

Sopeña, Federico. *Vida y obra de Falla.* Madrid: Turner Música, 1988.

Stein, Louise K., and Roger Alier. "Zarzuela." *The New Grove Dictionary of Music and Musicians.* 2nd ed. Ed. Stanley Sadie and John Tyrrell. Vol. 27. London: Macmillan, 2001. 755–760.

Steinberg, Michael P. *Listening to Reason: Culture, Subjectivity, and Nineteenth-Century Music.* Princeton: Princeton UP, 2004.

Storm, Eric. *La perspectiva del progreso: Pensamiento político en la España del cambio de siglo (1890–1914).* Madrid: Biblioteca Nueva, 2001.

Traubner, Richard. "*Die Herzogin von Chicago:* Jazz versus operetta." Liner notes. Emmerich Kálman, *Die Herzogin von Chicago.* CD. Decca, 1999.

———. *Operetta: A Theatrical History.* Rev. ed. New York & London: Routledge, 2003.

Turina Gómez, Joaquín. *Historia del Teatro Real.* Madrid: Alianza, 1997.

Tusell, Javier, and Genoveva Queipo de Llano. *Alfonso XIII: El rey polémico.* Madrid: Taurus, 2001.

———. "The Dictatorship of Primo de Rivera, 1923–1931." *Spanish History Since 1808.* Ed. José Álvarez Junco and Adrian Shubert. London: Arnold, 2000. 207–220.

Ucelay da Cal, Enric. "The Restoration: Regeneration and the Clash of Nationalisms, 1875–1914." *Spanish History Since 1808.* Ed. José Álvarez Junco and Adrian Shubert. London: Arnold, 2000. 121–136.

Ullman, Joan Connelly. *The Tragic Week: A Study of Anticlericalism in Spain, 1875–1912.* Cambridge: Harvard UP, 1968.

Uría, Jorge. "La cultura popular en la Restauración: El declive de un mundo tradicional y desarrollo de una sociedad de masas." *La cultura española en la Restauración.* Ed. Manuel Suárez Cortina. Santander: Sociedad Menéndez Pelayo, 1999.

———, ed. *La cultura popular en la España contemporánea: Doce estudios.* Madrid: Biblioteca Nueva, 2003.

Unamuno, Miguel. *En torno al casticismo.* 1902. Madrid: Alianza, 2000.

Valverde, Salvador. *El mundo de la zarzuela.* N.p.: Palabras, 1976.

Varela Ortega, José. *Los amigos políticos: Partidos, elecciones y caciquismo en la Restauración (1875–1900).* Madrid: Alianza, 1977. Madrid: Marcial Pons, 2001.

Vásquez, Roland J. "The Quest for National Opera in Spain and the Re-invention of the Zarzuela (1809–1849)." Diss. Cornell U, 1992.

Vidal Corella, Vicente. *El maestro Serrano y los felices tiempos de la zarzuela.* Valencia: Prometo, 1973.

Vilches, Jorge. *Progreso y libertad: El partido progresista en la revolución liberal española.* Madrid: Alianza, 2001.

Vilches, María Francisca, and Dru Dougherty. *La escena madrileña entre 1926 y 1931: Un lustro de transición.* Madrid: Fundamentos, 1997.

Vives, Amadeo. *Sofía.* 1923. Madrid: Espasa-Calpe, 1973.

Webber, Christopher. *The Zarzuela Companion.* Ed. Louise K. Stein and Roger Alier. Lanham, MD, & Oxford: Scarecrow, 2002.

——— and Ignaco Jassa Haro, eds. *Zarzuela.net.* www.zarzuela.net. Accessed 19 October 2014.

Weber, Eugene. *Peasants into Frenchmen: The Modernization of Rural France, 1870–1914.* Stanford: Stanford UP, 1976.

Weber, William. *Music and the Middle Class: The Social Structure of Concert Life in London, Paris, and Vienna between 1830 and 1848,* 2nd ed. Aldershot: Ashgate, 2004.

Williams, Rosalind H. *Dream Worlds: Mass Consumption in Late Nineteenth-Century France.* Berkeley: U of California P, 1982.

Wilson, Elizabeth. *Shostakovich: A Life Remembered.* Princeton: Princeton UP, 1994.

Young, Clinton D. "Theatrical Reform and the Emergence of Mass Culture in Spain." *Sport in Society* 11.6 (Nov. 2008): 630–642.

———. "Why Did Spain Fail to Develop Nationalist Opera?" *Bulletin of the Association for Spanish and Portuguese Historical Studies* 38.1 (2013): 117–137.

Zurita, Marciano. *Historia del género chico.* Madrid: Prensa Popular, 1920.

INDEX

Index